THIS MODERN WORLD

by TOM TOMORROW

Martin Hirst

Allen & Unwin
83 Alexander Street
Crows Nest NSW 2065
Australia
Phone: (61 2) 8425 0100
Fax: (61 2) 9906 2218
Email: info@allenandunwin.com
Web: www.allenandunwin.com

Cataloguing-in-Publication details are available
from the National Library of Australia
www.trove.nla.gov.au

ISBN 978 1 74237 057 6

Index by Puddingburn Publishing Services
Set in 11.5/14 pt Bembo by Post Pre-press Group, Australia
Printed by South Wind Productions, Singapore

10 9 8 7 6 5 4 3 2 1

*For my family, who instilled the values I hold dear,
and to Tiffany White, the mother of all creatures.
She still loves me, despite the many lost weekends.*

Contents

Preface

All that is established melts into air; all that is holy is pro-
faned, and man is at last compelled to face with sober
senses his real conditions of life and his relations with his
kind.

The Communist Manifesto

The bulk of this book was written over a period of two years between
the middle of 2008 and April 2010. In that time the world's media systems were caught up in a massive vortex of uncertainty and change. *News
2.0* captures the flavour of that period and sets it against an historical
background. In short: Where did the news media's crisis of confidence
and lack of commercial certainty come from and what are their likely
impacts?

A starting point for this book is the sense that the news media have
changed more in the last decade than they did in the preceding 30
years. A corollary is that they are likely to change again over the next 10
years. Therefore, it is impossible for a text like this to be completely up-
to-date. Important and relevant things may have happened in the time
between the manuscript going into production and today. Obviously,
that will be seen as a gap in the record, a hole in the text. My excuse:
there is no crystal ball.

However, I have tried to include enough data and analysis to (it is
hoped) make *News 2.0* useful to a general readership and relevant to
students of journalism and to the news media industry. In these pages I
have laid out some thoughts about why the public no longer seems to
trust most mainstream journalism and why the production of the news
commodity is no longer providing 'rivers of gold' in advertising revenues.
I have surveyed and discussed what some may call 'citizen journalism',
which I prefer to define as 'user-generated news-like content' (UGNC).
Where did UGNC come from and can it 'save' the media? I have not
tried to give a definitive response to this or other questions; nor to
suggest a sure-fire set of solutions. Predictions have a selfish habit of

being wrong. Instead, the last two chapters attempt to signal some possible futures—those that seem most plausible given that the world faces what the American media scholar Robert McChesney calls a 'critical juncture' in the history and development of global media.

If that does not satisfy you, I am sorry. However—as Marx and Engels wrote in *The Communist Manifesto*—it is our choices that will determine the future. As the power of social networking shows us, we can exert pressure on the global mediasphere, but we must begin from the reality of where we are today. Our starting point must be to 'face with sober senses' the 'real conditions' in which we find ourselves. We first have to make sense of, and come to terms with, the *present* by understanding that the turbulence of today is created by the rapidly approaching and inevitable media *future* disrupting the certainties of our media *past*. Armed with this crucial knowledge—facing our actual conditions with a clear head—we have a chance to make real a vision shared by many: a democratic media operating on the principles of public service and the public interest. Whether that is a future consisting of 'citizen journalism', a mix of big and small media in public and private ownership, or a situation very much like today, in which an unrepresentative group of powerful private corporations control most of what we can see, say, hear and read, only time will tell. All I am certain of is that our actions can now make a difference to this future. That *News 2.0* took almost two years to complete was both a blessing and a curse. It was a curse because I had nightmares about looming deadlines, all of which passed in quick succession and made the nightmares worse. It was a blessing because without the many delays and interruptions I would not have caught the Twitter wave and the iPad phenomenon, nor would I have seen the 'Witches of Facebook', the nasty trolls who infect social media sites with racist, sexist or homophobic ranting and who can—if not challenged—make our online experiences thoroughly unpleasant. All of these moments were crucial to the themes of *News 2.0*.

Before leaving this preface, it is necessary to make a small explanation regarding the methodology and theoretical framework for *News 2.0*. The term 'dialectic' is used throughout this work to describe an historically contextualized process where the clash and contradiction of binary opposites (two ideas or social forces—'good' and 'evil', for example) results in the creation of a third idea or force, which then further establishes a binary opposition with one or more ideas or forces

(Jameson, 2009; Merrill, 1989). As distinguished journalism scholar John Merrill writes, 'Paradoxes abound in journalism. But conflicts and disagreements in journalism are healthy, not unhealthy. Contraries contend and clash and that is good . . . No journalist steps into the same journalistic river twice' (p. 5).

According to the entry in *Keywords* (Williams, 1989), as a method of understanding, the dialectic requires a logical application of reason in order to investigate the truth 'by discussion' (p. 106). It is also a means of describing and analyzing 'the interactions of contradictory or opposite forces' (p. 108). This approach is a corrective to the tendency towards 'technological determinism'—the belief that the technology drives all other changes—and suggests that technological change is one social force that contributes to the conditions that produce several *potential* outcomes. As Canadian media scholar Vincent Mosco writes, it is the balance of power between social forces that determines the direction of change: 'power sets the pattern for the principal direction of production, distribution and use' (Mosco, 1988, p. 3).

While we can consider this the framework for a 'mutual constitution' approach to technology and social relations (Mosco, 2004), Jameson is careful not to give equal weight to the initial opposites as the dialectic does not exist outside of social reality. 'Any opposition can be the starting point for a dialectic in its own right' (Jameson, 2009, p. 19), thus the power of each side to influence the other is proportional to its real social power and can change as the balance of social forces changes. 'Dialectic' also refers to a form of theorizing that uses the idea of opposing and contradictory social forces to question, analyze and interpret real world events. It is a methodology sometimes referred to as 'historical materialism'. My work is clearly situated in this field, which takes the form of a 'political economy' approach.

Political economy situates journalism as a cultural and intellectual endeavour—encased in a set of social relations—that operates both within and upon ('mutual constitution') a series of economic, political, ideological and cultural constructs that work simultaneously to both preserve and undermine the dominant relations of production and broader social relations that mark out the capitalist mode of production. Physically, we see the play of these social forces in the duality of the news commodity. This simply means that news has a 'use value', the information it contains and an exchange value, its commercial value measured against other commodities. It creates a contradiction because the use value is based on the principle of 'public interest' while the exchange value is based on the private interest of the economic beneficiary in the exchange process (usually a unit of media capital; shareholders, etc.). This duality is also embedded in the contradictory class location of journalists as social actors whose actions are constrained by power that exists outside the newsroom, which is at the same time economic, political and cultural in scope.

A key theoretical problem in the political economy tradition is how to uncover, understand *and undermine* unequal relationships of power in society. In relation to the study of news and journalism, this question is framed clearly: 'on balance [does] the media system . . . promote or undermine democratic institutions and practices. Are media a force for social justice or for oligarchy?' (McChesney, 2008a, p. 12). It is therefore relevant to question the news media's role in the generation of hegemonic and oppositional discourse in the public sphere.

I was introduced to the application of the dialectic as a matrix of contesting social forces and power relations within journalism, and as a method for the study of journalism, by the conservative-libertarian American news scholar John C. Merrill. In his *The Dialectic in Journalism*, Merrill discusses the 'triadic movement' of social forces and ideas both within and outside the news production process that can have a determining influence on the work of journalists and on the content of news. After nearly 20 years of research and study in this field, I am certain that a dialectical approach—recognizing the interplay of social forces (including technology) and historically interrogating the material and social circumstances in which change occurs—provides a full and useful account of what is actually happening; it allows us to understand the 'real conditions' in which we find ourselves and provides the tools for us to 'grasp' that reality and to argue for change. The dialectic approach is also an important method for understanding another key concept employed in *News 2.0*, the 'digital sublime' (Mosco, 2004). The 'digital sublime' is a state of mind—an ideological world-view—that elevates digital technologies above their actual place in the social order. The 'technological sublime' is a form of determinism that creates a state of uncritical magical thinking in which technologies are mythologized with 'seductive tales containing promises unfulfilled or even unfulfillable' (Mosco, 2004, p. 22). By employing the dialectic—in both senses in which it is used here—it is possible to avoid the 'sublime'; to see beyond the limits of technological determinism and to examine the digital economy and the emerging digital cultural-political landscape in such a way that it exposes the 'profound contradiction between the idea of liberal democracy and the growing control of the world's political economy by the concentrated power of its largest businesses' (Mosco, 2004, p. 59).

This book would not have been written were it not for the constant inspiration and enthusiasm of my students and colleagues. Over the past 15 years I have taught in several universities in Australia and New Zealand and, briefly, in the UK. In each place I have been amazed by the willingness of both colleagues and students to engage with ideas and to argue. Together we've had many discussions around the convergence of computing, media and telecommunications technologies and the impact of this revolutionary change on what we know as news and journalism. I am always delighted with the insights that emerge from these conversations: examples of what Pierre Levy calls 'collective intelligence'. We could all do a lot worse than listen to young, energetic journalists; they *are* the future of news.

Tēnei tā kōrua pukapuka

I owe a word of thanks to my students in the School of Communication Studies at Auckland University of Technology. In particular: Vincent Murwira, Tamara Walker, Imogen Neale, Niko Kloeten, Andre Huber, Angela Norton, Amy Williams, Vaughan Lovell, Grace Homney, Matt Samra, Melanie Smith, Michel Sam Mathew, Jane Sisson, Aroha Treacher, Dylan Quinnell, Sarah Murray, Andrew Hughes, Turei MacKey, Alistair Grey, Bridget Mills, Kieran Nash, Lucas de Jong, Adrian Hatwell, Rebekah White, Josh Gale and Danielle Street. I would also like to thank Amberleigh Jack for her research efforts and the flow of emails pointing me to something relevant that I might have otherwise missed. My colleagues Greg Treadwell and Mark Hayes provided constant encouragement. I am grateful to A&U publisher Elizabeth Weiss for never losing sight of what this book is about and to my editor Ann Lennox for her care and her always useful suggestions. The manuscript reviewers provided valuable feedback and prevented me from allowing some silly errors to cloud my argument. Any remaining mistakes are my own fault. My AUT colleague Wayne Hope is a friend and intellectual sparring partner. Our 'politics in the pub' sessions are always enlightening and have left an indelible mark on this book.

Martin Hirst
Auckland
Aotearoa/New Zealand
April 2010

1

Convergence, journalism and News 2.0

Welcome to the brave first decade of the twenty-first century, a decade which will destroy more science fiction futures than any ten year span that preceded it.

Charles Stross

In the introduction to *Toast*, a collection of short stories, science fiction writer Charles Stross writes that a 'fogbank of accelerating change' seems to 'swallow our proximate future'. He also writes that the pace of change in the period from the late 1960s to the present has been faster than at any other time in history. He adds that today 'if anything, it's accelerating' and that technological change is 'one-way'. There's no going back. Stross speculates, as sci-fi writers are encouraged to do, that the world may be heading towards what mathematician and computer scientist Vernor Vinge describes as a 'singularity'. In astronomy, a singularity would occur when a star dies, creating a high-density black hole. It would be the end of time for anyone near the star at this moment as enormous gravitational forces suck surrounding matter into the vortex.[1] In Stross's fiction, and in *News 2.0*, singularity is used as a metaphor for a spectacular and almost catastrophic event that—in a sense—ends one period of history at a single stroke. But it's not the end of our world; in dialectical terms it's the beginning of a new phase of history. Stross writes: 'At the singularity, the rate of change of technology becomes infinite; we can't predict what lies beyond it' (Stross, 2003, p. 13). For cultural studies theorist Henry Jenkins, this singularity—the birth of convergence culture—is defined by the clash of old and new, particularly in terms of media forms and media platforms. 'Contradictions, confusions, and multiple perspectives should be anticipated at a moment of transition where one media paradigm is dying and another is being born,' Jenkins argues. What Jenkins means by convergence culture is the period in history (the present and our immediate future) during which the technological shift from analogue to digital forms of communication—letters to emails, for example, or books to e-readers—creates new patterns of thinking and social relationships that move and develop at greater speeds and over greater distances. Vast amounts of digital data can be accessed and processed in real time, physical time and space appear to shrink, national borders are being overridden by transnational communities and even virtual ones such as the online gaming world Second Life. Facebook, for example, is now described as the fifth largest 'country' on the planet.

In his 2004 novel *Singularity Sky*, Stross uses the character of Burya Rubenstein, a revolutionary leader and journalist, to further define singularity as 'a historical cusp at which the rate of change goes exponential . . . the suddenly molten fabric of a society held too close to the blowtorch of progress'. For Stross, one aspect of a technological singularity is the point at which computer intelligence begins to outthink the human brain. According to computing and robotics professors cited by Stross that point is likely to be reached around 2035, and 'we cannot possibly know what life will be like' once artificial intelligence (AI) gets beyond our ability to control it. There's no doubt that scientists are working on the concept of artificial intelligence, but can they produce a super-computer with thinking abilities as incomprehensible to us, as Stross describes it, 'as ours are to a dog or a cat'? Futurist and Internet pioneer Jaron Lanier is a sceptic who doubts such claims (2010, p. 26) We will find out soon enough who is right; but the point here is that Stross is right *enough* about the singularity thesis. The world appears to be on a path of technological change that is constant and speeding up, following 'Moore's law', which states that computer power doubles every 18 months. It is also clear that humans are no longer only analogue creatures; we are increasingly digitally equipped and the convergence of computing and communication technologies is almost complete. In that sense, perhaps we have already experienced a mini-singularity in terms of technology. Machines are getting smarter, but perhaps not quite in the semi-human AI way. Not yet, anyway. We've been operating in a digital world now for long enough for it to have far-reaching and non-reversible effects on our lives, on the ways we work and relax and on many of our cultural norms. The media is already talking on a daily basis about the new social values of digital 'cyberculture' in terms that media scholar Mark Deuze (2006) describes as 'an expression of an increasingly individualized society in a globalized world'. News organizations were among the first to embrace convergence, mainly for reasons of business economics, but as Australian journalism scholar Stephen Quinn (2005) observed, convergence highlights a series of contradictions between the commercial expectations of the news capitalists and the aspirations of working journalists. As we shall explore, this is often cited as a major element of the current crisis in the news industry and the practice of journalism. Only one thing is clear: as convergence culture grows organ-ically from the digital revolution, as Charles Stross writes in *Toast*, 'The future is not going to be like the past any more—not even the near future.'

This is already evident in popular culture, as media sociologists Shayne Bowman and Chris Willis note; ideas, products, trends, styles and social mores appear to 'accelerate their way from the fringe to the mainstream with increasing speed' (2003, p. 7). Media scholar Naren Chitty describes the impact of globalization on the news media in similar terms. He says that the global and the local are now intimately intertwined in the global economy and through globalizing cultural linkages such as Hollywood blockbusters, McDonald's, Starbucks, Nike and Gap. 'Globalization has made the local explode in the global and the global implode on the local' (Chitty, 2000, p. 14). The impact on the global media has also been profound. In his 2009 La Trobe University annual media studies address, the managing director of the Australian Broadcasting Corporation, Mark Scott, said that the media is in a state of 'transition and turmoil' and on a 'revolutionary road' that has turned the old certainties of the media industry on their head (Scott, 2009): 'Daily, doomsayers beat the drums for newspapers, free-to-air television, regional media and investigative journalism.'

Scott also mentioned the global recession as a major factor in the decline of media advertising revenues and bottoming share prices. The global downturn of 2008–10, he argued, had 'profound effects' on the global business of news and media. The shift was so sudden and the fall so steep that Scott did not appear hopeful of a significant recovery any time soon. 'Executives, particularly those in the newspaper business, wonder whether the good times will ever come back.' Perhaps, at one level, it's too late for the good times to return because cyberculture turns the mediasphere on its head. In Burya Rubenstein's terms, globalization has 'ripped up social systems and economies and ways of thought like an artillery barrage', a 'hard take-off singularity' (Stross, 2004, p. 163). In 2010 we saw the near collapse of once-strong economies in southern Europe—Spain, Greece and Italy—while emerging nations on the fringes of the former Soviet Union were torn apart by economic and political crises. Labour unrest in China pricked a hole in that nation's economic bubble and the global debt crisis engulfed Latin America. An oil spill in the Gulf of Mexico threatened not only the livelihoods of millions, but was also an ecological catastrophe of immense proportions. A troop 'surge' in Afghanistan and Iraq failed to relieve pressure on global superpowers fighting an unpopular war that, after nine years of conflict, seemed to be spreading into Pakistan, rather than receding. When globalization and economic crisis combine with the mini-singularity of digital technologies, we experience the resulting state of profound change as chaos and flux. As Stross has another character say to Burya Rubenstein at a critical point in *Singularity Sky*, 'Talk you of tradition in middle of singularity?' Well, actually: 'Yes'. We *have* to talk of tradition, because the present *and the future* are products of historical events and forces; the basic elements of convergence culture have been present in our world for most of the 20th century—the telephone, the television and (in the last 80 years at least) the computer. So we should not be surprised by the strength of convergence culture; it is the culmination of historically situated processes that have percolated through the filter of combined and uneven development for nearly a century. Technologies, economies and social structures do not all move evenly or at the same pace across the globe. At some points in time, advanced societies give less-developed parts of the world a 'leg up' through the transfer of knowledge and techniques of production; at others, advanced areas are held back, or even defeated by what might be considered—technologically and socially speaking—inferior systems of production. In the emerging world of convergence and globalization there is not one form of digital culture that sits snugly across all social formations, nor across all individuals and groups within one particular social formation.

The term 'digital divide' describes the chasm that separates those with good access to the Internet and other digital technologies on one side and those with little or no access on the other. According to global statistics for Internet penetration, as of 30 June 2010, just over a quarter of the world's population had access to the Web (a slight increase over 2008 figures). The highest penetrations were in North America (77.4 per cent) and Europe (58.4 per cent) and the lowest was Africa with 10.9 per cent, which is up from 6.7 per cent in 2008 (Internet World Stats, 2010). The digital divide highlights the fact that there is no linear progression from analogue to digital technologies, nor is convergence culture necessarily an improvement on the analogue past.

American media scholar Robert McChesney also talks in terms that resemble Stross's 'singularity'; he argues that globally the communication industry, journalism and even the very democratic fabric of society has reached a 'critical juncture'. This juncture—to some degree a product of the 'communication and information revolution'—has a number of possible consequences. McChesney argues (2007, p. 1) that it can be 'a glorious new chapter in our history', or 'we may speak of it despondently, measuring what we have lost', or 'we may end up somewhere in between'. For some it's a bright future of 'life-streaming', the practice of uploading a significant part of what you see and do to a social networking site to share with the world; for others it is a bleak future of surveillance and a total lack of privacy. There will also be economic winners and losers, for this is the nature of global capitalism.

We can never know the future with any certainty, and according to a former director of The Institute for the Future, Roy Amara, we tend to overestimate the effect of a technology in the short term and underestimate the effect in the long term. This has become known as Amara's Law, and it reflects the tensions and contradictions that run through our understanding of digital technologies, what Deuze (2006, p. 66) calls the 'scrambled, manipulated, and converged' mediasphere. It is reasonable to assume that we are, perhaps, passing through a technological and economic singularity in the era of digital globalization. The co-director of the Media Center at the American Press Institute, Dale Peskin, has described the recent past as an 'era of enlightened anxiety', a time of 'harsh truths and puzzling paradoxes' that we were 'thrust into' without much warning. We cannot know for certain the exact point in time when this change occurred. Indeed, sometimes the rate of change is too slow to be noticeable. A singularity takes time to build momentum and we can now see—with the benefit of hindsight—that the seeds of our digital future were sown in the 1930s when German engineer Conrad Zuse developed the first programmable machines using valves. The first tottering steps were taken in the years after the Second World War, when experiments began with giant super-computers (which were minnows by today's standards). In 1945 Vannevar Bush created the first hypertext language that eventually—some 45 years later—gave us the Internet. The world took more confident steps towards convergence in the late 1960s and early 1970s when computing power was increased, simultaneously miniaturised and coupled with telephony and satellites. By the 1980s, we began to run towards the digital future: IBM released the first PC and Apple launched its Mac range. By the end of that decade the world was connected to the Internet. Today, wireless connections enable computing 'on the go' and a simple phone is more powerful than the first generation of desk-top computers.

Web 2.0: The singularity arrives

> Web 2.0 is the era when people have come to realize that it's not the software that enables the Web that matters so much as the services that are delivered over the Web.
>
> **Tim O'Reilly**

We started to go truly digital in the 1990s, with mobile phones, compact discs, DVDs, Web browsers, email and ubiquitous computing in our school, work and leisure lives. The digital singularity—and point of no return—can be traced to the emergence of what we now call 'Web 2.0', a term describing the rise of social networks and powerful applications that can be accessed on mobile devices. The concept of Web 2.0 is generally considered to have risen out of the ashes of the dot. com crash of 2001. The major difference between Web 2.0 and its Web 1.0 predecessor is the level of interaction between users. Until the late 1990s the Web was static, or 'read-only'. Web 2.0 can perhaps be characterized as the 'read–write' Web; creating and uploading content is now much easier and does not require hours of hand-coding in hypertext mark-up language. Web pioneer Tim O'Reilly is usually credited with defining the term. Rather than seeing Web 2.0 as a new configuration of hardware, he prefers to call it a 'business revolution' in computing that recognizes the importance of the Internet as a 'platform' utilising applications that 'harness network effects to get better [as] more people use them' (O'Reilly, 2006). Social-media blogger Christopher Lynn (2008) describes Web 2.0 as 'platforms and tools that increase communication, collaboration and connection', a more socially oriented Web architecture and user-generated content creating a 'two-way exchange'. According to O'Reilly, some of the applications that make Web 2.0 possible and practical are: Google AdSense, file-sharing and bit-torrent technologies, tagging and sharing content, social networking and wikis, which are online documents that can be edited by several users at once. He adds that it is also about 'leveraging collective intelligence' and monetizing the clickstream—the record of our Web browsing. Increasingly Web-delivered services, such as shopping and banking, have come to include news in a variety of formats and across a variety of platforms. Indeed, news is going mobile, being accessed on phones, PDAs and wireless devices such as Kindle books, the iPad and other electronic readers.

The first predictions about the possible impacts of rapid advances in computing and Internet technologies began to be publicly aired about a decade ago. Some—like wearable computers—are still developmental and experimental, but digital downloads, the 'read–write' Web and touch-screen mobile phones are with us already, and the pace of change has not slowed down much, if at all. At the same time as the development of Web 2.0 began to gain traction, *Time* magazine named 'You' (and I guess, by extension, 'Me') as its person of the year. It was a gimmicky concept that included a special mirrored panel on the cover, instead of the usual portrait of a newsworthy person. Inside, a sizeable group of Internet entrepreneurs—bloggers and social-networking stars—were celebrated. It was an homage to the user-generated culture of the early 21st century, a culture that is described as 'convergent' by media scholar Henry Jenkins in his 2007 book *Convergence Culture*. The subtitle of Jenkins' book is *Where old and new media collide*. We are living through that collision today. Some are celebrating, declaring that a new age of democratic media is emerging. Others, such as reformed new-media spruiker Andrew Keen, are less enthusiastic. Keen argues that convergence has brought with it a flattening and thinning out of culture. He says we are living in a time where 'high culture' has been hollowed out and replaced with a narcissistic culture of the self. He believes that convergence presents us with a distorting mirror, one that makes all of us look beautiful and smart, when in fact we're losing all sense of community, identity and collective intelligence (Keen, 2007). Keen describes this as the 'cult of the amateur', and he doesn't like it. More optimistically, Mark Deuze (2006) prefers to think of convergence and digital culture as bringing about the remaking of human communication—a communication mediated by the convergence of computing and the ubiquitous screen. He sees this convergence as the extension of our *participation* in media-making and in the circulation (*remediation*) of information, but also our further involvement in the assembly and editing (*bricolage*) of mediated and remediated cultural artefacts. There is no doubt that convergence culture is a double-edged sword—we should expect nothing less in the world of the singularity—a time of uncertainty and rapid change.

The convergence singularity is not yet over, but at the close of the first decade of the 21st century most of us take for granted the microchips that power everything from cameras to cars to mobile phones. It's now a commonplace notion that we live in the 'digital age'. We hardly think about computers any more; they have moved us from what Canadian media scholar Vincent Mosco called the 'digital sublime' to the digital mundane. We experience digital living through new gadgets and applications. Often there is no choice; they are pushed at us daily in advertising and other forms of communication. Devices such as iPods, iPads, iPhones, Wii toys and the Xbox, laptops, in-car navigation systems, social network sites like Facebook and even the micro-blogging service Twitter no longer seem strange. It's become unusual not to have a high-end personal communication device or a Facebook profile—at least that's how it might seem in most affluent Western countries today. The World Wide Web is no longer just another form of mass media with a unidirectional messaging system; it is now interactive and home to massive amounts of user-generated content (UGC). While the world of Web 2.0—characterized by social networking—cannot be represented by a single site; the YouTube video-sharing site perhaps comes closest. YouTube is one of the world's most popular and heavily trafficked websites. In the first six months of 2006, when it was relatively new, YouTube's traffic grew nearly 300 per cent, from 4.9 to 19.6 million unique hits per month (Freeman and Chapman, 2007). By late 2009 YouTube was claiming up to one billion hits per day.

However, the change from analogue to digital culture goes deeper than exponentially expanding video viewing on YouTube. The digital age is also a time of cultural convergence that, according to Jenkins, crosses over everything: economics, politics, our social lives and even the way we think. This is now an unstoppable process and the pace of change is likely to quicken as more broadband cable and wireless 'hot spots' are rolled out around the world. Technical experts say the 'video-centric' nature of 'fast-pipe' broadband will further increase the multiple ways we use screens—as televisions and computers and mobile phones—and also increase the amount of media we consume: more news, entertainment, lifestyle and sport content pushed through converged screens and telecommunications devices (Canning, 2009). ABC boss Mark Scott says that fast broadband opens up a 'multi-channel, multi-platform world of the future' that offers exciting prospects for content-providers and advertisers. Other commentators are not so sanguine: one calls high-speed broadband a 'television killer' that will also render decades of media regulation 'outdated and irrelevant' (Day, 2009, p. 27). There's no doubt that both versions of a possible near future are valid. Opposing views are part of the process of combined and uneven development that typifies the playing out of the digital dialectic, a discussion that occurs in the media industry across the globe. There are utopian and dystopian aspects of convergence culture, and there will be winners and losers among both producers and consumers. Australian media commentator Mark Day says that the major players (governments and global media or telecommunications companies) are 'preparing to stake out the future battlefield', including the spaces in which social networking, marketing and advertising intersect. The reason is simple: that's where the money is going. Or, perhaps to rephrase that, these are the areas from where future profits might conceivably be generated.

It might seem that we are entering another 'golden age'; the power of almost limitless computing, linked to satellites, high-speed fibre-optic cable and cheap mobile telephony is supposed to make our lives easier. The optimistic outlook of the digital pioneers—the founders of the Internet and the inventors of the thousands of applications that we can access through our browsers—would have us believe that many of the world's problems can be solved by the application of 'digital thinking'. This was certainly the attitude that informed digital pioneers such as Vint Cerf, Nicholas Negroponte and Douglas Rushkoff, who predicted that the unfolding Internet age would promote a new era of global democratic politics. Unfortunately, as we are reminded on an almost daily basis, this is not always the case. The global economic crisis that bit into the world's financial markets in 2008, war, failed states, famine, environmental disasters, genocide, political and economic corruption, family and child abuse, poverty and lack of opportunity for vast sections of the world's population are part of our daily diet of news and information. The news industry has not been immune to the crisis that accompanied the global financial meltdown. Neither have journalists who throughout 2008 and 2009 were losing jobs and confidence in their futures in almost equal measure.

Does journalism have a future?

> There is no future for journalism without journalists and the trends are not good.
>
> **Vincent Mosco**

Mosco is rightfully pessimistic about the future of journalism: the trends *aren't* good. He's also right that without journalists there is no future for journalism. But, strangely, this is a contested notion. Many media scholars would disagree, citing the rise of so-called citizen journalism, crowdsourcing of the news and the explosion of social media as positive developments in the digital age.[2] Mosco would suggest that these utopian sentiments are manifestations of the idea of the 'digital sublime', demonstrating the myth-making potential of digital technologies when viewed outside of political or economic contexts. Mosco (2004) prefers to consider the situation dialectically: that is, from the standpoint of the 'mutual constitution' of technological and social forces existing in tension and affecting each other and which, ultimately, shape the age of 'News 2.0'. In this context the dialectic is represented in the process of combined and uneven development, in which technological change pushes economics and social forces in one direction, but the economic, cultural and social forces of global media systems also contribute to the final 'shape' of technologies and their deployment. Therefore, it would be premature and one-sided to think that social media technologies (Twitter, Facebook, YouTube, etc.) will overcome the news industry, or that collaborative efforts between amateurs and professionals (crowdsourcing) will replace the need for, or the corp of, professional journalists any time soon. Instead, the process of combined and uneven development signals that the news industry is compelled to engage with open source innovation (citizen journalism, etc.) in an attempt—so far successful—to secure its short-term survival and to push into the distant future the question of its own demise. This does not mean, however, that we can ignore the questions raised by the digital optimists about the apparent power of social media and Web 2.0 applications to significantly affect the future of journalism. This book addresses these questions from a perspective similar to that of Vincent Mosco and the political economists, and puts the issues into an historical context, albeit the limited context of the history of Web 2.0. Indeed, the history of News 2.0 is still being written. It is still being lived too. That is why the questions it raises are so important. At one level, as journalists or as consumers of news we still have time to intervene and shape the future because we are, as Robert McChesney argues, at a 'critical juncture'. The critical nature of this timeframe forces us to ask: Does journalism—as a trade, a craft or a profession—have a future? Can journalism survive the Internet? Should we worry if the news industry collapses entirely and what would this mean for democratic discourse and the public sphere? These are not just rhetorical questions; there are two trends that are having a profound effect on the news media and, according to some observers, could actually mean the collapse of the news industry and the disappearance of journalism as we know it.

The first issue we need to consider is the crisis of profitability in the global news industry that has seen scores of newspapers close and television lose its grip on audiences. Television is still the dominant medium, but it is under challenge from online gaming, social media and Internet-based news services. Advertising revenues across the mainstream media (MSM) are collapsing and online revenues are not yet strong enough to replace them. Coupled with the global financial crisis which began in 2008, this means that news organizations, including some of the world's leading media brands, are in trouble. Between 2003 and 2009, the share price of the company that owns the *New York Times* and the *Boston Globe* shrank more than 90 per cent: from US$50 to less than the US$4 cover price of a *Times* Sunday edition. The giant Hearst Corporation also considered closing the *San Francisco Chronicle*, a significant American news masthead. In March 2009, the *Seattle Post-Intelligencer* closed its print edition and the *Christian Science Monitor* ceased publication of its daily edition. Both organizations shed workers and announced that they would maintain an online-only edition. Thousands of journalists and newsroom staff around the world lost their jobs in 2008 and 2009. While the situation did turn around somewhat in the latter months of 2009, at the time of writing it seems this crisis is far from over.

A second consideration, which suggests that the news media has been hit by a 'perfect storm', is the exponential growth of alternative sources of news and news-like information via the World Wide Web. Significantly, most of this content is free and this has jolted editors and executives to consider the ways in which the news media and traditional styles of reportage may, or may not, adapt in the global convergence culture. The changes have been dramatic in just over a decade. In 1999 there were no blogs, only a handful of mobile-phone cameras and very few news websites with video or audio content. By 11 September 2001, technology had progressed to the point that amateur footage of the New York terror attacks was available within hours, but the bulk of the news was carried around the globe by traditional network television and news-cable stories. Three years later, when the 2004 Boxing Day tsunami devastated communities on both sides of the Indian Ocean, radio bulletins and news websites were carrying the news within minutes. Amateur video footage, cameraphone images and email reports from survivors came soon after and the whole world was fully aware of the scale of the disaster within hours.

Then, in July 2005, images of another terrorist attack—this time in London—were shot on mobile phones and emailed or text-messaged to media outlets within minutes of the bombs detonating on buses and underground trains. In February 2009, when bushfires ripped through the Australian state of Victoria, eventually killing some 200 people, news was delivered across a range of platforms (many of which did not exist in 1999) within minutes. News was sent as a series of short alerts to mobile phones; social networking sites such as Facebook quickly became forums for condolences and shocked reactions. The Twitter micro-blogging application was used as a two-way system for alerting ABC newsrooms about the location and direction of fire fronts and warning people to prepare for an approaching front. Within nine hours on 7 February 2009, 1526 reports were broadcast and 574 news website items appeared on the Victorian bushfires. All of this material was instantly available to a global as well as an Australian audience. Time and distance are no longer formidable barriers to the rapid spread of news—particularly bad news. It appears that 2009 was something of a watershed in this regard with anti-government uprisings in Iran and terrorist attacks in Mumbai generating huge interest in the power of social networks to compete with mainstream media as news channels.

The question of journalism's future is intimately linked—though in this book treated separately—to the future of news, particularly news in the form that we have known it for most of the 20th century. We can call the previous industrial model of news production and consumption 'News 1.0' to distinguish it from the new economic and cultural forms of news production and delivery that are emerging in the 21st century: 'News 2.0'. This term deliberately echoes the nomenclature used to describe the new forms of computing and communication convergence that has become 'Web 2.0'. The decline of the traditional (some say 'old') media and the parallel rise of the new (some say 'postmodern') media is a complex process. Only part of the answer to the questions surrounding the future of journalism lies in the digital technologies that can make any of us instant reporters—what we have come to know as the 'accidental' or 'citizen' journalist—a complete explanation only comes into view through the lens of political economy and rigorous cultural studies research.

It would seem self-evident that the majority of our experience of emerging convergence culture is mediated by digital technologies. After all, without these new and effective tools there could be no such thing as an accidental journalist. It is the mobile phone and the digital video camera, coupled with a wireless or broadband Internet connection, which bystanders and eyewitnesses use to capture events that can later be turned into news via television, websites and blogs. Now that YouTube is hosting 'live' television-like broadcast and narrowcast services, it is easy for anyone to create their own amateur news program on the Web with a potential audience of billions. Social networking sites, alongside the 'broadcast yourself' portals such as YouTube and Flickr, have changed forever the way that news is created and consumed. But to believe that this is a result only of digital convergence is to see only half of the picture. It is necessary to reject the notion of 'technological determinism'—the idea that technology is alone in driving the process of convergence and change in the digital age—in preference to a more complex and dialectical explanation. As noted earlier, the change we are experiencing is a process of combined and uneven development in which technology exists within a set of mutually determining social relations: technology does not and cannot exist in a vacuum outside the social, economic, political and cultural conditions under which it is invented, distributed, employed and integrated into our daily lives. Combined and uneven development simply means that the technological, economic, social and cultural forces that shape our society, and the direction in which it is moving, all impact on each other. Any one of these factors can act as an accelerant or a brake on development at any particular point in time. One example of this is the 'techno-legal' or 'techno-ethical' time gap (Hirst and Patching, 2007). This refers to the ways in which technology can enable a new process or function—such as digital file sharing—but without any legal or ethical protocols to regulate the function. As demonstrated in the famous Napster case, legal action taken by the global music industry against copyright-breaching downloads took years to resolve.

If you're someone who follows the news, or who has an interest in what's happening to the world's media, you're probably only too aware of the dramatic changes that have occurred over the past five to 10 years. To some, the news industry appears close to collapse and many influential people are suggesting that newspapers may cease to exist within another decade. More closures are likely if nothing is done to reverse their economic misfortune. This book puts the collapse of the traditional MSM into an historical perspective, one that takes into account the technology but also looks beyond digital gadgets to explore the economic, political, social and cultural factors that have contributed to this disastrous outlook for the news industry. It also examines another question: If the news industry is rapidly disappearing, what's happening to journalism and journalists?

---

[1] Other writers and futurists talk of the singularity as a point at which uploading of human minds and memory to a matrix of computers becomes possible.

[2] For example, Atton and Hamilton, 2008; Bruns, 2005, 2008; Deuze, 2006; Gillmor, 2006

2
Why is journalism in crisis?

> Journalism entered the twenty-first century caught in a paradox of its own making ... journalism is also under widespread attack, from politicians, philosophers, the general public, and even from journalists themselves.
>
> **Ian Hargreaves**

Ian Hargreaves is a professor of journalism at Cardiff University and had an illustrious career in British journalism; for 20 years he worked for the BBC, *The Guardian* and *The Independent*, among other postings. His book, *Journalism: Truth or Dare?*, published in 2003, explains the paradox he refers to above: the tense and contradictory relationships that exist between journalism, economics, popular culture and politics—or, in other words, the dialectical tensions between the public-interest role of the news media, the needs and desires of the news consumers, the profit motive of capitalism and the controlling power of the State. The exploration of this multi-layered relationship will take up a large part of this book, but the first task is to define and describe the crisis in journalism. It takes several forms, each of them distinct, but all interlocked.

In the Western world today, the public is losing confidence in the mainstream news media's ability to do a good job. There is the perception that journalists and editors are failing in their duty to promote and protect the public interest. This is one very important reason why alternative forms of news production—variously called 'citizen journalism' (Rosen, 2008), 'alternative journalism' (Atton and Hamilton, 2008) or 'produsage' (Bruns, 2008)—have generated so much interest in recent years. Readers, viewers and listeners no longer readily accept that what they are getting from their news sources is always reliable, accurate, fair and balanced. There is a feeling among some consumers and old-time journalists that newspaper reportage has been replaced by far too much opinion. To some extent this may well reflect the fact that newspapers can no longer compete with broadcast and Internet outlets to be 'first' with the news. In the face of competition from the immediacy of online news media, the role of newspapers has had to change in order for them to stay relevant. There's also a sense in which the news media is now seen as part of the global entertainment industry—a distraction, rather than a means of informing the public (Thussu, 2007). Critics argue that informative real news has been replaced by endless moral panics, celebrity news and emotion. It is titillation, not information. All of this negative opinion about the news media is compounded by technological change that appears to be beyond our control. In an age when anyone, it seems, can be a journalist, or at least act like one, the question is being asked: Do we need professional reporters any more? Though, it must be said, this is not a new question: it was raised just over a decade ago by New York University professor of journalism Jay Rosen in his book *What Are Journalists For?* He concluded that journalists don't just report the world, but that they are also 'part of the structure that holds it up' and that they make politics 'worth our time and trouble' (Rosen, 1999, p. 285). In other words, both journalists and a commonly circulating repertoire of news are important to the fabric of liberal democratic politics. In 1999 Jay Rosen thought that this role would be even more important as the tidal wave of information—some good, some bad—was unleashed by the World Wide Web, but he also thought it would lead to a new role for journalists, which would be to make our time spent with various media 'more productive' in terms of having a functioning civil society. Journalism, Rosen said, would play the role of inviting people to join in public events and civic conversations; hence, news needed to be 'current' and 'accurate' to work 'as a map, guiding us towards the places where public challenges are found' (Rosen, 1999, p. 297).

Today, it would seem, we need this type of accurate map even more as the embedding of the Internet and the World Wide Web in our daily lives produces economic, social, political and cultural impacts on traditional journalism and the mainstream media. The rise of do-it-yourself

(DIY) news and information makes sensible navigation through the maze of sites that make up the Web even more difficult. It has led some media-studies academics to suggest a new role for journalists: one as filters of information, rather than collectors, reporters and editors of original news. The thought behind this is that now that almost everyone can upload their own versions of 'news' to the Internet, the function of journalism is to act as an intelligent sifter of the billions of bytes supplied by amateurs. Australian media academic Axel Bruns calls this a shift from 'gatekeeping' to 'gatewatching', which he suggests might help avoid the 'somewhat patronising stance of industrial journalism' (2008, p. 73).

Bruns believes that the MSM model of journalism is wrongly premised on the idea that audiences cannot make intelligent decisions for themselves because they are 'too distanced' from the news flow. His cultural-studies colleague at Brisbane's Queensland University of Technology, John Hartley, argues in a similar vein that journalism must be reoriented to take account of the 'writing public'. The function of this reoriented journalism is to 'sift existing data ... not to generate new information'; a process he calls 'redaction' (Hartley, 2008a, p. 48). Further, Hartley suggests that it is now possible to imagine a society 'in which everybody is a journalist', but he adds that when it arrives 'the last people to know may be professional journalists'. This is an attractive argument at one level—it seems to suggest a more democratic world in which there is greater participation in politics and civil society; it also appears to speak to the general public disillusionment with professional journalism. But we also have to consider the alternative proposition that the overwhelming array of new content on the Web—particularly news as generated and disseminated through social networking sites—is also creating conditions under which there is information overload and a splitting of both markets for news and the public sphere itself. One of the most controversial themes in discussions of the Internet's impact on news and journalism has been what we might call the 'fragmentation' thesis. Economically, this is easily seen in the breakdown of large mass markets for news (particularly in radio, television and newspapers). In social and cultural terms it can be approached via the metaphor of the 'national conversation'. As the market is fragmented, so too is our community of common interest; our conversations take place in smaller circles that have little or no connection with each other. To some extent, as this continues, we lose our ability to generate a collective response to common issues. Supporters of the 'digital sublime' would argue that we are now talking to more people than ever before (via social media networks for example). Critics might counter with the argument that the conversations are scattered and focus more on personal (leisure-oriented) topics rather than issues with a high public interest (politics-oriented) quotient. Even more alarming is the so-called 'echo chamber' effect in which a small group of loud voices bounce around in cyberspace creating a lot of heat, but no light. A decade ago, Jay Rosen was worried that the civic and civil society that is generated around an imperfect news market was fragmenting; splitting into ever smaller and more arcane niche publics who seemed to spend less and less time talking to each other, outside small circles of like-minded individuals. He was right; the process of public atomisation has in fact increased since 1999. This is most evident in the 'Broadcast Yourself' mantra, which is the catchy marketing slogan adopted by YouTube. The fragmentation is also clear in the decline of mass newspaper readership and television viewing audiences in highly industrialized nations, where choice of media seems overwhelming at times and news consumption is decreasing overall.

Cardiff University media-studies academic Cynthia Carter points to the ways in which the 'lived culture of citizenship' is changing, particularly for teenagers and young adults. Her research demonstrates that many young adults are disengaged from the political process that 'largely ignores their interests' (Carter, 2009, p. 35). Blogger and Internet pundit Andrew Keen is one of the harshest critics of the DIY information world of Web 2.0, which he argues contains 'less culture, less reliable news, and a chaos of useless information'. His real concern—what he calls the 'chilling reality'—is the 'disappearance of truth' (Keen, 2007, p. 16). Keen's position is the diametric opposite of that put forward by John Hartley and Axel Bruns; rather than seeing a bright and democratic future, Keen sees a threat to the quality of public discussion and political discourse. What they all agree on is the fact that the pace of change is quickening and that we are faced with having to make some serious choices. This change appears perhaps as a dichotomy—do we embrace the chaos and uncertainty of DIY news, or do we rally around professional journalism and defend the current institutions of the mainstream media?

Unfortunately, it's not that simple. We may be at McChesney's 'critical juncture' in the history and development of modern communication systems, and certainly there are some difficult political decisions to be made, but, in a sense, the chance to continue business as usual has passed. The mainstream media and the production system of industrial journalism are changing and the embedding of digital technologies in our everyday lives—Vincent Mosco's 'digital mundane'—has a lot to do with it. The old media may not be dead yet, but it no longer has the vigour of youth as it did in the last decades of the 20th century. It is necessary to put the debate about News 2.0 into some perspective, though. It's not 'Chicken Little' time: the sky is not falling *yet* and mass media is not *yet* dead and buried. However, it seems clear that newspapers, radio and television are declining. One consequence of this is that the very function and professionalism of the news media—with its ethic of public interest—is now under question.

British media scholar Mike Wayne suggests that a series of inherent contradictions are in play within the global media economy; the key one involves the ways in which the emerging digital modes of news development and production are in a state of creative tension with the existing analogue social and economic relations of media production (2003, p. 39). The digital economy—not yet fully formed, but clearly beginning to dominate the old analogue economy—has led to what Wayne calls a 'general culturalization' of news production and a situation in which communication has come to hold a more central role in the general contours of the world economy. This can be directly related to the crisis of profitability in the newspaper industry, which retains a highly analogue form despite its growing online presence: digital production, reproduction and distribution of news, information and entertainment commodities 'abolishes at a stroke' a large proportion of the once productive labour formerly involved in their production (Wayne, 2003, p. 47). At the same time that this has a positive impact on the cost structures of media enterprises, it also cuts into their profits in a number of ways—such as a reduction in advertising revenues, for example. As McChesney points out, new technologies, rising labour productivity and a period of rising profit margins are not any kind of insurance against the vagaries of the business cycle of booms and busts in the capitalist economy. He writes: 'a high rate of accumulation [of assets] can itself lead to crisis . . . overexpansion of capacity . . . is an essential feature of a capitalist economy, [particularly] in the monopoly stage and in the current phase of accelerating globalization and new technology' (McChesney, 2008a, p. 301). Again, it is not hard to see this being played out on an almost daily basis in the global media economy; one of the key problems confronting large news organizations in many parts of the world is that they have been loaded up with unproductive debt as a result of asset-buying sprees when the economy was in better shape and when global telecommunications and media industries were being deregulated. Adding this debt burden to the steady decline in revenues and turnover is a recipe for disaster because 'the economic laws of motion of capitalism remain in force' (McChesney, 2008a, p. 304). It is also clear that dialectically the positive and negative impacts of the debt crisis are spread unevenly across the digital economy. One area of particular concern addressed in this book is the impact of the global downturn in the news industry—and associated questions of its future economic viability—on the roles and functions of journalists. News workers (journalists, printers, camera and studio operators, online technicians, producers, editors, advertising sales staff and distribution workers) are on the front lines of these changes.

Over the past decade a number of books by senior journalists, former journalists and academics have questioned the very idea of a profession or a craft of news production. Many, such as Ian Hargreaves, suggest that there is a paradox, or even a crisis. The paradox is the 'either–or' proposition that sets two potential futures in opposition to each other. In this context will 'professional' journalism continue, or will it be replaced by an ever-expanding field in which 'everyone' contributes their own journalism to the mix? The news industry's crisis has two aspects: economic and cultural. Some think it's too late to stem the impending disaster, or that it doesn't matter. Others want to find a solution, if there is one. We've known about the crisis for more than a decade, but the intractable contradiction at the core of the problem— the unresolved tension between the public-interest ethos of journalism and the insatiable appetite for profit that drives the global capitalist economy from crisis to crisis—has not been resolved. News is an informational commodity in our society; it circulates according to the logic of capital accumulation and its public interest use-value is always overshadowed by its economic exchange-value (Hirst and Patching, 2007). This argument is taken up in later sections of the book; but first: What does this mean for journalists?

What are journalists for? (Redux)

Journalists do not join the parade because their job is to report on the parade.

Jay Rosen

In 1999, Jay Rosen argued that contemporary American journalists were increasingly out of touch with their audiences, that journalistic analysis of current events was weak, and that reporters and editors based their work on some dubious assumptions about American political and civic life. Today, Jay Rosen is a prolific blogger, author and champion of what he has termed 'open source' journalism: collaboration between audiences and producers to create news that is available to everyone, everywhere. The analogy is to 'open source' software and operating systems such as Linux. Rosen's work in this area informs a large part of the debate that is currently raging about the shape and future of journalism in the 21st century. When Rosen posed his provocative question in 1999, he felt that the tremors of dissatisfaction had been reverberating through American journalism for at least the previous 10 years. At that time, Rosen's answer was to begin agitating for and developing the principles of what he called 'civic journalism'. Civic journalism was about reconnecting with the original roots of modern journalism—the close relationship between reporting and civic duty; in a sense, a return to the democratic foundations of what is generally termed the Fourth Estate model of journalism. Ironically, Rosen may well have unleashed a demon rather than a saviour. The idea of civic journalism is all but forgotten today, but it sowed the seeds of what, in the digital age, is often called 'citizen journalism'. This is a problematic term, but it has caught the popular imagination and today can mean almost anything—from blogs to *Wikipedia* and CNN's heavily branded *iReport*. It covers eyewitness accounts, in some instances blogs and even 140-character 'tweets', but is it too broad to have any real analytical meaning any more?

Rosen is credited with producing the most useful working definition of citizen journalism in 2008: 'When the people formerly known as the audience employ the press tools they have in their possession to inform one another, *that's* citizen journalism'. He also suggests that the strategy behind this definition is to 'eliminate any reference to the news media as pipe through which current information vital to the public has to flow' (Rosen 2008). Citizen journalism is used as a catch-all phrase, but should be more tightly defined and used alongside other terms such as 'amateur' and 'accidental' journalist, or even 'user-generated' *news-like* content. For now, it will suffice in the context of a discussion about the crisis in mainstream journalism.

The rise of citizen journalism, embodied particularly in YouTube's 'Broadcast Yourself' slogan, is itself now contributing to the conditions of crisis in which journalism continues to flounder. Rosen's experiments with open-source journalism projects are an interesting attempt to revitalise journalism from below and they don't always meet with approval from those in the profession. So far he has collaborated with *Wired* magazine and the American political blog *Huffington Post* on what he calls 'pro-am' assignments, in which amateur reporters collaborate with professionals to produce news that doesn't follow a mainstream model. A key premise of much analysis of the broad 'citizen journalism' movement is that it has grown out of a sense of dissatisfaction with the mainstream media and a recognition that, in many respects, the MSM has failed to live up to its 20th century promises.[1] In a sense, putting this dissatisfaction at the forefront of the conditions under which citizen journalism might flourish is unnecessary. Criticism of the mainstream news media is not limited to the margins, or to those with an activist bent.

Neil Henry's *American Carnival* has a subtitle that tells us exactly what he thinks is wrong with the news media today: *Journalism under siege in an age of new media* (Henry, 2007a). Henry is a former foreign correspondent and now a journalism professor at the University of California-Berkeley. Henry is African-American, and he devotes a chapter to a discussion of race in the American news media; it's not a pretty story. But it is Henry's vision of a failing system of journalism that is most interesting. Declining newsroom job opportunities, stagnant or falling wages for journalists and shifting consumption patterns are among his headline issues. So too is the rise of fake news from PR hucksters and the suborning of the public sphere of democratic discourse and true citizenship into a tawdry marketplace for second-rate emotions, cut-price celebrity and shoddy thinking. What we are now experiencing—the downside perhaps of convergence culture—is the almost complete marketization of democracy: 'exercising choice . . . restricted by market principles' (Fenton, 2009, p. 55). Neil Henry asks a very important question: In the 'New Media age', does professional journalism matter as much as it once did?

It's not hard to agree with Henry's argument that journalistic standards might be falling in the face of an unregulated free-for-all on the Web. In Henry's view we are in an age of 'transformation and disintegration' in which news reporters seem to be failing in journalism's mission to help sustain a democratic civil society (2007a, pp. 31–2). Neil Henry is a digital pessimist; he doesn't see a bright new future as Web 2.0 changes our lives forever. Instead he sees a world in which truth and public interest is no longer a strong 'cultural value' defining news. In an opinion piece for the *San Francisco Chronicle*, Henry (2007b) was at his gloomy best: 'a world where professional journalism, practiced according to widely accepted ethical values, is a rapidly diminishing feature in our expanding news and information systems, as we escape to the Web to experience the latest "new" thing.'

Another key text that sheds some light on the crisis in journalism is Philip Meyer's *The Vanishing Newspaper* (2004). It carries the subtitle: *Saving journalism in the Information Age*. Meyer is well credentialled to comment on the vanishing newspaper: he was a reporter and manager for more than 25 years before ending a distinguished academic career as emeritus professor of journalism at the University of North Carolina at Chapel Hill. Meyer's thesis is that the traditional business models that made newspapers attractive and profitable investments have been disrupted by technological change. Early in the text, Meyer notes that some of the most interesting and innovative new forms of news are being created by non-journalists—that is, by people who are not trained in news-gathering and writing and who are often 'ignorant' of the culture of professional journalism. Meyer attempts to develop a model of journalism for the future that can be both profitable and socially responsible, but he was an early critic of Jay Rosen's civic journalism movement, describing it as 'camouflage' for any 'vested interests' attempting to harness the 'power of the media' to their cause (Meyer, 1995). He was concerned that the traditional media value of objective reporting would be lost in a sea of biased opinion masquerading as news. Meyer's proposed solution was what he called 'objectivity of method', as opposed to 'objectivity of results'. He explained this as the application of a scientific method to journalism, arguing that is ideologically safe because 'it requires no departure at all from the enlightenment philosophy that gave us our stance of prickly individualism'. More recently, media scholars Chris Atton and James Hamilton have argued that what they call 'alternative journalism' is a fundamental challenge to the epistemology of journalism in the MSM. They argue that journalism based on 'cultural capital', rather than financial capital, might lead to the production of 'different forms of knowledge' that may challenge the ways in which traditional journalism structures our view of the world (Atton and Hamilton, 2008, p. 127).

In contrast to Atton and Hamilton's progressive views, Philip Meyer has fairly strong free market and libertarian tendencies and in his argument with the civic journalism movement he relies on the philosophers of bourgeois freedoms to denounce what he calls the 'easily-perverted field of critical theory', which he sees as lying behind civic journalism's attack on objectivity. In 1995, Philip Meyer was like the boy with his finger in the dyke: he knew he was doing the right thing, but also that the tide and current might eventually overwhelm him. He ends with an offered compromise: 'Public journalism and investigative journalism need one another, and if we recognize that we have a chance of preserving our cherished First Amendment traditions and responsibilities.' Perhaps the problem today is that we don't know who is going to pay for expensive investigative journalism in the future.

Lawyer and blogger Scott Gant (2007) takes a different view of the 'cherished' First Amendment in *We're All Journalists Now*. This book also comes with a helpful subtitle: *The transformation of the press and reshaping of the law in the Internet Age*. Gant is a partner in a Washington DC law firm and specializes in expensive corporate litigation; he also seems to share some of Philip Meyer's libertarian views about the sanctity of the free market, particularly the marketplace of ideas. Gant sees the problem as one of media organizations chasing audiences who are no longer 'turned on' by the news and as a result 'diminishing the breadth and quality of reporting'. He sees journalism rapidly becoming 'just another form of content', indistinguishable from advertising, public relations, marketing, blogs or entertainment. However, he also argues that the First Amendment right to freedom of the press does not just apply to the institutional media, but also to non-professionals who wish to publish their views, even the 'unabashedly opinionated'. It is, he says, particularly important to argue this now because of the eroding boundaries between 'professional and non-traditional journalists' afforded by the rise of digital publishing technologies. He concludes that the American legal system's keystone protection of free speech unfairly privileges professional journalists and creates a 'caste system'. Instead, it should recognize the equality of professionals and amateurs alike: 'It's time to recognize that technology has caught up with the First Amendment and truly made us all journalists now.' This is a strong argument, despite the fact that the many features that distinguish professionals from non-professionals might be in dispute. It is also a good example of the 'techno-legal time gap' (Hirst and Harrison, 2007): the dissonance between law and regulation and the power and applications of the technology. We will return to definitional arguments in a later chapter, as the question of who now qualifies to either call themselves journalists or to be considered as such by the wider community is a key feature of the crisis in journalism, particularly from the profession's position of self-interest.

Dan Gillmor's *We, the Media* also argues that everyone today is a journalist, or at least has the potential to be one. The subtitle also echoes Scott Gant's emphasis on the American Constitution and its lofty ideals: *Grassroots journalism by the people, for the people* (Gillmor, 2006). Gillmor's ideas neatly capture a key dialectic tension in journalism today, the dynamic between professionalism and amateur ideals. At times he appears to be championing a full-strength revolt against professional journalism, at others he is keen to retain the strong ethical and professional ethos of 'fairness, accuracy and thoroughness'. He argues the point that there is an ongoing need for a professional style of editorial control that reinforces the Fourth Estate values; then, a few pages later, he reverts to an enduring mythology of the digital age: 'the user is truly in charge, as a consumer and a producer'. Each of these authors tends to demonstrate a level of technological determinism in some arguments both for and against citizen journalism. This means that the technology—and what it can do, or enable—is essentialized and removed from the constraints of social forces and social relations of production. This has two detrimental effects on analytical thinking: a) it marginalizes or removes social relations from the field of analysis (Hirst and Harrison, 2007), and b) it ascribes agency and power to objects and commodities and sees them as the 'intrinsic properties' of the technology rather than 'the result of [unequal] social relations between people' (Wayne, 2003, p. 40).

In refuting technological determinism, Purdue University media scholar Lee Artz argues that technologies exist within a determining set of social relations, such that any technology is developed and used in ways that 'both reflect and [are] intended to reproduce that social formation, even as certain conditions of that formation change' (Artz, 2006, p. 36). This position acknowledges that technological change is a social force and that new technologies are necessarily a part of any 'revolution' in the relations of production. However, it puts at the heart of the change the important social tensions and the dynamic of a system of unequal class structures that are in a state of economic and political flux. This flux runs across the entire terrain of the capitalist economy, including communications and the news industry: 'the mediated production of communication exists within the totality of relations of production' (Artz, 2006, p. 47). This insight also informs an analytical framework for examining how the global media industry is attempting to incorporate many aspects of amateur and citizen journalism into its new digital configurations.

There is really only one point of agreement between Rosen, Meyer, Henry, Gant and Gillmor—the common belief that we are now living in a different time. Whether we call it the 'Information Age', or the 'Internet Age', or the 'Age of New Media', the 21st century is already a vastly different place to the late 20th century we've only just left behind. It is useful to characterize the present and near future as the 'Age of Convergence'. As Henry Jenkins puts it in the title of his 2006 book, we are now living in a *Convergence Culture*. Jenkins' subtitle also points to the crisis in journalism: *Where old and new media collide*. An important marker of this collision between 'old' and 'new' media is the issue of public trust. Who and what is more trustworthy from an audience perspective: the professional or the amateur, the journalist or the blogger?

Trust me, I'm a journalist . . .

> . . . to become a journalist is an act of character. For the public's ability to become a force in self-government depends upon the integrity of your work.
>
> **Bill Kovach**

Bill Kovach is senior counsellor on the Project for Excellence in Journalism, a research organization that evaluates and studies the performance of the news media, and he's right: the value of a journalist's work is measured by its public acceptance. The integrity of our daily news is a factor in its value and thus in public judgment of a journalist's character (Kovach, 2005). A key tenet of 20th century industrial journalism was that a journalist must be trusted, must be seen to be honest and ethical. The news was meant to be reliable and to give an honest, accurate and objective accounting of true facts in the public interest. The public mood today is that journalism has failed this character test. For Kovach, the problem has several root causes—a failure of leadership in newsrooms around the world, the 'thinning of professional staff' through cost-cutting measures, and a resultant failure to 'ask the right question at the right time'. In other words: a failure to challenge entrenched economic and political power, or to stand up to the purveyors of what, thanks to British journalist Nick Davies, we have come to call 'flat earth' news: news based entirely on public relations material, rather than endeavour and inquiry by independent journalists. Then again, it might not be surprising to learn that the public is wary of journalists when a survey of journalists themselves also finds that they don't think their colleagues are doing a good job. The Journalism in Color Survey of black, Hispanic and Asian journalists in the USA reported in March 2010 that most respondents felt that minority and diversity issues were not adequately covered in the American news media (News One, 2010). The survey, sponsored by the UNITY alliance of 10,000 journalists of colour in the United States, also found that more coverage of diversity is not always better coverage.

Journalists are not alone in being low in the public trust stakes. Surveys conducted over the past few years indicate that there is a general decline in the public's trust of many professions and institutions, according to reputable polling organizations in the USA and UK. The Harris Poll Confidence Index for 2009, for example, suggests that only 4 per cent of US respondents trusted the bankers and executives of Wall Street. Trust levels for financial institutions had fallen over 40 per cent in a year according to other measures (Hamilton and Jones, 2009). An Edelman Trust survey, also in 2009, indicated that only 23 per cent of British respondents trusted media companies; globally (based on the survey sample in 20 nations) the figure was only 44 per cent. 'With the dispersion of traditional media's authority and the rise of opinion journalism, trust in the institution as a whole has waned' (Edelman Trust Barometer and Strategy One, 2010, p. 3).

The Edelman report also recommends that media companies

recognize that trust has to be earned anew in a climate where other entities and individuals can generate their own news-like coverage and bypass traditional journalism. The decline of public trust in the news media is not necessarily new; surveys conducted annually over the past decade and in several nations show that the drop has been steady over that time. Academic studies also tend to confirm this trend. A recent research project (Donsbach, Rentsch and Mende, 2009) found that around two-thirds of the German public has little trust in its news media and that the gap is widening for younger generations.

The *Reader's Digest* magazine has conducted annual surveys of the most trusted people and professions for the past 15 years or so. In the 2008 New Zealand survey, the top-ranking journalist was retired newsreader Judy Bailey at number 15. TV3's current affairs host John Campbell was next at number 45, and the only other journalist in the top 100 was broadcaster and columnist Paul Holmes at 65. In the Australian survey of the most trusted professions, journalists were 35th out of 40— well below ambulance officers (1st), locksmiths (15th), hairdressers (21st) and bartenders (26th). Journalists were only two places above prostitutes (37th) and did marginally better than car salesmen (38th), politicians (39th) and in last place at 40th, telemarketers (M. Atkins, 2008; *Reader's Digest*, 2008a). In the 2008 New Zealand sample, journalists were 34th, psychics and astrologers were in 35th place, and 36th place went to real estate agents. The bottom three places were the same as the Australian list (*Reader's Digest*, 2008b). A 2004 Pew Center report on public attitudes to American newspapers found that overall trust in the largest US news brands was declining and that in general people trusted newspapers less than other media. The researchers concluded that this might have something to do with the visual nature of TV news being more appealing than newspaper text. The report found that people tended to think that the newspaper industry is motivated by commercial imperatives and that journalists are 'out of touch' with ordinary readers. The 'believability' of newspapers was tracked from 1985 to 2003 and in that time it fell by about 19 per cent, from 78 to 59 per cent. At the same time, the proportion of those who did not believe newspapers grew from 2 to 9 per cent (Project for Excellence in Journalism, 2004).

A 2005 survey found that around 60 per cent of Americans trusted the news media to report 'fully, fairly and accurately', a decline from the 'high-water mark' of 70 per cent during the 1970s (Love, 2007). In

2006, a similar report found that people were coming to rely more on the Internet for news because of the convenience factor. At the same time, the researchers found that audiences tended to trust the Internet more and also liked the greater diversity of opinion that it offered. The researchers reported that about 68 per cent of people who consume their news online believed 'almost all', or 'most' of what they found there. However, levels of trust tended to vary between established and branded news sites and individual sites, such as blogs. Seventy-nine per cent of respondents trusted major news brands, while only 12 per cent trusted sites hosted by individuals (Project for Excellence in Journalism, 2006). When the 2009 Pew Center survey was released it reported an all-time low in the American public's perception of the news media's ability to be accurate. Only 29 per cent of Americans believed reporters generally get the facts straight and 63 per cent said that news stories are often inaccurate. In particular, the report highlighted that many established old media brands are losing credibility, including such stalwarts as the *New York Times* and the *Wall Street Journal* (The Pew Research Center, 2009). Perhaps the most alarming figure is one reported in a British survey that showed only 3 per cent of respondents trusted journalists. When journalism professor and former editor Roy Greenslade reported this on his blog, he also posed a pertinent question: 'Why, I wonder, is the public so disenchanted with journalists?' One simple answer is that the news media has actually let the public down to such an extent that journalists have spoiled their reputations, almost beyond repair. It is possible to partially explain the reasons for this by referring to what is arguably the biggest story of the 21st century (so far): the global 'war on terror', which began in the immediate aftermath of the September 2001 attacks on New York and Washington DC and that has dominated the news media since.

If you can't trust a reporter, whom can you trust?

Lay all Judith Miller's *New York Times* stories end to end, from late 2001 to June 2003 and you get a desolate picture of a reporter with an agenda, both manipulating and being manipulated by US government officials, Iraqi exiles and defectors, an entire Noah's Ark of scam-artists.

Alexander Cockburn

Alexander Cockburn is the editor of *Counterpunch*, an online political newsletter. In August 2003, he wrote a scathing piece about *New York Times* reporter Judith Miller. According to Cockburn, Judith Miller had been using her trusted position as a senior *Times* staffer to actively promote the Bush administration's agenda of war in Afghanistan and Iraq. A month earlier, *Washington Post* columnist and prominent Bush supporter Robert Novak wrote that a well-known American diplomat, Valerie Plame, was also a CIA agent who had some role in hunting for alleged weapons of mass destruction (WMDs). Later, under Grand Jury questioning, Robert Novak named White House officials Karl Rove and Richard Armitage as his sources. The real story behind this drama was that Plame's husband, career diplomat Joseph Wilson, had publicly denounced as false the suggestion that Saddam Hussein was attempting to purchase uranium from the tiny African nation of Niger to make nuclear weapons. Rove, Armitage and White House official Scooter Libby had then used their friends in the news media to attack Wilson and attempt to silence him by making veiled threats about his wife. They knew that outing Plame as a covert CIA operative was illegal and might put her life in danger, but they were prepared to do it in order to maintain the lie about Iraq's nuclear ambitions. Judith Miller also wrote about Plame in the *New York Times*, and on 6 July 2005 she was jailed for refusing to tell a Grand Jury investigation the source of her information. She was released on 29 September and the next day testified that her source had been Scooter Libby. Libby was sentenced to 30 months in jail and fined $250,000. On 2 July 2007, George W. Bush commuted the jail term, calling it 'excessive'. In 2010 this story was made into a movie, *Fair Game*, starring Sean Penn and Naomi Watts as the diplomat/CIA couple Joe Wilson and Valerie Plame. Alexander Cockburn described Judith Miller as a 'willing cheerleader for war' and it seems clear that she was prepared to use discredited and unnamed sources in her efforts to actively assist the Bush administration. It is little wonder that, when stories such as this emerge, news consumers might have reason to feel cheated and become disillusioned.

The whole WMDs saga that provided justification for the 2003 war in Iraq has been shown to be a lie. However, unlike the news parody of America's *Daily Show*, it was news that had been faked in an effort to deceive the public into supporting what was, at the time, a very unpopular war. The American, Australian and British governments continued to press the case for WMDs, despite it being clear that the intelligence basis for their assumptions was inaccurate. In October 2002, President Bush gave a speech in Cincinnati in which he argued hard that Iraq possessed chemical and biological weapons and was seeking nuclear weapons. The speech was widely reported by a willing-to-believe American press and backed up by columnists, commentators and television talking heads across the nation. The speech was reprinted by many news organizations, including CNN, CBS and the usually sceptical British *Guardian* newspaper; the Fox network carried the speech live. In many news reports the speech was described in positive words: 'purposeful', 'stern but subdued tones'. Writing in the *New York Times*, columnist Todd Purdum (2002) described the tone of the speech: 'using simple metaphors and concrete examples in a fatherly reminder and a president's ability to rise above elite diplomatic debates . . . Mr Bush did not so much offer up new evidence against Iraq as weave together known facts in a new and plain-spoken effort to persuade the public . . . [he] cast the threat in unadorned language'. Unfortunately, the 'facts' were mostly lies. They were deliberate and cynical lies that the Bush administration continued to repeat to the media at every opportunity for the next three years; though, to be fair, the news media did eventually begin to fight back. Then there were the newer lies, such as President Bush's 2005 assertion that the United States does not use torture. Administration officials continued the denials for two more years and they were often reported as fact in the news (Gollust, 2006). It has since been revealed that American soldiers and civilian contractors from Abu Ghraib to Guantanamo Bay have committed war crimes, including sanctioned torture of detainees (Physicians for Human Rights, 2008).

Prior to Bush's October 2002 Cincinnati speech, the American public was keen to see the United Nations inspection teams given more time to find the WMDs that Saddam Hussein had allegedly stockpiled, but within months the tide had turned. By March 2003, the American public was behind its president and supported the war. In part this is due to the largely uncritical reporting in the mainstream media. Sympathetic reporting of the Cincinnati speech helped the administration's case by playing to a sense of vulnerability in the public psyche. Framing the Iraq story within the 'terror frame'—emphasizing Saddam Hussein's alleged links to nebulous terrorist groups and with ties to rogue regimes in the Middle East—served to generate fear and allegiance to the governmental and military powers that were perceived to be doing something about it.[2] From September 2001, sections of the American, British and Australian news media and in other 'coalition of the willing' nations wittingly or unwittingly became part of an effective propaganda exercise to sell the invasion of Afghanistan and Iraq. In September 2003, six months after the American invasion, it was clear that no WMDs were ever going to be found. However, when the Iraq Survey Group's interim report was published confirming that they were not there, the US and British governments continued their spin campaigns. CIA spokesman Bill Harlow told Reuters that the report had not reached any 'firm conclusions' and that nothing would be ruled 'in or out'. It was as a result of the lies told by government and often repeated uncritically by the news media that a decline in the public's trust of journalism became stronger, particularly in relation to news about the ongoing conflicts in Afghanistan and Iraq. No doubt this contributed to the general decline in public trust of the news media.

In 2007, a Pew Center survey asking Americans who they trusted for news about military conflicts, particularly the Iraq war, found that only 38 per cent had more than a 'fair amount' of trust in the news media. Sixty per cent had 'not too much' or lesser trust in the news media. This was a sharp decline from a similar 2004 survey that showed 81 per cent had a 'fair amount' or greater trust in the news media's coverage of war and only 15 per cent having 'not too much' or lesser trust. Interestingly, the figures included data from 1991, when 85 per cent had a 'fair amount' or greater trust in the news media and only 13 per cent had little or no trust. This is significant because in 1991 the American military was also involved in a war in Iraq. The key thing to note here is how far public trust in the news media's coverage of war fell between 2004 and 2007. We can surmise from this that there is perhaps a direct link between the public's trust of government when a war is unpopular and their trust in the news media to report it accurately. The Pew Center report also highlights the linkages between public trust of government and the news media. The number of respondents who felt the war was going well in 2003–04 reached 90 per cent of the sample; by 2007 it was down to 40 per cent. The report, *Who do you trust for war news?*, concluded that four years into the Iraq war both political and media institutions had a much lower public confidence rating than they did in March 2003. Perhaps this is not surprising when we know that both CNN and the *New York Times* were used by the American government to plant false stories in the public eye to bolster its case for a war in Iraq. The case of *New York Times* reporter Judith Miller and conservative syndicated columnist Robert Novak shows that this was a widespread tactic of the Bush White House and that some reporters were more than willing to be collaborators in the deception. However, it's not just the reporting of the 'war on terror' that has disappointed the news-consuming public. There have been other high-profile scandals involving journalists and the news media: Jayson Blair and Stephen Glass are two examples. Both Blair and Glass invented—in other words, made up—news items and interviews for two prestigious publications. In Blair's case it was for the *New York Times* and Glass for the *The New Republic* magazine. When Blair's deception was discovered, the *Times* was brutally shaken and several senior editors were sacked. The public's lack of faith in the mainstream media also goes some way to explaining the popularity in the US of Jon Stewart's *The Daily Show* and other satirical programs that lampoon the news industry. It really is no wonder, then, that a cynical public might turn to non-journalists for their news. It might be faked, but at least it's funny.

When too much (fake) news is barely enough

Are we prepared for the global, 24-7 fake news cage match that will dominate journalism in the twenty-first century?

Robert Love

In 2005, when the war in Iraq began to unravel for the 'coalition of the willing', the American government launched a $300 million initiative to generate positive news stories from the beleaguered nation. A conservative columnist was also hired by the Bush administration on a $240,000 annual salary to write good news stories about the controversial *No Child Left Behind* education reforms. The global warming/climate change debate has also been skewed in some cases by scientists and experts recruited to discredit opponents and confuse the public. In another high-profile case of deception, a publicist called Karen Ryan was hired by the US Department of Health and Human Services to produce video news releases (VNRs) extolling the virtues of the administration's Medicare plan. These VNRs were used by news stations across the US with virtually no editing and often without any acknowledgment of their source. As Robert Love (2007) wrote in the *Columbia Journalism Review*, 'it may be fair to say that the nation's capital has been giving Comedy Central a run for its money as the real home of fake news'.

When the *New York Times* can seriously ask if the cult comedian Jon Stewart is the most trusted man in American journalism, then you know the news media are in trouble. In 2007, Stewart was ranked fourth in a public survey of who Americans most trusted as a television news anchor. Stewart's late-night satirical show, *The Daily Show*, broadcast on the Comedy Central cable network, was one of the most highly rated television programs for political news during the 2008 US Presidential election. However, Stewart claims that his show is not journalism. He told PBS interviewer Bill Moyers that the writing team sees itself as 'a group of people that really feel that they want to write jokes about the absurdity that we see in government and the world and all that, and that's it' (Kakutani, 2008; Project for Excellence in Journalism, 2008).

Perhaps the funniest and most outrageous of recent fake news shows was *Da Ali G Show* and the characters of Borat and Bruno, invented and performed by British comedian Sacha Baron Cohen. In his Ali G alter-ego, Cohen managed to talk his way into some very biting interviews on serious topics with people who had no idea they were being ambushed. As Borat, Cohen became a global sensation as the boorish Kazhak reporter who was ineptly trying to find the very best in Western culture to help his homeland prosper. Ali G and Borat both had an innocence that masked Baron Cohen's sharp intellect and often probing line of questioning. Similar programs, such as the *Colbert Report* (also on Comedy Central), the *Chaser's War on Everything* in Australia, *A Wonderful Country* in Israel, *Have I Got News for You* and *Spitting Image* in the UK highlight the fact that being mistrusted and parodied is a global problem for journalists. Satirical news shows also strike a chord with audiences because they come at the truth from a different angle. The gloss and spin of politicians is removed as they are mercilessly lampooned and their statements recast in ironic and often accurate send-ups.

So while audiences might be turning away from the mainstream news media, it seems they are not necessarily losing their interest in news and current affairs. Satirical news shows actually ask a lot of their audiences. Viewers must be up-to-date with the current real news in order to get most of the jokes. Haifa University lecturer David Alexander has studied *A Wonderful Country* and says that it is the 'deep involvement' of Israeli citizens in the political life of their country that makes the show so popular. Stewart's *The Daily Show* has become a real cultural and political force in America that has a measurable impact on the national conversation and which, according to the Project for Excellence in Journalism, is 'getting people to think critically about the public square'. Some media studies academics go so far as to suggest that the popularity of the fake-news genre signals the end of the news genre as a viable form in the electronic public sphere and that it reflects widespread audience disillusionment with television as a reliable information source (Druick, 2009).

Satirical news shows are not new to television; in fact they are almost as old as the medium itself. In the early 1960s *That Was the Week That Was* on the BBC was a popular vehicle for David Frost and other comics. The writing team included John Cleese, Roald Dahl and Peter Cook. From their earliest incarnations, these programs have provided audiences with a brief respite from the focus on doom and gloom that tends to dominate the daily news agenda. They provided a cultural breathing space and a few laughs. Even so, *That Was the Week That Was* could also at times be fearless in exposing the hypocrisy of British politics and interviewing establishment newsmakers with an acid tongue. This is the tradition that *The Daily Show* now carries on; it works because of its keen sense of the absurd and because, according to the *New York Times*, it is attuned to the 'cognitive dissonance [that] has become a national epidemic' in the United States and many nations (Kakutani, 2008). The popularity of these shows is another audience reaction to a mainstream news industry in crisis—an industry that is no longer entirely believable. Satirical fake news shows bring this home to the audiences with laughs and insights that they don't get from evening news bulletins, or their daily newspapers. Stewart does not hide his own politics behind a façade of fairness and balance. He has been quoted as saying that he was looking forward to the end of George W. Bush's presidency 'as a comedian, as a person, as a citizen, as a mammal'. Audiences seem to like this honesty and don't seem to mind the openly partisan positions that Stewart takes. In the end, says *New York Times* critic Michiko Kakutani, the motivation for the show is not so much to express partisan support for one political party or another but, rather, 'a deep mistrust of all ideology'. Unfortunately for the mainstream news media, journalists and journalism now also appear to be subject to this same public mistrust.

Faking it is easy

> ... the visual image has always been a weapon. The dif-
> ference today is two little inventions, the Internet and
> Photoshop.
>
> **Tracey Barnett**

During the Gulf of Mexico oil spill crisis in 2010, global petroleum giant BP was pinged for faking an image of its Houston command centre to make it look busier than it really was (Rothman, 2010). The picture was distributed to the news media and became another PR hit against the beleaguered multinational. While faked news photographs are not new, it is true that digital manipulation of images—using techniques such as 'cloning' figures in and out of images—is now much easier. As New Zealand commentator Tracey Barnett points out, the news-data flow is also now two-way. The traditional gate-keeping function of editors in the newsroom is sometimes compromised, particularly when news organizations are feeding off the Web: 'If news sources from the Web are now flowing both ways, who's minding the backwash?' (Barnett, 2008). The backwash can be significant and lead to further embarrassment in the newsroom. In 2007 a New Zealand viewer sent in a photoshopped image of a tornado that she said had crossed the coast near the North Island town of New Plymouth. The image was used by both major TV news services in their evening bulletins before the fake was discovered. Such singular incidents, carried out as a relatively harmless 'hoax', are a concern, but they are not the major problem when it comes to faking news. In the last few years there have been several more serious incidents of fake news getting wide distribution before the hoax was uncovered. In 2008 a fake story about Apple CEO Steve Jobs being seriously ill was uploaded to CNN's *iReport*. It circulated widely, causing stock prices to tumble until the rumour was corrected. In the same year, a 13-year-old boy was wrongly reported as using his father's credit card to hire prostitutes and in 2009, at the time Michael Jackson died in June, several other celebrities were also prematurely killed off in hoax news reports that circulated in reputable outlets. Indeed, anyone can now create their own fake news bulletin by using an online news-clipping generator at the Fodey.com website. By entering a headline and a small amount of 'copy', it is possible to create an image of a newspaper that contains your 'story'. You can then download an image of your clipping and post that wherever you like on the Web, thus creating a virtual 'paper trail'. This is relatively harmless, but even so the website contains a disclaimer and this advice: 'Please do not use the names of real persons or newspapers'.

Is this hoaxing of newsrooms becoming a serious problem, as Barnett suggests? Is it another nail in the coffin of journalistic trust now that we can no longer believe our eyes? The issue of veracity and verification of news and information has become a big issue in the age of citizen journalism. A 2008 study of Australian news editors by journalism scholars Colleen Murrell and Mandy Oakham highlighted their concerns about taking advantage of user-generated content (UGC) in their news products. Most of the senior editors interviewed by Murrell and Oakham said they had to allocate scarce newsroom resources to monitoring UGC because of the legal and ethical risks it might pose and also because of the possibility that it could indeed be fake. Similar results were found in a New Zealand study by postgraduate student Vincent Murwira. His interviews with senior news professionals also elicited the response that in many cases handling UGC was more trouble than it was worth (Murwira, 2009).

Attempts to hoax newsrooms and journalists for fun are undoubtedly a problem, but of more concern must be any deliberate attempt to influence the news agenda for reasons of personal, commercial or political gain. According to British journalist Nick Davies, corporate and government attempts to control the news agenda is a growing problem. In his 2008 book, *Flat Earth News*, Davies documents cases of deliberate attempts to plant false news stories in the media and argues that the profit-motivated corporate structure of the news media invites the invention of news items for purely commercial purposes. He also outlines cases of deliberate government misinformation designed to mislead journalists and news audiences. His research shows that as much as 80 per cent of British news comes from tainted sources, mainly the public relations industry (Davies, 2008a). A similar study in Australia, released in March 2010, also found that a high proportion of news was generated from media releases. The project, *Spinning the Media*, found that in some papers the proportion of PR material was close to 70 per cent. Surprisingly, some of the editors approached for comment were realistic about the situation: they might not like it, but they were stuck with it (Crikey.com and ACIJ, 2010). While we might describe PR-generated news as 'fake', it does have at least one foot in reality. The events, people and issues promoted by PR companies exist and may even have some relevance to the news agenda, but what about news that is deliberately made up and designed to mislead in order to promote a commercial or political interest?

A famous American case of fake, politically motivated news is the so-called 'Swift boat veterans for truth' campaign against Democrat candidate John Kerry during the 2004 US Presidential election. The veterans claimed that John Kerry had lied about his military record during the Vietnam conflict and on that basis they claimed he was unfit to be commander-in-chief. Eventually the group's lies were uncovered, but not before some damage had been done to Kerry's reputation. In his 2008 book *True Enough*, Farhad Manjoo argues that the veterans were successful because of the fragmentation of news sources in the digital age; by scattering their false messages widely and establishing an online presence, the group was able to multiply the number of sources for their lies and create a false sense of truth and urgency. Kerry's enemies had a clear political motive for their actions—to derail his election bid—and they did so as private citizens, but the stakes are much higher when government agencies attempt to mislead news organizations. In October 2007 the US Federal Emergency Management Agency (FEMA) arranged a hastily called news conference to talk about its handling of a wildfire emergency in California. Unfortunately, no journalists were on hand to attend. This did not worry the FEMA officials, they simply rounded up some agency staff members to sit in a room and be videotaped asking questions of FEMA deputy head Harvey Johnson. The scam was eventually exposed by the *Washington Post* and Johnson was forced to apologize. What is mind-boggling about this incident is why an organization like FEMA might think it's acceptable to fake a news conference. Perhaps it might be explained as a one-off mistake, but the record indicates that this tactic was seen as an acceptable practice right across the administration of President George W. Bush.

In *American Carnival*, Neil Henry describes the state of journalism in the United States in terms of a series of freak shows, balancing acts and sideshow alley tricks 'awash in Orwellian terminology'. His chapter on fake news is aptly titled 'World of Illusions'. He devotes some pages to the 'Karen Ryan' story—the saga of how a federal government agency employed a PR firm to produce VNRs that appeared to be real news stories. The series of covert advertisements for the administration's controversial Medicare legislation even ended with a news-style sign-off: 'In Washington, this is Karen Ryan reporting'. It is not really Karen Ryan's fault that she became the public face of this scandal; she was a freelance journalist doing a paid job. The real villains of the piece were the government officials and PR company executives who knew exactly what they were doing. But Henry also sheets home some of the blame to a corporate television news industry that had downsized staff and cut production budgets to the point that it came to rely on VNRs to fill the gaps between the real advertisements.

The Medicare VNRs were distributed in a commercial arrangement by CNN Newsource alongside its regular (and presumably real) news stories. Thus, the material came into local television news stations across the country without any clear identification as to its origins; at least 40 stations played the VNR as news. What Neil Henry is pointing to with this example is a wider malaise afflicting the news industry, and not just in the USA. Around the world, boundaries between news, PR, entertainment and advertising are blurring. These shifts are signified by the term 'advertorial', which blurs the line between editorial content and advertising; information programming is being fused with entertainment to give us 'infotainment' and 'reality TV' is far from real, mostly being constructed as voyeuristic soap operas and game shows that trade on the humiliation of the participants. Not even documentaries are safe: on one hand we have 'mockumentaries' (some of which are quite funny) and 'documercials' in which actors and celebrities pretend they're not really selling us more stuff that we don't really need and that doesn't really work.

To understand why all this is happening we have to go beyond the moral issues of right and wrong to examine the structural causes that create the symptoms of a distressed media system. In medicine, you not only have to relieve the symptoms of an illness, you have to treat the underlying pathogens or problems that created them. The examples of fake news created by the PR industry and hungrily swallowed by poorly resourced newsrooms suggest that economic factors play some part in creating the crisis of credibility and trust discussed in this chapter. In fact, the very structural deficiencies and problems that define capitalism as a mode of production are a strong influencing factor in the poor state of health in which the news industry finds itself today. As John Nichols and

Robert McChesney (2005, p. ix) argue, the logic of capitalism 'makes it rational to gut journalism and irrational to provide the content that a free society so desperately requires', and this goes some way towards explaining the conditions of crisis in the news media today.

So where do we go for answers?

Trust is a rare and highly valuable thing in media.

Jim Spanfeller

If audiences are not totally disengaged from the news agenda, why are journalists and journalism so unpopular? The distrust of politicians and of news journalists seems to go hand-in-hand, which means we will have to look beyond the walls of the Fourth Estate to find answers to the question about why the public trust in the news media is falling. Part of the answer is obviously to be found in the work of Nick Davies and other critics who point out that the commercial structures of the news industry lend themselves to fake news being created for commercial purposes. Another piece of the puzzle is explained by the exposure of government news management used to mislead the public for base political reasons. It's not surprising that news consumers are cynical; they have learned to distrust the news—and journalists—because of the sheer volume of lies and fake news that has been uncovered. But it is important to separate the news industry from journalists in order to understand both sides of this trust equation.

This chapter started by noting that while many of us may not like the way that news has been presented to us and that the Internet creates the technological conditions for us to move into more personalized media consumption, we still have some basic need for news and information. Therefore, it is sensible to argue that we still need journalists in one form or another. On one hand, we might still need professional journalists with training and ethical codes to ensure that our news is of a high standard; on the other, there's a growing legion of non-professionals—widely defined by Jay Rosen as those who used to be the audience and who now have some basic production tools. The following chapters will examine both sides of this expanding reportorial community in an attempt to offer some answers and suggestions for how journalists can recover their reputations and earn back the trust of audiences. However, it is first important and useful to outline what's happened to the economics of the news media in the last decade or so and why so many commentators and industry leaders were worried that the news industry may have appeared to be on the verge of collapse in 2008–09.

---

[1] See, for example, Atton and Hamilton, 2008

[2] For more analysis of the 'terror frame', see Hirst and Patching, 2007; Papacharissi and de Fatima Oliveira, 2008; Schaefer, 2006

3

Globalization and the news industry crisis

History plays pranks with all rigid forms and fixed routines.
All kinds of paradoxical developments ensue which perplex
those with narrow, formalized minds.

George Novack

The convergence of computing, telephony, television and text is part
and parcel of that economic, technological and social phenomenon that
we've come to know as 'globalization'. As Mosco notes in *The Digital Sublime*, the technological condition of convergence was one precondition
for the revolution in telecommunications and for media globalization.
But the microchip is only one aspect of the process of dialectic change,
flux and what Vincent Mosco calls the 'mutual constitution' of historical
trends, technological change, social forces and ideas. It is also a process of combined and uneven development—change does not occur
at a uniform pace in all places at the same time. Change on a global
and historical scale takes time—the Industrial Revolution, for example,
was 100 years or more in the making. There is an incremental, gradual
movement and then, when the conditions are right, a qualitative change
that is irreversible. As Charles Stross noted: the future comes crashing
into the present. But the future may land across the world unevenly; the
impact in one nation or region or branch of the global economy may
not be replicated in another, at least not on any scale of simultaneous or
instantaneous occurrence. We can see this easily in the uneven way that
digital technologies are taken up across the planet.

In many industrialized countries—particularly those at the core of globalized capitalism—most of us take broadband Internet access for granted. We have access to hundreds of television channels that never satisfy, more magazines than we can read, endless numbers of FM radio stations that play high-rotation music of almost every genre, wall-to-wall talkback on the AM frequencies and more bytes of digital information than any one person could ever digest. In a sense we are media-saturated, so perhaps it's no wonder that we are starting to turn off newspapers that no longer seem so relevant. In less affluent parts of the world, however, particularly in Africa, the Middle East and Asia, there is actually growth in newspaper circulations. In nations with poorly developed or no access to broadband services, and in those where average incomes are low and people cannot afford televisions and computers, the low-tech printed page is still a major source of news, alongside radio, which is accessible on cheap transistors. The division between the media rich and the media poor is one obvious example of combined and uneven development in relation to the impact of technology on people's lives and their access to news. Another is the uneven development of technologies and social relations in the broad field of communications and in the particular field of journalistic production.

The process of combined and uneven development was first theoretically established by Karl Marx in his works Grundrisse der Kritik der Politischen Ökonomie (Outlines of the Critique of Political Economy) and Das Kapital where he noted that the development of capitalism creates both pockets of wealth and large pools of poverty. Marx called this the general rule of capital accumulation, and he believed that the general dynamic of social change—in particular, the transition from one mode of production to another—was also part of the historically grounded process of combined and uneven development.1 In the 20th century it was the Russian revolutionary Leon Trotsky who advanced the theory of combined and uneven development, noting that not every nation had to go through all the stages of the Industrial Revolution. Instead, he argued, advanced capitalism could be 'imported' into nations that came into contact—through trade or conquest—with the more progressive and productive mode of production. In his History of the Russian Revolution Trotsky states: 'Savages throw away their bows and arrows for rifles all at once, without travelling the road which lay between those two weapons in the past.' The Marxist theoretician George

Novack advanced the concept of combined and uneven development by establishing the parameters for two types of 'combination'. The first involved the less advanced society absorbing the new mode of production, or at least elements of it, without any fundamental damage to its own social structure. The second is more destructive, as elements of the less advanced society are incorporated into the world of the advancing capitalist mode of production. Novack argued—and the world today confirms his analysis—that the weaker and 'backward' social structures would eventually be pulled into the orbit of the more 'advanced' mode of production (Novack, 1972, p. 107). Two small examples illustrate this, though many more could be cited. After the Opium Wars (1839–42 and 1856–58) and the Boxer rebellion (1900–01), China was compelled to take up industrialization and to become incorporated into the world market for trade and commodity production. China moved rapidly through the stages of the Industrial Revolution. It moved from small-scale iron ore smelting during the 'Five-Year Plan' phase of the 1950s to the 'Four Modernizations' under Deng Xiaoping in the 1970s and an outward turn to the world economy in the 1980s to full integration into globalized capitalism by the late 1990s (the 700th KFC fast-food restaurant opened in China in 2002), becoming the world's largest producer of household garbage in 2009 (Bradsher, 2009) and the second largest economy in terms of Gross Domestic Product (what the national economy actually produces each year). Today, China is a global superpower and rapidly moving to the centre of the world economy, at the expense of the United States in particular. The second example is India, which has become a telecommunications and computing hub for the world, based on a plentiful supply of cheap labour. To a large extent, too, India has skipped over the development of a fixed-line copper-wire telephone system and moved very quickly from having almost no telecommunications infrastructure to having one of the world's largest mobile-phone networks. Despite these changes in India and its integration into the networked global system—the fourth largest national economy—culturally and socially it does not resemble any of its major trading partners. It might be argued that the United States and India are today much closer in cultural terms than they were in the 1970s—and Bollywood certainly rivals Hollywood in the competition for global eyeballs—but that would be a mistaken assumption based only on superficial features. There is a certain amount of sharing of cultural norms and values—notably, American television and music are popular in India, but Bollywood culture has also had a big impact on Western societies, including the British and American film industries and musical subcultures (Thussu, 2007). The process of combined and uneven development is often marked by such cultural 'borrowings', but the economic and social dynamics of American and Indian capitalism are vastly different. The result of combined and uneven impacts of globalization—in both India and China—has been rapid social change and political instability. Of course, since the events of Tiananmen Square in 1989, the remnant Stalinist regime in Beijing has been able to keep a repressively heavy lid on the social pressure cooker. India's more open society—though rigid in terms of caste and class—is fracturing under the pressure to provide more wealth for a burgeoning middle class and to deal with the massive divide between rich and poor that globalization is not really closing. According to social geographer Mike Davis (2007) we are rapidly moving to a situation he describes as a 'planet of slums', a world where cities are divided into areas of extremes of wealth and poverty and more than a billion city-dwellers inhabit 'postmodern slums': 'Instead of cities of light soaring toward heaven, much of the twenty-first century urban world squats in squalor, surrounded by pollution, excrement, and decay.' Marxist theoretician David Harvey notes that the combined processes of digital convergence and globalization have not led to a reciprocal convergence in living standards across the world. He adds that globalization's promise of a better world 'has not materialized' (Harvey, 2006, p. 69).

In terms of geography, time and distance, the process of combined and uneven development can be seen in the articulation of what has become known as the 'digital divide': a series of broken promises. In its simplest and most direct form, the digital divide refers to the disparities in access to information and communication technologies (ICTs), but it also means variations in digital literacy—the ability to physically use and conceptually manage ICTs: 'access is meaningless unless people actually feel able to make use of such opportunities' (Selwyn, 2004). The concept of the digital divide provides a reality check when considered against the 'techno-enthusiasm' of those who over-sell the democratic potential of online participation and Web 2.0 technologies. While the term was originally used to refer to variations in access and literacy between nations (the global North–South divide, for example), recent research has shown that this global variation in access to computing and telecommunications resources has both intra-national and inter-national consequences and both socio-economic and cultural aspects. These include disparities of access and literacy based on income, gender, ethnicity and geographic differences. Further research has also suggested that the gap between the digitally enabled and the digitally poor has not closed significantly, despite almost a decade of government initiatives, countless surveys, policy shifts and regulatory reforms.[2]

In the context of the digital divide and the combined and uneven development of communications capitalism, the role of the traditional form of media (radio, television and print) remains central to the development of meaningful public spheres—the social space in which important debates and issues can be democratically decided—and to democratic change in many parts of the world. Conversely, it is difficult for initiatives in citizen journalism to gain a foothold in regions of the globe where poverty is still endemic, a situation that places large popu-lation groups on the wrong side of the digital divide. As Guillen and Suarez contend, when only approximately 10 per cent of the world's six billion inhabitants have good access to ICTs, and are literate in their use, the role of governments is a determining factor in shaping and implementing citizens' access to news and information sources across all platforms. Thus, the political complexion of government in any given social formation is a crucial variable for both the journalistic field that pertains to that nation and also the relationship between the field of journalism and the broader public sphere (Guillen and Suarez, 2005).

Globalization and nations—where does journalism sit?

> To meet the realities of a new world, journalism must ground its efforts by asking its basic questions again: What is journalism, and what is it for?
>
> **Sidney Callahan**

One of the key debates within studies of globalization and the media is whether or not the national mediasphere and the nation-state are still important for journalism and journalists (Callahan, 2003; Deuze, 2007). On one hand, scholars such as Anthony Giddens have argued that the power of the nation-state is fading in the face of global corporate pressure and multinational institutions such as the World Bank and the International Monetary Fund. Others, such as James Curran, offer an alternative explanation that posits the still important power of the nation state as a central element of globalization. It seems that Curran is right; the nation-state cannot be dismissed as being without power, because communication systems are still, in significant respects, national, despite their links to global networks. Infrastructure, cultural content and audiences are all nationally constructed; nation-states are influential in shaping media systems, in particular the regulatory and legal frameworks within which national and trans-national media operate, and the nation is still a very important marker of difference in language, political systems and cultural traditions. Robert McChesney would add to this list the fact that many forms of communication, in particular mass-media forms, are also heavily subsidized by the nation-state, meaning it still plays a pivotal role in local, national and global communication. In *Media Work* Deuze (2007) argues that the pull of the nation-state, and therefore of national mediaspheres, is weakening and for scholars such as Ingrid Volkmer the starting point for analyzing the shift to a globally networked public sphere is Marshall McLuhan's much-misunderstood notion of a global village. Volker extends this idea into a global news network that emphasizes both cross-border similarities and cross-border differences by constituting 'parallel' news flows—one national and several trans-national—that may contradict each other in terms of framing and ideological context and, by extension, then begin to reshape national public discourse (Volkmer, 2003, p. 12). The dialectics that set these trends in motion are still in process and we can only guess at how they will eventually resolve.

One region where this process of combined and uneven development of local, national and trans-national news flows is most evident is the Middle East. In many Arab nations much of the urban population has at least some access to international news services that sit uncomfortably alongside more controlled local and national news agendas.[3] In the decade since the Qatar-based Al-Jazeera network began operating, the mass media in Arab nations has undergone massive change. In Iraq and Afghanistan—both under direct American influence—state-subsidized, but semi-private, media have been established to give legitimacy to the flawed process of regime change. In Iran, the heavily censored state media has come under sustained pressure from thousands of bloggers—both local and outside the country—who are critical of the regime. In some of the Emirates, Saudi Arabia and Egypt, despite still-tight government regulation, a commercial and relatively free mass media is slowly emerging. As many scholars have noted, one positive impact of convergence culture has been a slow, but steady, push-back against repressive regimes and restrictive media laws in some nations; while in others repression of the media is increasing. It is important to acknowledge this, but at the same time to treat such changes with caution. As many global journalism and freedom of expression groups argue, many Middle Eastern nations are still dominated by closed national media systems. For example, the international news workers' protection group Reporters sans Frontières (RSF) rates many Middle Eastern nations high on its list of dangerous or difficult situations for journalists and the news media.

The variations between nations and nation-states as to how they regulate journalism and how journalism is practised are no surprise, given the global process of combined and uneven development. There is no single 'model' of journalism, and local or national variations in culture and the expression of journalism are to be expected (Hallin and Mancini, 2004). Therefore, we should not expect the crisis in the political economy of the news media, or the crisis of confidence, trust and professional ethos in journalism, to be evenly spread across the globe. There are, according to Hallin and Mancini, four dynamics at work which—when combined with a process of uneven application—create the conditions in which the twin crises in news media and journalism exert themselves: *modernization, secularization, commercialization* and *technological innovation*. These factors exist both within national media systems and as external (global) forces that also exert pressures within and across borders, forming combinations that constitute a series of interlocked and mutual antagonisms. For Volkmer this situation provides the setting for trans-national news flows to bypass nationally based regimes of censorship in a process she identifies as 'reciprocal communication'. This process renders 'obsolete' traditional journalistic distinctions between domestic and foreign news agendas, creating a new dialectic of cultural tensions between local, national and global news flows which 'increasingly impact on public participation, notions of political identity and "citizenship"' (Volkmer, 2003, p. 15). Volkmer concludes, rather hopefully, that an increase in the flow of global news, which can easily jump borders and national control regimes, creates the conditions under which 'critical content' can be made available to a new global political network. At the same time, some scholars are arguing that traditional journalism has for too long focused on the national and is losing touch with a society 'that is global as well as local' (Deuze, 2008, p. 4). This provides a background and context in which news flows can trickle upwards from non-traditional local sources into global news flows. Indeed these 'bottom up' journalistic forms are seen as one possible answer to the digital divide—whether these forms are independently produced, or produced in concert with professional journalists—in the global cultural economy (Deuze, Bruns and Neuberger, 2007).

Good journalism is expensive

> The major contradiction within the operation of the journalistic field lies in the fact that the journalistic practices that best conform to journalists' ethical codes are very often simply not profitable.
>
> **Patrick Champagne**

The good news is that in 2010 news consumption was increasing; even young people were spending more time with newspapers than they were five years ago (Dodd, 2010). The bad news is that spending money on journalism doesn't make media shareholders rich. The global news industry and news audiences are today facing a difficult to overcome contradiction. If, as a society, we continue to demand quality, hard-hitting and investigative journalism, who is going to pay for it? The political economy of the industrial news system appears to be no longer sustainable in the face of the global economic meltdown and the migration of eyeballs from the printed page to the interactive screen. This impacts on journalism and is one of the causes of the crisis in public confidence and trust in the news media. The other cause of the crisis—and something that many journalists and academics were hoping was also part of the solution—is the technological shift and the rise of convergence culture. These factors are key aspects of McChesney's critical juncture—the point of no return. He believes that we have at best one or two generations (a maximum of about 30 years) to sort this out. Some proposed solutions seem like a rehash of what has so obviously failed; others are innovative and different and others still are radical, wild and highly imaginative. They all deserve some consideration. Finding a solution, or solutions, that create the conditions for some form of sustainable journalism and news is important to maintain or expand some semblance of a public conversation. Nationally based news companies lived with the expense of serious journalism for most of the 20th century because their bottom line was protected by rates of return on investment way above the systemic average (Meyer, 2004). This is no longer the case and the global news market operates on different value assumptions. As Adrienne Russell (2009) suggests: 'We presently enjoy a mix of big-budget, shoestring-budget and free reporting. The fear is that big-budget reporting will disappear.' It is disappearing; expensive and detailed investigative reporting is one of the first casualties as newsrooms are downsized to keep profit rates healthy. In order to regain and retain a healthy quantity of expensive public interest journalism, the news industry—and the alternative journalists—need to find ways to underwrite their endeavours (Ellis, 2010). A key proposition is how to monetize the clickstream on user-generated news-like content sites like YouTube, which, though not one that might be automatically associated with journalism, are formative examples of how Web 2.0 and social media technologies are impacting on global news flows and enthusiastic theorizing of 'bottom up' news 'produsage' (Bruns, 2005, 2008).

---

[1] For a fuller explanation of the origins of combined and uneven development in political economy, see Bond, 1999; Novack, 1972

[2] For a fuller explanation of the digital divide, see Guillen and Suarez, 2005; Rice and Katz, 2003; Selwyn, 2004; Wilson, Wallin and Reiser, 2005

[3] For a detailed discussion, see Ayish, 2002; Bahry, 2001; el-Nawawy, 2003; Johnson and Fahmy, 2008; Khouri, 2007; Lynch, 2003; Martin, 2006; Mellor, 2005, 2008; Miles, 2005; Pintak, 2009; Pintak and Ginges, 2008, 2009; Rugh, 2004; Schleifer, 2004; Shapiro, 2005

4

The end of the mainstream?

Somewhere around the time television got big . . . the newspaper birthrate fell close to zero; after that, every death was one step closer to extinction.

David Von Drehle

In the first few months of 2009, obituaries were being prepared for a number of American newspapers and British media commentator Roy Greenslade was mapping the closure of regional newspapers across Britain. On 17 March, the *Seattle Post-Intelligencer* closed after 146 years of continuous publication. The west coast city's other daily, the *Seattle Times*, was also struggling, prompting some, like *Time* magazine's David Von Drehle, to suggest it could become the first large US city without a daily paper. For Von Drehle (2009), the eventual death of newspapers, coupled with the rise of online opinion sites, could lead to the 'fact-starved day when the loudmouths have only themselves to talk about'. From late 2008 a number of newspapers around the world began dropping their print edition and becoming online only. City University's Neil Thurman and Merja Myllylahti conducted a study of the Finnish financial daily *Taloussanomat* when it abandoned newsprint in December 2007. The paper was facing declining sales and growing costs, so the decision to move online only was driven by financial imperatives. However, *Taloussanomat* did not enjoy strong growth in online traffic, noting that at best it was 'modest' and, at worst, 'very poor indeed'. It certainly was when compared to the UK *Guardian*, which increased online traffic by over 30 per cent in the same period (Thurman and Myllylahti, 2009), though it must be noted that *The Guardian* is a global publication in English, while a Finnish-language financial publication would have a rather niche audience. *Taloussanomat*'s income fell by 75 per cent when the print edition was dropped, but costs were also slashed by around 50 per cent. Thurman and Myllylahti reported that the company was happy with the savings overall, but suggested that the online business model—coupled with different viewing habits by readers—did not automatically lead to an increase in online advertising revenue. Other revenue streams opened up for the publication, including mobile content and opt-in email newsletters, as well as the on-selling of content. Ultimately, the study concludes that overall traffic to the *Taloussanomat* website did not increase sufficiently to make the switch immediately profitable: 'most of *Taloussanomat*'s former print readers were probably already consumers of the online product, so going online-only did not propel existing readers online, nor attract a significant number of new users'.

Less than two years later, the company that owns the *Taloussanomat* brand announced the merger of the financial website with the mass-market tabloid *Ilta Sannomat* newspaper it also owns. The company wanted to achieve savings of around 30 million Euros, but according to Mikael Pentikäinen, President of Sanoma News, it was only halfway there in May 2009. 'The programme launched in January [2009] will save us about EUR 15 million, but unfortunately that is not enough. New actions are called for in order to keep the foundation of the company sound, in order to be able to invest resources in further development and in order to continue securing the prerequisites of independent journalism' (Mikael Pentikainen, quoted in WebWire, 2009). According to Neil Thurman, the attempt to gather in the remaining 15 million Euros entailed another 14 journalists and the managing editor of *Taloussanomat* losing their jobs (Andrews, 2009).

The movement away from daily print editions raises an interesting philosophical question: When does a newspaper stop being a newspaper? For example, the *Christian Science Monitor* stopped publishing a daily print edition in April 2009, while offering a weekly subscription print product ($140 per year), a subscription email newsletter ($5.75 per month) and a free online version. The *CSM* described its shift from daily print to online editions as a response to falling subscriptions. Judy Wolff, chairman of the Board of Trustees of The Christian Science Publishing

Society, said the company planned to 'take advantage of the Internet' to deliver the *Monitor*'s journalism 'more quickly', improve its 'timeliness and relevance', and to 'increase revenue and reduce costs'. '"We can do this," she said, "by changing the way the *Monitor* reaches its readers"' (Quoted in Cook, 2008). There is a certain cost in giving up the daily print edition—the advertising revenue it generates—and in October 2008 it was unclear how the *Monitor* planned to deal with this. There are three key strategies outlined in Judy Wolff's comments: improving timeliness and relevance, increasing revenue and reducing costs. The first is not really questionable. Of course continuous editorial updates are timely and relevant. But how was the *Monitor* planning to increase revenue? Obviously by reducing some costs—newsprint, delivery and fewer editorial staff—but this does not necessarily work to increase income unless there is also an increase in online advertising.

According to an analysis piece in the *Los Angeles Times* around the same time—some eight months out from the move—the *CSM* strategy was risky because online advertising revenue could not be guaranteed and the paper would be taking an immediate hit in subscription income. Unlike most daily newspapers, the five-day-a-week *Monitor* received the bulk of its revenue from mail-out subscriptions, not advertising. The new weekly magazine, to be published from April 2009, was one way that the company hoped to maintain its print presence, but it was expected to bring in only a fraction of the $9.7 million circulation revenue the daily edition generated annually. To compensate, the publication would have to increase online advertising dramatically (Hiltzik and Hsu, 2008). In October 2008, the *CSM* seemed hopeful, but realistically the paper's management was also facing huge challenges. To some degree, the position also seemed to be overly optimistic and just a little hopeful about the traffic that would be directed to the website and the number of subscribers who would transfer from the daily to the weekly print edition. In the end, Judy Wolff was left with nothing but a plea to readers: 'If you are a current subscriber, we ask you to stay with us. If you do not subscribe, we hope you will subscribe to the *Monitor* now as it embarks on its second century.' A lot of 'ifs' and 'buts' to qualify the hope. Perhaps the plan should have been a 'wing and a prayer' for the *Christian Science Monitor*. In March 2009, just weeks out from the relaunch online, the Poynter Institute's Rick Edmonds asked *CSM* editor John Yemma how the transition was going. Yemma said that staff had been cut by about

20 per cent and that there was both excitement and apprehension in the newsroom: 'We have a plan. We have a narrative other than doing-more-with-less. That gives us some hope. Of course, we need to succeed at our plan and reach a level of sustainability'. In April 2010, the *Christian Science Monitor* responded to my email request for an update on how the organization's new business model was working. The response was fairly upbeat: March 2010 figures for unique visitors and pageviews were both up well over 60 per cent on the March 2009 figures. The weekly print edition had 77,000 subscribers and had grown steadily since April 2009, and the Daily News Briefing had attracted 3000 new subscribers since its April 2009 launch. *CSM* spokesperson Abe McLaughlin said that financially the company was 'moving steadily toward sustainability' and was less reliant on the Church for funding. All this was done, McLaughlin said, with 'relatively small' staff cuts over the same period. John Yemma was also upbeat when interviewed by David Hirschman in March 2010 for the *Media Bistro* blog. Yemma talked about how the new model had created newsroom efficiencies, allowing the weekly print edition to be more of a news 'magazine' and the Web to be updated on a more frequent basis (Hirschman, 2010). I can't help wondering how long this experiment will last.

In the last few years, the main problem that caused the *Christian Science Monitor*, the *Seattle Post-Intelligencer* and other titles to reduce their print schedule, or to shut down completely, was that the cost structure for publishing newspapers had become unsustainable. In *The Vanishing Newspaper*, Philip Meyer suggests that newspapers may disappear by 2043 when they 'run out of readers'. *New York Times* publisher Arthur Sulzberger nominated 2012, while futurist and media blogger Vin Crosbie predicts 2021 as newsprint's use-by date and Microsoft CEO Steve Ballmer believes it might be 2018. That's a spread of about 25 years: a short time in the history of newspapers, which goes back 300 years or more. Ballmer actually went further than predicting the death of newspapers by 2018. He told the *Washington Post* that by that date—less than a decade away—all news and information would be delivered in byte and bit form, not on analogue paper. Brave predictions, and we'll know soon enough. Philip Meyer persuasively argues that the business model in newspapers represents an old and tired form of production and investment that can no longer manage costs and profits effectively; though he notes that until very recently the traditional rate of return on newspaper investments has been artificially high. The core prob argues, are the inefficiency of the newspaper market and the fact t. once unassailable mass-market model has also been disrupted by a.gital technologies. Meyer outlines one business approach in a mature industry—such as newspapers—to the inefficiency and disruption caused by change: 'A stagnant industry's market position is harvested by raising prices and lowering quality' (Meyer, 2004, p. 10). Ultimately, this is a self-defeating strategy: 'Once harvested, the market position is gone.'

Do trees have a future?

The economics of the newspaper business demand change to survive.

***Detroit Free Press* media release**

The 'strategic and innovative' changes announced by the publishers of Detroit's main daily newspapers, including the *Free Press*, were: dropping three days a week of home deliveries, downsizing the print edition on those days and hoping that advertisers would either move to the other three days or advertise online. The news release issued by publisher David Hunke included a suitably anodyne chunk of marketing-speak:

> Today, consumers are more empowered than ever before. In order to serve them well, we must find ways to be more nimble. That means we have to change the way we deliver that news—not just in subtle ways, but in fundamental ways.

Around the same time as Hunke made his consumer-driven comments, another American newspaper was also moving to reduce its daily editions and shift to a more online role. *The East Valley Tribune* in Mesa, Arizona is a long way from the major markets, but it too was feeling the pinch. The *Tribune* announced it would continue to print a giveaway edition on four days and reduce newsroom staff by about half. According to publisher Julie Moreno, the paper had suffered declining revenues and had been unable to 'trim costs fast enough to offset that drop despite three rounds of layoffs'. As Rick Edmonds wrote on his Poynter Institute *Biz Blog*, there are risks associated with this strategy. For example, advertisers might reconsider their commitment to the paper and reader reactions are even harder to predict. Edmonds himself also went on the record in 2007 saying that he felt newspapers might last another five to ten years or perhaps 'a bit longer'. The problem in predicting the future with any certainty is the process of combined and uneven development—or, in this case, combined and uneven decline—in the news print industry. While some titles and companies remain profitable, on margins of between 10 and 20 per cent, others are experiencing falling revenues and mushrooming costs (Edmonds, 2007). According to Rick Edmonds, 'Killing the print edition only makes sense if the savings are greater than the loss of print advertising revenue as some choose not to follow along'. In 2007 the picture was far from crystal clear for Edmonds: '[O]ne could hypothesize a future in which the daily print paper has died but the Sunday paper with its robust revenue stream and popular packet of inserts continues as a viable business.'

It might be premature to say that print is dying, but can it survive for much longer? According to Meyer, the decline in newspapers has been slow but steady for the past 50 years. Nonetheless, newspapers have survived the arrival of both radio and television. Perhaps, then, we need to be cautious about predictions of an imminent collapse. Meyer places the beginning of the decline of newsprint in the 1960s when newspapers were already a mature industry but most were still family owned and usually local to one city or town. In the 1960s, the US publishing group Gannett began to buy up newspapers, shutting some and forming natural monopolies with the others. Similar trends were apparent around the world. This is an historic process seen in many maturing industries in which large national or international firms absorb smaller, struggling companies, reducing local competition and leading to cost savings as infrastructure and other assets can be shared across the group. By the mid-1980s, this strategy had lifted operating margins from around 10 per cent to nearly 25 per cent across the print news industry. Robert McChesney attributes at least part of this shift to the relaxation of US media regulation from the 1970s on, particularly around the cross-ownership of print and broadcast outlets, which led to 'wave after wave of media deal making' (McChesney, 2008b, p. 39). Such patterns emerge across the English-speaking world. For example, it was in the 1960s that Rupert Murdoch began his march towards moguldom after taking over a small family business in the Australian city of Adelaide on his father's death. As Meyer notes, the real impact of this shift was an illusory growth rate that pleased the bankers and investment brokers, but actually harmed the long-term future of newspapers. Meyer argues (2004, p. 15) that more 'forward-thinking' news bosses may have been on the harvesting path in order to gather in resources for investment in new media, particularly from the mid-1990s, but the diffusion of share ownership to individuals and institutions who demanded a steady return on investment led most to view the future only in terms of 'maximizing short-term profit', not holding on to market share. As former editor Gavin Ellis (2010) pointed out, for most of this period proprietors ignored falling reader and circulation figures while raising advertising prices. This approach, which began to gain some momentum in the 1990s, has its roots in the shift from editorial principles to the principles of managerialism and marketing that began in the 1970s. American media researcher Derek Underwood pinpoints the change to a February 1989 meeting of the American Newspaper Publishers Association in Miami. It was, he says, a turning point 'in convincing editors that they must remake their newspapers in the name of better reader relations and improved customer service'. What this meant in practice was shorter stories, more news briefs and a focus 'on people rather than events' (Underwood, 1993, p. 5). McChesney supports this view, and adds that as news-gathering became 'more explicitly directed by market concerns' (2008b, p. 39) the focus of journalism became softer and real political coverage suffered. Unfortunately, this did not stem the outward tide in readership and market share.

The financial problem—while it exercised minds in boardrooms and newsrooms—was actually social and cultural. More working mothers, more distractions keeping youth away from newspapers and television news, a more mobile working population and shifting ethnic demographics are just some of the non-economic factors that contributed to a declining audience reach throughout the 1980s and 1990s. Well before the Internet revolution, newspapers were losing out to specialist magazines, cable television, video and home-recording, computer games, direct marketing and other forms of media that were competing for people's attention. On top of all this, says Underwood, the recession of the late 1980s ate into newspaper profits as retailers cut back on their advertising spend. The outcome, after 10 years of soul searching and research by newspaper executives was a change in thinking: newspapers would no longer be mostly about the big issues and stories of the day; they would

become a 'product in the marketplace' that attempted to offer readers a total lifestyle package. However, this did not work either, and so
American newspapers were on a merry-go-round of change, respond-
ing to each new research report that urged another shift in course. The
only thing left intact at the end of the 1980s, says Underwood, is that
marketing had become 'ingrained' in newspaper cultures, along with an
army of financial advisers, graphics teams, marketing consultants and 'a
new breed of corporate editors'. Newsrooms were continually being
'reshaped' to 'dovetail' into the new corporate goals. It seemed, at the
time, that there was nothing left to do other than continue the strategy
of harvesting the goodwill of the brand until, inevitably, it ran out and
the newspaper had no option other than to fold. Newspaper executives
and shareholders should be learning from recent history and strategizing
ways of maintaining their assets, but it rather seems that panic, not clear-
headed thinking, is the order of the day.

Are newspapers really dying?

Death Row? Not quite.

Peter Kirwan

There are plenty of indicators that the number of newspapers and newspaper jobs in the United States has declined over the last few years. It is
clear that the trend in circulation and paid sales for newspapers in most
of the Western world has been downward since about 2003, particularly
in the US (Choire, 2009). There are similar scenarios in the broadcast
and print news industries in many countries, including the United Kingdom, Australia and New Zealand. Peter Kirwan argues that to avoid
total collapse, British newspaper owners 'must strike a precarious balance between cutting costs and investing in the future' (Kirwan, 2009a).
At the end of July 2009, a rumour circulating among London journalists
was predicting that *The Observer*, one of Britain's oldest surviving newspapers and long a staple of the UK quality news market, was going to
be closed. According to a report in *The Times*, the *Observer*'s owner, the
Scott Trust, was divided over whether or not to retain a weekly magazine with the same masthead or close the paper down because it was a
financial drain on the company's finances. The *Observer*'s circulation had
declined from a high of 1.3 million copies in 1979 to 440,000 in 2009

(O'Connell, 2009). The company was in trouble, despite the widely held belief that being managed in perpetuity by a trust fund would shield it somewhat from market forces. According to news reports in the UK, the Guardian News and Media Group—publishers of *The Guardian* and *The Observer*—lost a huge £89.8 million in the trading year that ended in March 2009. In the 2008 financial year it made a healthy profit of £306.4 million (Silk, 2009).

The anecdotal evidence supports the thesis of collapsing newspapers, but collating and analyzing the data on newspaper circulation and readership is a mammoth task and the most detailed figures—published by the World Association of Newspapers—are, not surprisingly, upbeat about the future of newspapers globally. In its 2008 *World Press Trends* report, the WAN argues that the newspaper industry—in both print and online versions—has a bright future. Paid circulations and readership both grew in the period 2003–07 according to *World Press Trends*, despite an obvious decline in the United States, Western Europe and other industrial nations (WAN, 2008). We might expect WAN—the global peak body for the newspaper industry—to be optimistic, but it is notable in the *World Press Trends* report that free titles—particularly in some large American and European cities—were the fastest growing area of circulation and readership. According to the 2008 WAN report, newspaper circulation globally rose 2.57 per cent in 2007, but the 2009 report shows that circulation rose only by 1.3 per cent in 2008. The 2009 report also contains a sobering 'reality-check' comment from WAN president Gavin O'Reilly: '. . . this growth is taking place in the developing markets of the world and masks a continued downward trend in the developed markets'. O'Reilly goes on to criticize what he calls the 'doom and gloom' merchants infected with a case of 'wilful self-mutilation' who are bemoaning the 'death' of the newspaper industry. To some extent O'Reilly is right, and the figures produced WAN's 2009 report tend to back his claims:

- 1.9 billion people read a paid daily newspaper every day.
- Newspapers reach 41 per cent more adults than the World Wide Web presently does.
- More adults read a newspaper every day than eat a Big Mac every year.

These facts and figures might give the newspaper industry some hope, but the trend is downwards; between 1984 and 2004 newspaper circulation in the US dropped from 64 to 53 million (figures cited in Ahlers, 2006). On a global scale, however, this is offset by rises in circulation and readership in some countries. Figures for the US and UK are dropping steadily and therefore most commentary from the Western areas of the world is pessimistic at best. It seems much of the circulation increase comes from non-English-speaking areas, namely Africa (+6.9 per cent), South America (+1.8 per cent) and Asia (+2.9 per cent). Even the areas showing a loss are not showing dramatic circulation falls, with Australia, Oceania and Europe decreasing by 2.5 per cent and North America dropping 3.7 per cent (WAN, 2009).

It's the US that seems to be suffering more than the rest as far as paid circulation goes, and this is borne out by the job losses and closures documented by Erica Smith's *Paper Cuts* website. According to Audit Bureau of Circulation figures, total US newspaper circulation decreased by more than 7 per cent in 2008. Interestingly enough, the figures released for individual newspapers showed decreases throughout the top 25, with the exception of the *Wall Street Journal* (+0.6 per cent). *USA Today*, the *Wall Street Journal* and the *New York Times* are still the three largest papers in the US according to circulation figures, it was the tabloid papers that had the most significant drops in circulation. With the New York *Daily News* dropping by 14.3 per cent and the *New York Post* by more than 20 per cent on 2007 figures, it could be argued that consumers are happy to read their tabloid news free online but still prefer to pay for 'real' news. The *Post* itself, however, claimed the drop in circulation was due to an increase in price, from 25 cents to 50 cents. While the *New York Times* fared better than many of its city rivals, the paper still suffered a 3.6 per cent drop in circulation, with a daily reach of an estimated 1,039,031 readers. Importantly for the *Times*, however, despite the decrease in circulation, its 2008 price rise led to a slight increase in revenue (Arango, 2009).

Certain newspapers saw declines in circulation in both Australia and New Zealand, although the decreases were far less significant than the US and UK. In fact, Rupert Murdoch's flagship *The Australian* increased its circulation figures between 2007 and 2008 (from 133,000 to 136,000). Other papers, including *The Telegraph* and the *Sydney Morning Herald*, showed slight decreases, though minor compared to the drop in circulation that US and UK news reports have suggested. While, as a whole, the WAN figures for 2008 showed a decrease in Australian circulation, the drop was a mere 0.9 per cent, with more than 20 million newspaper sales each week (Newspaper Works, 2009). New Zealand's three major papers, the *New Zealand Herald*, the *Dominion Post* and the Christchurch *Press*, all showed a loss in circulation figures from 2007 to 2008, with the *Herald* losing about 14,000 buyers, dropping to 180,939 (Newspaper Works, 2009). In August 2010, the *Herald* was trumpeting its status as New Zealand's 'most read' newspaper, with a daily readership of 600,000. But buried in the story was the fact that audited circulation was 'holding even . . . at just over 170,000' (New Zealand Herald, 2010). Did someone mention 'spin'?

It clearly pays to be cautious with circulation and readership figures, but a reported rise in circulation in Asia is not a new trend, with China and India clear leaders in the WAN 2007 figures. The year 2007 showed a 1.9 per cent global increase, although this figure drops to just 0.04 per cent if Asia is excluded (Press Trust of India, 2007). In Brazil, newspaper circulation has grown steadily since 2001, with a 10.5 per cent growth in capital cities and a 25 per cent growth in tabloid papers. The country's traditional papers, however, have taken the biggest hit, showing a 25 per cent overall drop (Menezes, 2009).

Though the paid circulation figures of newspapers did not show a great change, the circulation of free newspapers dropped significantly according to the 2009 figures compiled by Piet Bakker, a professor in Amsterdam who tracks circulation figures on his blog site *Newspaper Innovation*. According to Bakker, European papers have been hit severely by circulation drops, with a 10 per cent fall since 2008. In the first half of 2009, 14 European titles closed. Globally, circulation figures have dropped by about 9 per cent, though as with paid circulation figures, free paper circulation in Asia is still rising (Bakker, 2009). In August 2009, James Murdoch announced the closure of News International's free London afternoon paper, *The London Paper*, and rival free-sheet *Metro* cut 30 jobs around the same time. According to industry gossip, this was a signal that the free afternoon papers were failing; *The London Paper* was reported to have lost as much as £21 million in the 2008/09 tax year (Reuters, 2009).

It is interesting that throughout 2008, in countries such as the US where there has been a drop in paid circulation, there has been an overall increase in readership—combining print and online reach—of about 8 per cent. Of these readers, 52 per cent of the online audience claim they spend the same amount of time online as they do with a print paper, and 82 per cent of the online audience claim they do not read online news exclusively and have read a printed paper in the same week (Bollenbache, 2009). Though the Internet may not be solely to blame for circulation falls, it is likely it plays a major part. In the first three months of 2009 more than 73 million unique users visited newspaper websites according to research from WAN. The figure at the same time in 2008 was 10.5 per cent less, at around 65 million (Arango, 2009). The UK's highest-rating site in 2008 was *The Guardian*, with 18.7 million unique users, while a number of news sites showed considerable increases, such as the *Mail Online*, with its highest ever figures of 18,712,533, an increase of 100 per cent from May 2007. While the US and UK newspaper sites are doing well in the online readership surveys, the *Times of India* recorded an online readership of 159 million unique hits, which is considerably more than the *New York Times* (142 million), *The Sun* (UK) (142 million) and the *Washington Post* (61 million).

While online audiences are undoubtedly growing, in the last few years masthead-branded online sites have not shown the same revenue potential as their print counterparts. In the first half of 2009, Newspaper Association of America (NAA) numbers showed a decrease in both online and print revenue, with total figures dropping by more than 16 per cent to less than $38 billion. As the full picture for 2009 became available, it was clear that the downward trend in circulation, readership and advertising continued. In the UK, *The Daily Telegraph* dropped 9.8 per cent year on year, *The Guardian* fell 16 per cent, *The Independent* dropped 11 per cent and *The Times* dropped 16.9 per cent. Looking at UK paid-for sales only, the *Financial Times* dropped 8.8 per cent to an average of 79,864 sales per day (Ponsford, 2010). For the 100 leading American newspapers, the average fall in the second half of 2009 was more than 10 per cent; total newspaper sales fell to around 44 million copies, lower than at any time since the 1940s. In the same period, advertising revenues fell by more than 28 per cent (Perez–Pena, 2009). It seems the biggest question facing newspapers is not so much who is buying the papers, but who is (or in many cases who isn't) buying the ad space.

Will downloads kill the video stars?

The music industry does like to insist that file sharing—aka illegal downloading—is killing the industry, that every one of the millions of music files downloaded each day counts as a 'lost' sale, which, if only it could somehow have been prevented, would have put stunning amounts of money into impoverished artists' hands. And, of course, music industry bosses' wallets. But we won't mention that.

Charles Arthur

Video didn't kill the radio stars, as the '70s pop band The Buggles sang, but it is possible to argue that downloads might kill the radio *and* the video stars. But funnily enough, *Guardian* blogger Charles Arthur (2009) thinks it's video-gaming that is denting sales in the music industry, not illegal downloads. Given the historical blending of media forms and platforms it's unlikely, but broadcasting has gradually moved from an analogue base in the 20th century to a digital base in the 21st. It is also slowly moving from broadcasting to narrowcasting, targeting smaller, niche audiences with tailored content. This should, theoretically, open up a whole new universe of opportunity for broadcast journalism; but it's not necessarily having this effect. Why? Part of the answer is that localism is both a strength and a weakness of radio in the digital age. The digital revolution has made radio more portable and also allowed audiences to time-shift information and current affairs broadcasting through downloads and podcasts. Recent American studies indicate that a large number of 18–24-year-olds are now listening to individual play-lists on iPods and other MP3 format players and perhaps only listening to the radio in their cars (Albarran et al., 2007). The Albarran study of American undergraduates also suggests that for any use other than finding news and information, young adults prefer the iPod or down-loads from music sites over listening to the radio. The study concluded that the radio industry will have a difficult time recapturing its young audiences when variety and choice are their key motivations for audio consumption. A second impact of convergence has been the formatting of network programs across what were once local stations, which has tended to alienate some audiences. Consolidation of programming and stripping out of local content is another cost-saving measure that allows for one radio signal to service several geographically distant markets (Sauls and Greer, 2007). Around 2004, the new subscription service satellite radio networks in the US were being hyped as the next big thing in digital broadcasting, offering a mixed-business model that included some advertising revenue. But, even then, industry analysts recognized that profit margins would be tight and the fight for subscribers fierce (Green, Lowry and Yang, 2005). In 2007, shares in Sirius, a leading satellite-radio provider, were trading at $3.54, but in March 2010 the company was fighting to retain its NASDAQ listing as its share price fell below $1.00, even though the network had over 18 million subscribers. News reports suggested at the time that Liberty Media—a global media and satellite company—was looking to take over Sirius.

The key discussion here is again based on arguments from political economy, which examines the issue from economic, cultural and socio-political perspectives. As the profitability of radio declines, strategic mergers between existing operators—to consolidate investment in expensive equipment—are being suggested as one solution to rising costs. Ultimately, though, the audience gets squeezed through these transactions. As Robert McChesney has argued, digital technologies have accelerated the process of change, in particular cost-cutting and resource-sharing in networked radio and in television news; but more broadly there is a process of technological and business discontinuity under way that impacts on the entire broadcasting industry (Ahlers, 2006). In the early years of convergence, CNN and the Fox network were able to remain profitable. The operating profit for the Fox network in the US tripled in 12 months from September 2001. The other advantage gained through cross-media ownership in broadcasting is the ability to cross-promote assets in other media. For example, news reports and other programming can be used to promote films, concerts and musical acts owned by the same parent company. This seems logical from a business perspective, particularly if you are Fox or Viacom or Disney. Media political economist Eileen Meehan (2007) calls this the 'synergy' methodology that works to integrate oligopolies with each other to maintain overall profitability at the expense of real competition.

So, if readership and circulation figures seem to indicate that newspapers are not going to disappear overnight, even though advertising revenues are dropping steadily, what about radio and television? If it's difficult to find clear and objective data on newspaper circulation and readership, attempting to source accurate figures about broadcast listening and viewing is even harder. For media companies the ability to tell a positive story and prop up the advertising rate card is more important than providing accurate circulation and ratings data. According to some sources there are more than 21,000 television stations around the world and nearly 45,000 radio stations. Unfortunately, while this might seem like a consumer paradise of choice, the political economy of broadcasting—like that of the print media—has steadily seen global conglomerates develop to dominate regional markets using the successful 'Hollywood' model of amassing huge libraries of content and on-selling costly high-value productions into the global marketplace (Waisbord, 2004). As Mike Wayne points out clearly in *Marxism and Media Studies*, the tendency towards monopolisation in the global capitalist economy is evident in the shrinking number of giant media corporates that now dominate global production and distribution of news and entertainment worldwide. The American 'Big Five' have carved up the national free-to-air and subscription television markets across North America (Meehan, 2007), but the same methods are used globally and for a large international media company, such as Murdoch's News Corporation, the ability to synergistically repackage content across many national platforms (Fox in the USA and Australia, Sky in the UK and New Zealand, Star in China, etc.) is a very important business tool.

Television is also different because it already had a trans-global distribution system in place prior to the emergence of the digital economy. There are national distribution channels, but also cross-territorial channels, dominated by a few large global companies that on-sell content or format templates that can be given a local flavour (Chalaby, 2003). Despite global synergies, in some countries national networks are losing market share. For example, in the US between 1980 and 2004, nightly audiences for evening network news bulletins fell from 53 million to about 27 million, a drop of 51 per cent over 25 years (Ahlers, 2006). It is the cross-territorial distribution networks that now dominate global television. For example, in 2003, the French-based Pan-European network Arte was in 60 million European households, CNN International in 84.7 million households, BBC World in 56.4 million households and MTV in a staggering 92.4 million households. The figures from 1997 to 2002 give an indication of the scale of growth in those years; satellite and cable channels had an average reach of 33.5 million European households in 1997 and an average reach of 47.8 million households in 2002. Between 1988 and 2002, advertising revenues for these trans-national networks increased by a factor of 20, from 31 million to 628 million Euros. On a global scale the leading trans-national broadcast networks also have a huge reach: BBC World 94 million households, CNN International 172 million, Discovery 222 million and MTV 382 million households (Chalaby, 2003). A 2009 study predicted there would be more than 370 million pay TV subscribers worldwide in the next few years (ABI Research, 2009). Any global business would love to have that level of market penetration and the scale of the trans-national television market underlies the importance of the media industry to the world economy. It also highlights the dialectic between commerce and civil society, particularly in the ways that trans-national television—delivered via satellite and/or cable technologies—has transformed some aspects of public life in parts of Asia, Africa and the Middle East.[1] Indeed, some scholars suggest that one positive aspect of global trans-national television is the expansion of cross-cultural and multi-cultural programming (Keane and Moran, 2008). However, in more mature markets the tendency has been towards monopoly and cross-media ownership. For example, in Japan the introduction of satellite services has led to changes in regulation and business practices where analogue 'spectrum scarcity' is replaced by 'abundance' of digital broadcast channels (Kwak, 2008).

The latest technological addition to trans-national television distribution is to link the television screen to an array of interactive value-added services, such as live gambling on horse racing, football and other sports. This could be a potential goldmine for News Corporation, which has a stake in interactive wagering in 15 or more markets from Hong Kong to California and Latin America. It is also another way in which the clickstream of computer users can be monetized by linking their television screens and credit cards via a server and set-top black box. Wide-area distribution that spreads the cost and the risk, coupled with the technology to manage account betting by consumers, is attractive as a new revenue source for key players in global television (Kruse, 2009). The transition from analogue to digital, and from national to global platforms for broadcasting television signals, has also shifted the dynamics of power—not only are distribution channels now important, it is vital for the key players to also control a library of content. In this environment control of sport content has become a significant battleground in the competitive television market (Hutchins and Rowe, 2009).

Television networks, whether terrestrial and national in scope or trans-national, are not immune from the declining numbers of eyeballs that are regularly viewing their broadcasts. To some extent large global players can move with their audience by offering set-top boxes that encourage time-shifted viewing. The downside is that the same device can also be used—and increasingly is—to skip through the advertisements at high speed. All news media, and big media generally, are confronted too by the generational shift in consumption patterns. A lot more media consumption today is on portable devices that can access content over the telecommunications network. Overlaying all of this is the uncertain economic future and the global differentials that mark the process of combined and uneven development across the world's media industries. Television is still the dominant news and entertainment medium and newspapers will be around in one form or another for some years to come. But the future is convergence—in particular the melding of the computer screen with the television and the mobile communication device (because it's so much more than a phone). CNN's news website, for example, claims more than 75 million unique visitors per month. However, for the moment—like at other times of 'critical juncture'—the only constant is change, even if it's not to everyone's taste. Ben Grossman, a journalist himself, laments the lowering of standards (as he sees it) inflicted on television news by cost-cutting and by the ubiquity of the Internet. He says there is no doubt that traditional journalism is 'under siege', before adding: 'The more poignant query is whether the medium is evolving or devolving. We all like to say it is the former. But let's be honest: We all deeply fear it's the latter.'

The issues Grossman says he encountered while watching a TV news bulletin centred around amateur footage in two stories (one from YouTube) and then he was even more offended when, in a third item, 'the interview subject was actually holding the microphone' (Grossman, 2009). What Ben Grossman found so disappointing—the use of YouTube and amateur footage, the talent holding the microphone—are aspects of the emerging News 2.0 model that incorporates user-generated content and amateur reporters. It is an aspect of convergence culture, and we either learn to live with it or bury our heads in the sand. Media executives are quickly scrambling to make up lost ground—they have begun to understand that technological convergence brings with it both threats and opportunities. Networks are outsourcing, looking at cheaper Web-based distribution models and 'viewing the Web as the next battlefield for eyeballs and ad dollars, looking beyond the cable news networks' (Weprin, 2009). Their short-term approach is to attempt to harness the power of Web 2.0 to the advantage of their corporate goals. As they do this there are impacts on the quality of journalism, as Ben Grossman discovered one night in Los Angeles. The news industry might not be dead yet but, in the scramble to maintain the life-support of profitability, might it still kill journalism?

---

[1] For details, see Bahry, 2001; Martin, 2006; Miles, 2005; Pintak and Ginges, 2009; Thomas, 2003

5

Is this the end of journalism?

Not journalists, but churnalists.

Nick Davies

If Nick Davies is right and we're now living in an era where 'churnalism' has replaced real journalism, then reporters and editors have a big job ahead of them to regain the public trust that has been lost. Part of the problem is, as Davies has pointed out, structural—the capitalist nature of the news industry works against full disclosure, overly critical discussion, truth and public interest; but it also has something to do with the very culture of journalism as it has been practised since at least the 1950s. It's useful to start with this decade because it is the recent history of journalism that is important. While some reference will be made to earlier journalistic cultures, the issues that news workers are facing today stem directly from the changes that have occurred in the real age of mass media—that is, from the time when the contours of the 20th century mediascape were formed: the age of radio, television and the mass-circulation modern newspaper. It was also in this period that the Fourth Estate became the dominant way of thinking about the news media, even though the term itself comes from the 18th century.

The Fourth Estate model requires a particular type of journalistic organization and culture in order to function with any real sense of purpose. For most of the 20th century the organization and culture of journalism was bound up with the mass-industrial model of news production that we've seen is now failing, if not in terminal decline. A 2009 report for the Reuters Institute for the Study of Journalism suggests that digitization of news production and distribution has the potential to 'hollow out the craft of journalism' (Currah, 2009). Under such circumstances, there will be little time for original and expensive investigative journalism, which is at the heart of the Fourth Estate role of the news media. Even more alarming, notes the report's author, Dr Andrew Currah, is that news-gathering is being outsourced: 'not only [to] trusted wire agencies, but also [to] the public relations industry' and to citizen journalists. A new model of outsourcing was gaining traction in 2009: the so-called 'content farms' where armies of freelance 'reporters' are paid about US$5 per item to write short 'articles' in response to common queries on Google and other search engines that are then uploaded to websites such as *eHow*, *answerbag* and *Travels.com* (*The Economist*, 2010a). By the end of 2009 a number of content farms' operations were within the top 20 websites in North America (MacManus, 2009). Not only do these operations swamp the Internet with what Dan Gillmor calls 'mediocre content', Andrew Currah sees this brave new future of journalism as another form of industrial reporting, one in which news workers become 'prisoners of the screen: cogs in a highly demanding news factory'. However, it is a news factory where time and resource constraints contribute to a loss of diversity in news sources; a greater reliance on cheap (if not totally free) amateurs and user-generated content and a greater distance between the reporter and the world outside the newsroom. Therefore, Currah argues, reporters are less likely to 'capture the complexity' of news stories, or to contextualize 'facts, events and stories'.

Is the Fourth Estate finished?

> There can be no higher law in journalism than to tell the truth and to shame the devil.
>
> **Walter Lippmann**

The Irish-born philosopher and statesman Edward Burke (1729–97) is widely attributed with coining the phrase Fourth Estate to refer to the gallery of reporters who haunted the Palace of Westminster during sittings of the English parliament. Unfortunately, there is no direct record of his words, but the Scottish essayist Thomas Carlyle referred to them in the following terms in his 1869 book *Heroes and Hero-Worship*:

Whoever can speak, speaking now to the whole nation, becomes a power, a branch of government, with inalienable weight in law-making, in all acts of authority. It matters not what rank he has, what revenues or garnitures: the requisite thing is that he have a tongue which others will listen to; this and nothing more is requisite.

Carlyle wrote these words in 1841, but the term Fourth Estate came into common usage through a number of sources. Irish playwright and poet Oscar Wilde used it, like many others, in a sardonic way when he wrote in his 1891 essay 'The soul of man under socialism':

Somebody—was it Burke?—called journalism the Fourth Estate. That was true at the time, no doubt. But at the present moment it really is the only estate. It has eaten up the other three. The Lords Temporal say nothing, the Lords Spiritual have nothing to say, and the House of Commons has nothing to say and says it. We are dominated by Journalism.

In the same paragraph, Wilde argues that the 'tyranny that [British journalism] proposes to exercise over people's private lives seems to me to be quite extraordinary'. Clearly he was not a fan of 19th century British journalism, and even suggests that perhaps the British public get the journalism they deserve: 'The fact is that the public have an insatiable curiosity to know everything, except what is worth knowing. Journalism, conscious of this, and having tradesman like habits, supplies their demands.'

Wilde continues by describing that there are obviously some, motivated by base instincts and perhaps even starvation, who will write salacious stories, but ends by suggesting that there are also reporters whose motivation is more honourable: 'It is a very degrading position for anybody of educated men to be placed in, and I have no doubt that most of them feel it acutely.'

The Fourth Estate is a flawed model for journalism today[1] and Wilde's stinging criticism rings a bell for us. However, stripped to its bare essentials, the Fourth Estate model was really about upholding and advancing the interests of a growing bourgeois public. This is still the core of professional journalism: the question is really about whether or not it can survive in the age of News 2.0 when it seems to be under a three-pronged threat from bloggers, amateurs *and* corporate greed. An attempt to breathe new life into the Fourth Estate model was initiated in the mid-1990s and one of the leading proponents of this cause was the Australian journalist and writer Julianne Schultz. In her 1998 book *Reviving the Fourth Estate*, Schultz argued that by reclaiming the values of Carlyle and the early champions of free and independent journalism, perhaps journalism could be saved from itself. However, it has really come to nothing and, by her own admission, Schultz recognized that attempting to revive the Fourth Estate was a thankless, even hopeless, task given the commercial pressures that dominate any democratic ideals that journalists, reporters and editors might harbour about their work. There's general consensus among media sociologists that journalism is a commodity when it lands on the news stand—in the same way that a new car is a commodity when it hits the showroom—but there's little clarity about what this actually means. It's obvious to most commentators that it implies 'a number of market-led restraints' (McNair, 1998), but to others it means the unfettered circulation of ideas: 'we are speaking of a market, offering choice' (Horne, 1994).

In this 'free markets' version, the *myth* of the Fourth Estate is an effective ideology that masks the symbiotic relationship between the media, the ruling class and the state. When it is challenged, 'the media's real agenda—commercial success and maintenance of the status quo—is revealed' (Schultz, 1998, p. 55). Professionalism can blind reporters to the assumptions that underpin their daily practice and to their own objective situation as 'churners' of the dominant ideology. The ideological spectacles, worn so comfortably by some journalists and with irritation by others in the media, tend to blur the vision and take the class antagonisms of capitalism out of focus. The late Greek Marxist Nicos Poulantzas noted that this class-blindness 'gives rise to specifically corporatist forms of trade-union struggle; this competitive isolation is the basis of a complex ideological process that takes the form of petty-bourgeois individualism' (1975, p. 291). This ideology—expressed in the ideals of the Fourth Estate and journalistic professionalism (Hirst 2010)—can only be challenged under conditions of extreme crisis: events (so far unforeseen) that would push industrially organized 'grey collar journalists' (Hirst, 2003) closer to the ranks of the proletariat, where their economic condition would appear to place them in relation to other workers and to capital itself. While these implicit class relations are not always obvious, they underpin the social relations of news production that have existed since the late 19th century.

The age of industrial journalism

> Professional journalism emerged not to the opposition of most media owners, but to the contrary, with their active sponsorship ... It made sense for media owners to grant some autonomy to journalists because it gave their product more credibility and worked to enhance their commercial prospects.
>
> **Robert McChesney**

As journalism emerged as a distinct discipline of labour in the late 19th and early 20th centuries, a systematic pattern of 'how to do journalism' developed within the social relations of the news industry. Newspaper offices were in fact news factories. For many, this was seen as the beginning of professionalism in the reporting of news—based on an emerging ideology of promoting balance, accuracy, fairness and objectivity as key values for reporters. Industrial journalism grew into a production system that foregrounded news as a commodity and that was predicated on an assembly-line methodology. This involved the systematic collection of relevant facts, with an emphasis on official sources, the use of an inverted pyramid template and a 'standardized product, able to be distributed as a self-contained unit' (Bruns, 2008, p. 81). This pattern suited media capital, because it allowed owners and managers to create a format favourable to advertisers, and throughout the 20th century it was evolved along similar lines to the ways in which generalized labour developed in the capitalist economy. This 'constant drumbeat for profit' and a 'concern with minimizing costs' (McChesney, 2008c, p. 37) has been a major influence on the ways that journalism has been practised for at least the last 150 years. The commercial model also operates hand-in-glove with an implicit ideological agenda that Herman and Chomsky (1988) characterized as 'manufacturing consent'.

Traditional work practices and routines in the field of journalism and news-gathering developed in the context of a need for newspaper owners to guarantee a return on their investment and a political return—a complacent working class. They set about systematically organizing news production to meet these needs by guaranteeing a regular supply of the commodity 'news' to audiences and a regular supply of commodified 'audiences' to advertisers. It is the general commodity form of capitalism that gives industrial journalism its shape, content and social position in the class structures of the system (Taylor Jackson, 2009). News, as a form of communicative action, employs the productive technologies of printing, broadcasting and Web publishing within a set of social relations that are at the same time both fixed and in constant flux. They are, in a capitalist world, necessarily class relations that are shaped by 'the outcomes of nego-tiations, battles, or alliances among class forces' (Artz, 2006, p. 23). Like all industrial production, journalism occurs within social relations that legiti-mize and normalize market forces economically, culturally and politically. The published or broadcast-news commodity is distributed through com-mercial channels and is surrounded by advertising, and this serves both an economic and an ideological purpose in relation to journalism. This is the duality of the news commodity—the dialectical tension between private profit and public interest (Hirst and Patching, 2007). It is this clash of social relations that makes news a 'contested commodity' (Taylor Jackson, 2009). It seems to make the market both a rational and indeed the *only* form of social organization that can support a free press.

By the late 19th century, advertising had become the social glue that helped to keep the capitalist economy ticking over. If consumers didn't know that certain goods were for sale in certain locations and at certain prices, how could they plan their consumption? In other words, how would they know where and when to shop and how much to budget for their purchases? But also, how would they know how to con-sume—to indulge in 'retail therapy'—if advertising and popular culture didn't intrude to disguise and commodify humanity's real relationship with labour and natural resources? Newspapers developed as a means of circulating commercial information—everything from stock-market movements to shipping news and the availability of everyday goods and services for the household—but they also became vehicles for the trans-mission of ideologically loaded information—creating the conditions of 'hegemony': normalized and mostly hidden relations of subordination and domination.

Mass-media capitalists have made a lot of money from advertisers but, with rare exceptions, most people would not buy a newspaper just for the advertising it contained. The adverts need to be broken up with useful, or at least interesting, bits of non-commercial information. In this context, a formula for deciding what information might become news and how to gather that information and then present it in a useful form to readers became necessary. Throughout the age of industrial journalism, newspapers and broadcasters were driven by deadlines because the advertising content needed to be fresh each day; so too, then, did the news. In the 19th century, to make the production of newspapers as efficient and cheap as possible, the formula for turning random bits of information into news needed to be tightly controlled, manageable and able to fit within the daily cycle of deadlines. It's no surprise that the space left in the pages of a newspaper once all the advertising is placed became known as the 'newshole'. Each new day required that this newshole be filled with fresh information. By the mid-19th century, the most efficient way to do this was, in some cases, to buy copy in bulk from a wholesaler—a news agency such as Reuters (founded in 1851), Associated Press (started in 1846) or UPI (begun in 1907). In other cases, when news was not able to be supplied in this bulk format, newspapers had to hire their own reporters. Most reporters were assigned to cover local news from the area in which the newspaper circulated because the agencies were either national or international and could supply plenty of news from other places, but rarely of the right sort to satisfy an audience's interest and curiosity about events that were happening in their city, town or neighbourhood. By the early years of the 20th century, the industrial model of news production became the dominant form for the mass media, based on advertising revenues and some income from sales (for newspapers). Reporters, sub-editors and printers were the backbone of this industry—a mix of white, grey and blue collar workers. The main 'thinking' work was done by journalists who had to craft the content that would fill the newshole and make the product attractive to consumers. Thus we can begin to understand the process of journalism as an act of creative intellectual labour and journalists as collectively a group 'occupying a contradictory position between capital and the "traditional" working class' (Wayne, 2003, p. 7).

Public intellectuals of the everyday

Under capitalism, the elaboration and dissemination of ideas become specialized within a particular category of

people who monopolise premium modes of knowledge . . . a
group torn in a three-way split between labour, capital and
the petit bourgeoisie.

Mike Wayne

A political-economy approach to the sociology of journalism leads,
almost inevitably, to examining the work of reporters and editors from
the perspective of class (Wayne, 2003), and this remains an important
issue in the discussion of alternative forms of journalism—such as citizen
journalism and the integration of user-generated content (UGC)—into
the mainstream media system. If we are to abandon the industrial model
of news and journalism, or if it is going to be destroyed by 'journalism
from below', then what is going to replace it? This is obviously a crucial
concern for *News 2.0* and it is expressed in the question 'Can journalism survive the Internet?' But before this question can be answered, it
is imperative that the current structure, strengths and weaknesses of the
industrial journalism model are clearly understood. Journalists perform
an important intellectual function for capital—the normalizing, extension and re-imaging of hegemonic ideology—but they do so as wage
workers. That is, they are technically and structurally part of the labouring
classes. But, crucially, their work is part of capital's 'command and control
structure' (Wayne, 2003, p. 18), embedded in a very hierarchical division
of labour within the 'cultural industries' (news and entertainment media,
publishing and so on). It is this duality of the news commodity that creates most of the ideological tension in journalism and the news.

The hegemonic ideology of 'professionalism' in the media's ranks
would suggest that journalists are part of the 'middle class' and perhaps
some well-paid hacks are close to being members of the 'elite'. The 'grey
collar' argument is that the majority of journalists are workers, but the
dual nature of the news 'product' allocates them to contradictory class
locations with resulting ambivalence in their self-realized world-view.
There is in fact an emotional dialectic at play that drags news workers in
the direction of one or the other of the major social classes. They vacillate
and sometimes change sides, but they also reflect and expose, to the careful
reader, listener or viewer, the unsolvable contradictions within the system
as a whole, whether economic, legal, social, cultural or political. Writing
from an Italian prison between 1926 and 1935, the Marxist intellectual
and newspaper editor Antonio Gramsci clearly identified journalists as

intellectuals and the media as 'organizations of intellectual dissemination'. He wrote in 1916 that 'the bourgeois newspapers tell even the simplest of facts in a way that favors the bourgeois class and damns the working class and its politics'.[2] Nothing much has changed. News and journalism continue to have a class-based ideological function today. The difference now is that class contradictions do not appear as sharp as they did in the period 1900–45. However, political economy critiques clearly demonstrate that the interests of the ruling class dominate the news agenda and that news coverage (like much of popular culture) legitimizes and normalizes the hidden power of the economic elites (see, for example, Herman and Chomsky, 1988; McChesney, 2000, 2007; Wayne, 2003).

All journalists, either consciously or unconsciously, will hold a set of cultural and political attitudes towards the subject of 'news'. This may range from an uneasy feeling about some ethical dilemma they might face, to an understanding of the place of journalism in the world and, in the best cases, the ability to question and be reflexive about all the social relations that weave around and through journalism. These elements, as George Orwell put it in his 1946 article 'Why I write', form an 'emotional attitude' common to certain cohorts of journalists and other news workers. In concluding his essay 'Marxism and Postmodernism', the American Marxist scholar Frederic Jameson returns to two important themes that are relevant to a discussion of the class nature of industrial journalism: 'proletarianization on a global scale', and 'something mysteriously called 'cognitive mapping' of a new and global type'. But 'cognitive mapping' is in reality nothing but 'a code word for "class consciousness" of a new and hitherto undreamed of kind' (Jameson, 1998, p. 49).

Jameson's 'cognitive mapping' is Orwell's 'emotional attitude'—it is what the British Marxist Raymond Williams called the 'lived experience' of ideology, it is 'class consciousness'. The concept of 'grey collar' journalism—news workers existing between 'blue' and 'white' collar labour—encompasses a range of emotional attitudes, ideologies, consciousness and political positions that are contradictory and, for some news workers, confused or confusing.

Journalists know their world is changing; the questions for them are really how and why. The 'how' is expressed through the trend for journalism to become cross-generic and cross-platform; we see this in the blurring of boundaries between fact and entertainment and between producers and consumers, between newspapers, television and the Internet. It is evident in the growing phenomenon of 'infotainment' as a genre in its own right and the growing attention that we're all paying to blogs and social media. The cross-generic and cross-platform nature of contemporary journalism is a manifestation of the emotional and technological dialectics of our epoch: in this case the dialectics of what Frederic Jameson (1991) has described as the 'cultural logic of late capitalism', or the 'condition' of postmodernity. In a very interesting study of journalism's modes of production, Peter Berglez of Sweden's Orebro University describes the ongoing digital transformation of capitalism in these clear terms: 'increasing production, exchange, distribution and circulation of "cultural" commodities and services (of information and knowledge)' and all new industry 'interwoven with the continuing rise of new information technologies (ICT's)' (2006, p. 15).

The news industry is clearly affected by these dialectical pressures, which are generated at the very core of the production system, and all of this is happening at a time when the complex global system appears more 'fragile and irrational'—a state of *de-permanence* (Berglez, 2006).You only have to look out of your window to confirm this, or watch the news. At the same time, there is a countervailing pressure towards some form of stability; otherwise, suggests Berglez, the world would simply collapse. That it doesn't is due to the power of an alternative discourse of *permanence*. Ideological permanence (hegemony or manufactured consent) is constructed in the news discourse through the process of *reification*, its central function being 'to transform social material reality into seemingly everlasting "things" with fixed properties' (Berglez, 2006, p. 18). Journalistic modes whose production practices are dominated by capitalist relations of production will tend towards the production or reproduction of such reified discourse codified in the use-value pole of the dialectically bifurcated news commodity. It is the duality of the news commodity that allows it to hold the contradiction—between permanence and flux—in place. This is also an important point to make in relation to the impact of Web 2.0 on journalistic practices. These changes are the result of an insoluble link between the culture of the newsroom and modes of alternative news production and 'transformations in the capitalist mode of production and the logic of capital accumulation' (Hanke, 2005, p. 45). It is the insoluble link between the economic base of the news industry concerned with 'ownership conditions, profit motives, the mode of production etc.' and the superstructure—which circulates hegemonic and discursive ideological elements of the culture of late capitalism and shapes the public sphere 'for the survival of capitalism' (Berglez, 2006, p. 18).

What the promoters of many varieties of alternative journalism are all trying to do—in one way or another—is to actually break this link. Knowingly or unknowingly, what the pioneers of citizen journalism, collaborative professional/amateur (pro-am) projects, e-zines and community broadcasting are doing is attempting to subvert the dominant paradigm—even if just a little bit. Take, for example, the fairly conservative entrepreneurial reporter model now being heavily discussed in North American journalism schools. Students are being encouraged to go 'start-up' and to launch themselves into the digital marketplace (Glaser, 2008). At the same time, around the world, more senior journalists are moving out of mainstream jobs and re-inventing themselves in niche roles. In January 2009, former *New York Times* west coast reporter Sharon Waxman launched *TheWrap* to go independent in the crowded Hollywood gossip and soft-news market (Deahl, 2009). In a story covering Waxman's launch, *MarketWatch* blogger Jon Friedman wrote that it appears to be a growing trend: 'The allure of being your own boss and making a difference has inspired many journalists-turned-entrepreneurs to launch Web sites and leave behind the relative safety of writing articles and publishing books.'

At the other end of the entrepreneurial scale, Atton and Hamilton propose that all modes of alternative journalism have an anti-capitalist sentiment at their core. They are all pushing against the material forces of the news industry while simultaneously attempting to undermine the hegemonic power of so-called professional journalism. Supporters of the 'end of journalism' thesis who promote either entrepreneurialism or citizen journalism and those who wish to defend the continued existence of a cadre of professional journalists—and those in between—are all grappling with points along this dialectical thread. With this principle in mind, it is time to interrogate arguments about the reinvention of journalism—perhaps one way in which it might survive the Internet.

It's journalism, Jim, but not as we know it

Journalism will be reinvented, but judging by what is currently done in journalism schools and in the name of journalism studies, the last people to know may be professional journalists.

John Hartley

The reinvention of journalism, according to John Hartley (2008a), involves a shift in the editorial function of newsrooms—from the gathering and publicizing of new information, to what he calls 'redaction'. Redaction is the process of collating, sorting, ordering and editing information that is generated elsewhere, but it can also mean editing to conceal, such as when documents are blacked out in freedom of information requests. When, as in the case of Google's news search engines, this redactive function is taken over by an algorithm and not done with the intellectual intervention of a person, perhaps we should no longer call it journalism. This day is coming: already at least two projects are underway to automate the writing of news using an algorithm that mimics the basic structure of a news narrative (Bunz, 2010a). We have seen a number of examples of this redactive editing process emerging over the past few years, particularly in newspapers as they move away from their traditional print/text formats to more interactive and online products. For Hartley, redaction involves newsrooms becoming filters for information flows generated out in the audience or 'produser' communities, as Axel Bruns calls them. We also see it working in a more traditional format in collaborative 'pro-am' news websites such as *NewAssignment. net*, *ProPublica* and the now defunct *Assignment Zero*, which has been described as a 'spectacularly successful failure' by some of its supporters and early adopters (Lawton, 2007). However, it is perhaps a little unfair for John Hartley to suggest that professional journalists may be the last to know about journalism's reinvention. In some cases they have led the way and are on the 'front foot'. It would be more accurate to argue that newspaper companies and mainstream broadcasters have actually—if not always successfully—moved to embrace digital technologies and convergence. In doing so, they have also recognized the benefits of sophisticated content-management systems (CMS) developed by the open-source software movement and they have started to move away from the now outdated 'shovelware' applications that saw them simply push copy online from other sources.

One recent UK example is the Trinity Mirror group, publishers of titles in Birmingham and other centres. According to the company's editorial director, Neal Benson, the move online is a response to the twin pressures of a revenue downturn in the print industry and the growing availability and acceptability of online news (Thompson, 2008b). There are many other media companies—in print and broadcasting—who have taken similar steps. In some, such as the TV3 newsroom in Auckland, multimedia editors are sitting on the news desk alongside journalists and producers. In a well publicized move in 2006, *The Guardian* newspaper opted for a 'Web-first' strategy that has since been copied by many others. In this approach, stories are not necessarily held for the morning edition of the paper, but are put online almost as soon as they're finished. For *The Guardian*, the 'Web-first' strategy was aimed at developing the masthead's global online readership and was initially used for breaking foreign and business news while some exclusives were held back for the print edition. In each case, the motivation has been the need to respond to the Web's hunger for copy and incessant/non-existent deadlines. It also has a commercial/competition imperative—the desire to be 'first' with news and not be beaten by major competitors. *The Guardian* faced some mild criticism at the time; the Poynter Institute's Steffen Fjaervik suggested it was in fact only a halfway move to the 'speed model' (first on the Web) of publishing, as the paper would be keeping back some exclusives. Fjaervik described this as the more traditional 'value model', where exclusives are published first to whatever medium holds the most valuable audience. However, with the rate of decline in newspaper readerships and advertising, it might be argued today that the 'value model' and the 'speed model' are coalescing on the Web.

New York University journalism academic Jeff Jarvis attended a March 2007 *Guardian* staff meeting where further editorial and strategic changes were explained to reporters. He commented on his *Buzz Machine* blog that the shift to 24/7 publishing on the Web would impact on staff roles and responsibilities. According to Jarvis, the editor-in-chief of *The Guardian*, Alan Rusbridger called for more 'flexibility' from journalists and editorial staff and noted 'that means that jobs will change'. At the Trinity Mirror Group, the job changes meant a radical overhaul of the copy preparation process. Instead of a five-step process that included sub-editing and page design, it became a three-step process and reporters were re-designated as 'multimedia journalists'. Copy would be gathered, pasted into 'heavily templated' webpages and then published. Thompson noted that 'Trinity have merged the news editing and production function into one'. Multi-skilling is becoming the occupational norm in newsrooms worldwide. As well as saving time, such redactive measures in the newsroom also increase the productivity of individual journalists by reducing the time it takes to get a story from the 'finding' state to the point of publication. In New Zealand and Australia, the redactive function of copy-editing and placing has been outsourced by both the APN and Fairfax media companies. Since mid-2007, an outsourced editing house, PageMasters, has managed a contract to sub-edit and lay out a growing number of pages for major New Zealand titles the *New Zealand Herald* and the *Dominion Post*, as well as regional magazine and suburban titles owned by the publishers. A similar move by Fairfax in Australia in August 2008 was described on the *Editor's Weblog* as a 'key factor' in a decision to reduce staffing levels by over 500 positions (Thompson, 2008a).

In another interesting twist on the staff cuts, redundancies and news load-shedding that is plaguing the news industry globally, organizations are recruiting amateurs to fill the void and also to hold readers and attract new eyeballs to websites. In September 2008, the Trinity Group's *Teeside Evening Gazette*, based in Middlesborough, UK, announced a bold plan to recruit up to 1000 locals to write for 22 'hyperlocal' postcode-based news websites. According to *Gazette* editor Darren Thwaites, a business reason for the hyper-local move was 'monetizing' the sites (Oliver, 2008). Today, most large cities and towns have a number of very local newspapers that are heavily subscribed to by local businesses and that cover what we used to call the 'parish pump' news, referring to the place where locals would often gather to exchange their own form of 'news', usually titbits of information and gossip, which travelled from person to person. Not all newspaper reporters and editors liked the old-style parish pump approach to news. British writer and journalism academic Andrew Grant-Adamson had an early job on the *Buxton Advertiser* in the Peak District of England. In a 2007 *Wordblog* post he outlined why parish pump journalism was not popular with reporters: 'It seemed old fashioned and we fought for brighter newspapers which seemed more in tune with an age when increasing car-ownership was taking people greater distances from home in search of entertainment.'

Parish pump news today is often very parochial and, one could argue, of low news value outside of a very small area, but 200 years ago it was the cultural and political lifeblood of many communities. However, in a full circle return to localism, there are some journalists today who argue that a return to, or a stronger emphasis on, local and 'hyperlocal' news is in fact one way to save the newspaper format. Hyperlocalism is also something that's been adopted by professional and accidental Web journalists. Grant-Adamson makes the point that proximity has always been a prominent news value and he argues that the 'unlimited' space available through Web publishing means a return to localism is not a bad idea and perhaps long overdue. Certainly large media organizations are taking the idea seriously. In March 2008, the Trinity Mirror Group extended its network of hyperlocal news websites right across the nation. At the time of the launch, regional managing director Georgina Harvey said that the 22 hyperlocal news sites 'are closer to the community than any newspaper could hope to achieve'. This push outwards from the newsroom for the collection and generation of news content is another feature of Hartley's redactive editorial culture. The role of journalists in these situations is to manage and massage the content rather than to instigate news stories. This is another aspect of the digital dialectic that is impacting on the social relations of news production. As newsrooms shrink and remaining reporters find themselves with less time to be on the 'beat' ferreting out news, there is a greater reliance on media releases coming into the newsroom and also on amateurs recruited (at little or no cost) to be the eyes and ears of the news operation. The positive side of this arrangement could be that more local content makes it onto the news agenda; the downside is that it is unverified information that may be no more than PR or low-value gossip.

Hartley describes one impact of digital convergence as the genesis of a 'read-write' culture in which the differences between audiences and producers of media are blurring, or disappearing completely. This is in fact a very volatile fault line energised by two contradictory and mutually constituted social forces: the rise of the DIY culture of user-generated content and the slow but continuing collapse of the traditional media certainties in print and broadcasting. These dialectics appear to be embodied in digital technologies that we mostly perceive in the form of commodities or services online. This constitutes an aspect of the 'digital sublime'—the mythology of cyberspace as somehow driven by pure technical innovation and beyond the scope of human agency. As Vincent Mosco argues, these myths are not just a distortion of reality, they also constitute a 'form of reality' that 'give meaning to life' (2004, p. 13). In other words, they are part of the ideological framework in which we come to understand what is going on in the world around us. Unfortunately, we only ever get a partial view from this perspective; the real power and social forces that shape reality and drive society in the direction of convergence are hidden and need to be exposed in order to challenge the hegemonic world-view of capital. Thus, Mosco argues, a political-economic viewpoint must be employed to understand the dialectic between 'digitization' and 'commodification' that provides the foundation for the 'technological sublime' (2004, p. 154).

It is important to understand that the emergent convergence culture that Henry Jenkins describes has not sprung into being, ready-formed, at some definable point in the recent past. It is, as Jenkins suggests, a 'kludge'—an incomplete, unpolished work in progress. He goes on to argue that the shifting paradigm—from analogue to fully digital—is creating 'anxieties and uncertainties, even panic'. An important aspect of the heartache and panic felt in many newsrooms today is that the work of professional journalists is devalued in the eyes of the public and in the eyes of the business managers who control the finance and capital of the media industry. Factors we've already encountered—declining public trust, downsizing of newsrooms and the rise of amateur journalism—are the main contributors. However, the whole conceptualization of journalism as a profession is also partly to blame. The ideology of professionalism prevents news workers from fully understanding the social forces and the processes of political economy that are rocking their world.

Professionalism in journalism is a form of occupational ideology that McChesney argues creates an 'inability' for journalists to critique 'the system as a whole' (McChesney, 2008b). However, like all ideological constructs, professionalism in journalism has material aspects. This takes the form of a set of social relations that appear to explain, but actually mask, real social forces that dialectically bring into conflict centres of power within the newsroom and between the newsroom, the economy and popular culture. In common usage, professionalism has come to mean a particular and efficient attitude to work. We talk of professional bus drivers and carpenters, dentists and dog-walkers.

Professionalism also has certain cultural meanings within its constructed occupational categories. It is widely assumed that journalism is a profession because it shares some of these sociological characteristics that are found in dentistry, the law or branches of medicine. Journalism has core values that are often expressed in explicit codes of ethics and revolve around the public-service role of the news industry, which is seen to be a defining feature of professionalism. Journalism also has a distinct body of knowledge and a range of technical skills—from shorthand to a supposed facility with language (Hirst, 2010). Thus, it is argued, journalism has a particular intellectual and quasi-scientific claim to being a profession. However, as we've seen, this is no longer a sacred cow, nor can it be taken to be inviolable and permanent. There is, then, a normative power to the ideology of professionalism that appears to place news workers in the position of neutral observer whose loyalty is to an abstracted notion of the public interest. In this context, the argument about journalism as profession seems moot. There is an institutionalized set of core values and there is a distinct body of vocational and intellectual knowledge that appears to define journalism as a separate and unique occupational grouping. This line of thinking can also be extended to outlining the main features of what is widely regarded as a crisis in journalism today. It appears as a crisis for the profession itself, marked by several clear trends set in motion by forces internal and external to the newsroom.

The culture of the traditional newsroom is being undermined, not only by external forces such as the emerging DIY convergence culture, but by shifting work practices in the newsroom itself—the so-called 'backpack journalist'[3] and the emergence of new job descriptions such as 'multi-channel editors' and 'super-subs'. The professional journalist no longer has a monopoly, or exclusive control, over the body of knowledge that constitutes the profession. This tension between the now fading and discredited industrial model of journalism and the emerging sub-field of 'journalism from below' represents a volatile fault line within the ideology of journalism at the moment and it is highly contested both in theory and in practice. Similar contradictions exist for journalists in relation to their ideological perceptions of professionalism and their contradictory class location within the capitalist mode of production. Professional journalists no longer have exclusive access to the means of news production—digital technologies and the Internet have created a talented and growing pool of amateur reporters and editors who can, and do, bypass the traditional news gatekeepers and institutions.

A full analysis of the several paradoxes of professionalism is crucial to understanding the political economy of journalism. In sociological terms a profession has a particular relationship to capital, to the means and forces of production and to the mode of production. In line with the dominant normative paradigm in global journalism scholarship,[4] most approaches to the issue of professionalism in journalism do not embrace a political economy perspective and are, therefore, analytically crippled. As media economist James Hamilton points out, the news industry lends itself to analysis based on political economy because of its commodified form and the 'general characteristics of information goods': digital commodities (music downloads, etc.). On the other hand, the normative approach rests on similar assumptions to most forms of journalism—that the free market is by far the best model of social organization, despite its obvious faults. Therefore, there is an ideologically limiting and hegemonic discourse, in both journalism and journalism scholarship, that characterizes market relations as taken-for-granted and ultimately inviolable. While the debate today about the professional status of journalists is real and at times acrimonious, it cannot be properly theorized without reference to the political economy of what constitutes a profession and whether or not journalists fit this problematic profile. Without the lens of political economy, researchers and scholars are reduced to an uncritical acceptance of market forces as the normative background to the field and they are encouraged into a technological determinist view of the current situation (Wasko, 2009; Hirst, 2010).

In a technologically determinist frame, the new digital production tools are seen as a major cause of disruption in the field. The problem is characterized as being the DIY aspect of convergence culture. Put another way, technological determinism would suggest that it is the ability of what was once the 'audience' to effectively become the new 'producers'—which is embodied in the cultural commodity form of the technology—that is driving the crisis. However, there is an alternative and more complex explanation that puts the relations of production at the heart of the current crisis. In this framework, the driving social force is not the technology itself, but the need of media capital to reorganize itself and to rescue some of its declining profits. In other words, the declining rate of extraction of surplus value from the news production process (less profit on each individual purchase of a news commodity) has necessitated a classic response from capital: an attempt to increase the rate of surplus value by lowering production costs (outsourcing to DIY reportage and UGC) and intensifying the rate of exploitation (making those journalists who are still employed more productive, even if the quality of the product suffers). This response from capital to a period of economic crisis is not new. In the 1970s, American Marxist Harry Braverman developed his thesis of the proletarianization of white collar labour to explain how large sections of the so-called middle classes were effectively members of the working class. It is feasible to apply this analysis to journalists to arrive at the concept of the 'grey collar' news worker, which situates the production of news within the political economy of capitalism and journalists within a class-differentiated social schema.

The application of digital technologies has altered many of the social and cultural aspects of everyday journalistic practice. However, the economic fundamentals remain: 'Across the mediascape, advertisers want audiences delivered to them in predictable quantities and at standard and comparably efficient costs' (Schiller, 2000, p. 137). Perhaps now is the age of what Dan Schiller has called 'digital capitalism': a system of 'universal commodification' and what Canadian political economist Nick Dyer-Witheford (1999, p. 4) calls 'the contest for the general intellect'. As a form of intellectual labour, journalism is caught up in this contest; the opportunities and threats unleashed by digital technologies are the front line of this struggle. Further, it is on the terrain of this struggle that the new phenomenon of alternative forms of journalism—from Bruns' 'produsage' to all other forms of what is commonly referred to as citizen journalism—must be located. If the broad field of journalism is in a phase of transition, then the sub-fields of alternative journalism must be considered within this framework too. As Nick Dyer-Witheford writes, the information age does not transcend the laws of motion that govern capitalism, but rather constitutes the new terrain of struggle 'between capital and its laboring subjects'. In some senses it appears to be a struggle between human and machine in which more and more sophistication of technology (the embodiment of knowledge within machines) is threatening to 'all but eliminate' the need for human labour. This is no longer a science fiction fantasy but is rapidly becoming science fact; so-called newsbots can now aggregate news and push it towards us based on the search terms and parameters we enter. However, there is also the seed of further transformation held here in the dialectical couplet between technology and labour: 'by setting in motion the powers of scientific knowledge and social cooperation, capital undermines the basis of its own rule' (Dyer-Witheford, 1999).

We are not yet at that point in history—the technological singularity has not yet translated into a moment of more profound social revolution—but what does seem clear is that journalists can no longer hang on to the restrictive practices and beliefs that sustained the ideology of professionalism for the past 50 years. John Hartley makes the point that the practice of journalism and the meaning of journalism have to be 'understood as the same object of study', and this underlines the importance of a political economy approach. To some extent we can see the current situation as a power struggle involving social forces that drive the news industry—media capital and media labour—but also connect with contradictory social forces—social media and alternative journalisms—in part driven by digital convergence and its cultural manifestations.

There is a contest for the future under way—though it is perhaps not primarily between industrial and alternative journalism. It involves the evolution of communication technologies—in this case and most importantly the convergence of the computer, global telecommunications infrastructure and the ubiquitous screen, all of it driven by the microchip. But it is a process that takes place within social relations that create complex interactions between capital's 'drive to extend commodification' and our 'democratic aspirations for free and universal communication' that can 'be determined only in further struggle and conflict' (Dyer-Witheford, 1999, p. 72). That struggle will occur on a terrain determined by the interplay of social and economic forces—technological convergence and the response of engaged social actors; we can begin to map some of that terrain across Henry Jenkins' 'convergence culture'. As we focus in on the future of journalism we can also see the contours of this dialectical struggle in the tension between loosely described 'professional' journalism and its 'alternative' counterpart playing across an increasingly global mediascape.

---

[1] See, for example, Hirst, 1997, 2009e; Schultz, 1998

[2] For more on Gramsci's discussion of journalism, see Forgacs, 2000 (1988); Forgacs and Nowell-Smith, 1985b; Gramsci, 1992a, 1992b

[3] See, for example, Heaton, 2003; Pavlik and Feiner, 1998; Stevens, 2002; Stone, 2002

[4] See, for example, Weaver and Loffelholz, 2008

6

Journalism in the age of YouTube

With more and more people carrying around devices that capture video—from digital cameras to mobile phones—YouTube is set to become an essential destination for watching and sharing these experiences.

Chad Hurley

The launch of YouTube on 28 April 2005 may well be remembered as the singularity event that changed the world, signalling the arrival of convergence culture. Over the last few years the video-sharing website has become part of our everyday life experience. It is perhaps one of the (now many) places in cyberspace that has come to define a generation. Generation Y and the 'Millennials' generation (born between 1982 and 2000) are the first groups of 'indigenous' social networkers. It was online gaming designer and digital consultant Marc Prensky (2001) who coined the term 'digital natives' to describe the generation of teenagers and university students who in many nations have rapidly colonized social networking sites. This term now defines the experience of convergence culture for these demographics. However, it seems that the widely accepted ability of the digital natives to be adept 'produsers' (Bruns, 2008) of digital content, beyond their own circles of friends and acquaintances, may well be a myth of the 'digital sublime'. My own survey of New Zealand journalism students in April 2010 shows that while more that 95 per cent are active 'Facebookers', very few are producing and uploading original content for a more general audience (Hirst and

Treadwell, 2010). Despite this caveat, YouTube is no doubt important and within 18 months of its launch the site was certainly attracting the attention of journalists and journalism scholars. According to Professor Jeff Jarvis of New York University, every young journalist should become familiar with video-making, podcasting and uploading to social networking sites such as YouTube because these new skills represent the 'story-telling' methods of the future and will 'improve' their reportorial outputs. What makes YouTube so popular? It is a simple three-step formula: YouTube makes it easy to watch videos, it makes it easy to upload video and it makes it easy to share video with others. There is no need for users to have any techno savvy with compression rates or coding—YouTube takes care of all of these issues with a simple series of mouse-click commands.

YouTube was founded by three young men who had been working for the online transaction company PayPal, Chad Hurley, Steven Chen and Jawed Karim. In the early days of development, YouTube grew rapidly and new features were added almost weekly to enhance users' experience and to increase the functionality of the site. The YouTube business model is a free service to users that relies on banner advertising, sponsorship and partnerships with content providers for its revenue stream. However, the business has been criticized, and has faced several lawsuits, for alleged copyright breaches by users. The lack of strong editorial control over user uploads means that, from time to time, the company is forced to delete content when copyright holders become upset over infringements, which some analysts believe makes YouTube an unstable investment proposition. However, according to YouTube's legal team, infringing clips only have to be taken down if someone complains, so the company does not maintain any brief to remove material pre-emptively. In December 2008, YouTube was also forced to take down all clips featuring artists on the Warner Music label; a similar dispute with the PRS group also blocked premium music content on YouTube in the United Kingdom.

On 23 July 2005 YouTube developed a new application for the social-networking site MySpace that allowed users to show their favourite videos on a customized profile page. New channels were added to YouTube a few weeks later to help users sort through the growing number of videos being posted. YouTube videos are now routinely embedded on many websites and blogs with a templated code that makes the sharing of content even easier. One of the earliest news mentions of YouTube was a wire service article by Elizabeth Neus of Gannett News Service carried in several American news outlets. News of YouTube reached the Australian media on 3 September 2005: a news brief about new gadgets in the *Sydney Morning Herald*. In November 2005, YouTube announced a US$3.5 million funding deal with Sequoia Capital and early the following year Google bought YouTube for US$1.65 billion. On 20 May 2008, YouTube launched its Citizen Journalism channel. In April 2009, YouTube announced a deal with Universal Music to launch a new service to showcase global music artists on the label.

Today YouTube is entrenched as a social media site. It has secured commercial deals with many MSM news providers and has leveraged copyright and content deals with movie studios and record labels. In the process it has also had a fair share of legal battles, but its success has spawned many imitators across the globe; the Chinese site tudou.com is thought to rival YouTube in that country in terms of popularity and uploaded videos.

Social networking is the face—or perhaps the screen—on which convergence culture plays to a global audience that is both consumer and 'produser' (Bruns, 2005, 2008). There are some—the digital optimists—who believe that social networking will further unravel the MSM's ailing business models. They argue that peer-to-peer sharing of content—including information that might on the surface seem to be news-like—almost totally negates the need for professional journalists and their traditional gatekeeping role of selecting and verifying news content. However, others do not share their optimism nor their certainty, and encourage a more cautious approach. The laws of combined and uneven development suggest that UGC sites will eventually be sucked into the monetized clickstream of global media capital. The history of YouTube tends to support this view.

YouTube and the news: A day in the world of media convergence

> Note to future mobile phone-video-journalists . . . don't be such a pussy . . . get in the middle of the action!
>
> **Comment on YouTube video of UCLA**
> **tazer incident, 2006**

This comment was posted on the YouTube website in response to a shocking video of a young UCLA student being attacked by campus police with a tazer. The story and the mobile phone-video images captured by an eyewitness made the Australian television news three days after the incident. They appeared in a news bulletin remarkable for the number of issues it canvassed around the questions of media convergence—the use of YouTube material, commentary on an *Indymedia*-style media event when activists protested at a meeting of the G20 group of rich nations being held in Melbourne and 'celebrity' as a news value. In other ways, though, the bulletin represented a 'business-as-usual' approach to the production and delivery of television news. What was very interesting about this bulletin was the juxtaposition of technological, contextual and social convergence and divergence. The bulletin contained elements that reflected a number of interesting issues and trends that lead us towards an understanding of how news producers are learning to operate in the age of YouTube. Notably, it was a bulletin that, for the first time in Australia, contained video footage shot on a mobile phone and uploaded to YouTube before it was broadcast anywhere else. The increasing use of images recorded on mobile phones by an eyewitness who first circulates the footage via YouTube and which is then picked up by the MSM, as shown in the UCLA tazer story, is an example of amateur or accidental journalism being incorporated into more traditional news production cycles. The tazer incident story also carried strong indications that the 'surveillance society' is being normalized through media discourse (Andrejevic, 2007; Haggerty and Ericson, 2006); it is moving from the digital sublime to the mundane, or everyday.[1]

The UCLA tazer incident has become one of the defining moments in the evolution of journalism in the age of YouTube. What it signified was something unusual and fairly unique, but that now is commonplace and unremarkable: the completion of a feedback loop that starts with social media, initiates an MSM media event and then returns to social media as the story is re-cut, re-posted, mashed up and discussed in blogs and social networking sites. It is worth looking at this story as it is a paradigm case study of how convergence and social media began to impact on the mainstream media in the first few years of the 21st century.

If you search for the phrase 'cops tazer student' on the YouTube site, one of the most prominent results is a seven-minute video of an unprovoked attack on a UCLA student by campus police late in the evening of 14 November 2006. The footage—though grainy and mostly of furniture, backs of heads and occasionally the officers attacking the student—is harrowing because of the brutal soundtrack. The student, 23-year-old Mostafa Tabatabainejad of Los Angeles, screams in obvious agony several times. He shouts 'Stop!' and can be heard clearly demanding his rights as the security personnel continue to shock him with tazer blasts. Other students can be heard calling for the attack to stop and it emerged later that the officers had threatened them with the tazer if they interfered. The cops are screaming at the man on the floor, ordering him to get up. When he can't comply (the tazer causes paralysis) they hit him with it again. This story was covered very critically in the UCLA student journalism outlet the *Daily Bruin* and many other student papers. The video footage and commentary was circulating in cyberspace, on YouTube and in blogs, as well as in the local media, almost immediately. Los Angeles network station KNBC was reporting it the next day. However, it was not on Australian television until three days later. One of the student editors on the *Daily Bruin*, Anthony Pearce, told me how the story was broken in their online edition and how it became a major news item picked up from their initial reporting:

> I'll tell you now the whole thing happened rather fast. Our online story (we broke it) was up very early in the morning on Wednesday and by later in the day it had several thousand YouTube hits and was all over the local media. By late Wednesday and Thursday it was all over the national media, including the *LA Times*, the Associated Press, MSNBC and CNN. Eventually it worked its way up to CNN International. Throughout the whole process, more local papers in the UK and Europe picked it up, either from the AP story or through YouTube. It has been, and continues to be, quite an adventure.

At the time, this story was widely discussed in blogs and then on programs such as the *O'Reilly Factor* on CNN: other students, commentators and reporters canvassed the merits of the police action; they asked if the Iranian-American student was targeted because of some weird unspoken racial profiling, whether he should have just handed over his ID, even if he had been asked for it. In some reports there was a mention that Mr Tabatabainejad might be Muslim and had been stopped on that basis. The various blog posts and comments generated by the student media's coverage show the strength of feeling and argument that this incident generated in the blogosphere. But it is the remarkable journey of the amateur footage, as outlined by Anthony Pearce, that really high-lights the existence of a new feedback loop between the social networks of youth subculture—in this case YouTube and online student news sites—and the mainstream media and back again to the students' own social media sites. The 6.53-minute mobile-phone video has been posted and reposted to YouTube several times, along with grabs from news pro-grams on Los Angeles TV, MSNBC and the UCLA campus-based *Daily Bruin TV*. There is an interesting referential loop between the YouTube community and the networks. On 18 November, the UCLA authorities' response to the incident was front page news in the *Los Angeles Times* and also made it into the *New York Times* online edition, though only as a wire service piece about Mr Tabatabainejad's civil rights lawyer, who had previously acted for Rodney King, who was the subject in a police brutality case in Los Angeles in 1991, filing a brutality suit.

However, a search of the *Sydney Morning Herald* online database and Factiva, a business information and research tool, on 18 November 2006 produced no hits for the keywords 'UCLA' and 'taser' or 'tazer'. The story did not seem to be big news in the Australian mainstream media. A search on the terms 'UCLA' and 'student' at the news.com site in 2006, both as a site search and a Web search using the supplied engines, offered only sponsored links. A search using 'taser' and 'tazer' located one story from the previous year of police in Pittsburgh using a tazer against anti-war protestors, and nothing on the UCLA incident. The UCLA story made the Channel 10 news program, broadcast in five major Australian cities, because of the graphic soundtrack and footage that was available via YouTube, but its absence from the print media shows that a real dissonance between social media sites and commercial newspaper edi-tors existed in 2006. But four years later, this gap has been substantially closed. The MSM is today all too aware of the importance of follow-ing the social networking habits of tweens, teens and 20-somethings in order to turn their cultural habits into useable fodder to fill news-holes. In 2006, the use of phone footage from YouTube signalled the beginning of the MSM's attempts to commercialize and commodify the social media potential of UGC and social media sites. That this is now a commonplace—through ventures such as CNN's *iReport*—indicates that something substantial has changed in the past few years between the emergence of YouTube and the UCLA tazer incident in what is now unremarkable use of amateur video in television news bulletins.

The themes of *News 2.0* were developed in response to the UCLA tazer story in light of the 'age of YouTube' but, of course, it's not just YouTube, it's social networking and the interactivity of Web 2.0 coupled with the interlocking crises of commercial viability and journalistic credibility that have created the links between social media and the MSM. Today we can see that it's a major cultural shift that is affecting and changing the way in which we see the world. We have crossed some kind of threshold, a point of no return—the 'singularity' of Stross and the physicists. It is a process of change that *appears* to be driven by technology—by the shifting of our technological paradigm from analogue to digital—but it is also a process of change that is profoundly social and that takes in all the relations of production and all of the social relations that make up our society. It was YouTube that initially created the conditions for the emergence of 'amateur', 'accidental' and 'citizen' forms of journalism and also powered the social media revolution. It led to some theoretical innovation too; most notably the 'wisdom of the crowd' thesis—the idea that user-generated content and collective media production from below would somehow overwhelm the mainstream media with profound consequences for culture and politics.

How smart is the crowd, really?

> Social networks are primary conduits of information, opinions, and behaviors ... In view of this, it is important to understand how beliefs and behaviors evolve over time, how this depends on the network structure, and whether or not the resulting outcomes are fully efficient.
>
> **Benjamin Golub and Mathew Jackson**

A forceful idea embedded in the whole concept of Web 2.0 is that the collective wisdom of a crowd can solve problems and initiate solutions that might not be so obvious to a single expert working alone (Golub and Jackson, 2007). The idea of crowdsourcing—the creation of amateur content on digital platforms that is freely accessible—got a huge boost in the news in June 2009 when the UK's *Guardian* newspaper used the technique to help its reporters evaluate nearly half a million pages of documents on parliamentarians' expenses. According to a *Guardian* programmer, it was the game-like interface of the software, developed for the paper's online archive, that began to attract readers' attention (Andersen, 2009). Readers were given a ranking, based on the number of pages they reviewed and commented on, which reflects the 'karma point' system used on many social media sites; 'karma points' allow users to rank and rate their peers. Accruing karma points leads to the establishment of a user hierarchy as a form of peer-reviewed social ranking for those who post more interesting material. The crowdsourcing experiment seemed to go well for *The Guardian*, which had fallen behind its competitors on the MPs' expenses scandal story, but as one cynical blogger suggested, crowdsourcing is a polite way of getting readers to do the work of reporters (foibl.es, 2009). The same blogger also noted a mistake (and there were others) that crept into the coverage when one *Guardian* reader misread the handwriting of one MP on a document. The MP threatened a defamation case over the misleading article that followed. A few weeks later, and perhaps encouraged by the positive media coverage *The Guardian* garnered for its crowdsourcing experiment, the Associated Press launched its own version to enhance its coverage of a normally stodgy Washington event—Congressional hearings on the appointment of a new Supreme Court judge. According to AP's Director of Strategic Planning Jim Kennedy, the news agency was looking to rejuvenate (in the sense of make more youthful) its image and its products. 'We are looking to do things beyond writing stories, taking pictures, and shooting video. This big question here is: can a news agency have these kinds of interactions even as it supplies content to our customers?' (quoted in Crouch, 2009).

While crowdsourcing began in the subculture of open-source computer coding, the idea has been applied to online information repositories such as *Wikipedia*, to software development—particularly in online gaming—and also more recently to social networking and to reportorial activities, such as newsblogs and citizen journalism. The model for this style of 'open-source' journalism is the peer-to-peer publishing capability of the Web 2.0 environment that allows for a collective approach to gathering and editing information and which leads Mark Deuze (2008) to conclude that journalism 'is coming to an end'. There have been several experiments with what has become commonly known as 'crowdsourcing' in blogs, *Wikipedia*, etc. In some research there is a perceived tension between the common good—the provision of content for all to access and contribute to—and the private good—the attention that uploaded content attracts, translated into attention and a brief boost in public recognition for its creator(s). One YouTube study, conducted by researchers at the Hewlett-Packard social media laboratories in Silicon Valley (Huberman, Romero and Wu, 2008), shows that the more attention a person's content receives, the more likely they are to upload more content. They add that this applies only to a small proportion of total contributors; more than 60 per cent of contributors do not upload content regularly. The study concludes that there is a strong correlation in crowdsourcing activity between the attention a person's contributions receive and their overall level of productivity. A 2009 study of the role of crowdsourcing in mainstream news production refers to the practice whereby outsourcing 'tasks traditionally performed by employees are outsourced to a large network of people, recruited through an open call' (Muthukumaraswamy, 2009). Muthukumaraswamy's study examined several ways in which the outsourcing of production might work within a journalistic context—that is, how mainstream news organizations have adopted the practice. Others, for example Axel Bruns, imagine that crowdsourcing may well eventually replace the 'somewhat patronizing stance' of professional (or industrial) production of news. Bruns' theories of open source journalism are typical of one strand in this debate that privileges the values and processes of 'gatewatching' over the practices of the more organized and professional reportorial community that still operates within the bounds of the news industry. For Bruns (2008) crowdsourcing is the 'hive mind' of citizen journalism that enables a 'monitorial citizenship' based on knowledge sharing and collaboration. However, these claims are easy to dispute in terms of the actual reach and impact of non-industrial journalistic websites. It is a simple exercise to highlight a small number of (mainly American) blogs and non-industrial journalistic projects that have attracted media attention, or have a high profile because of a handful of incidents that have given them notoriety, but it is harder to make any kind of empirical case that it is the rise of the blogosphere or 'citizen journalism' that is bringing the business model of industrial journalism undone. Crowdsourcing the news has limited application, despite the popularity of the phrase.

We now almost accept the idea of 'the wisdom of the crowd' as an aphorism—it seems absurdly simple and right that a number of people all considering the same problem will find an answer more quickly and with better results than an individual—but the idea really only gained currency when James Surowiecki's 2005 book, *The Wisdom of Crowds*, was published. Surowiecki's observations began with his fascination with 'prediction markets' such as betting fields for Oscar nominees or presidential candidates. He noted that predictions were often made with a high degree of accuracy. What Surowiecki then did—and what made his ideas seem so right and influential at the time—was to apply this idea to some of the things happening in and around the Internet. For example, he suggested that Google's very successful search engine was, in fact, built on the wisdom of the crowd—the 'collective intelligence' of users whose choices powered the Google algorithms (Sunstein, 2004). The wisdom of the crowd is based on four principles:

- diversity—each person has their own private views;
- independence—individuals act alone;
- decentralization—individuals have their own specialized knowledge; and
- aggregation—there is a mechanism for collective decision-making (Smedinghoff, 2007, p. 40).

However, according to legal scholar and White House adviser Cass Sunstein, there is a basic problem with Surowiecki's thesis: 'he does not provide an adequate account of what makes crowds wise or stupid'. Sunstein makes the valuable point that crowds are generally only wise 'if their members actually know something about the relevant questions'. In response to one of Surowiecki's own anecdotes about NASA, Sunstein wittily suggests that the collective wisdom of NASA would not be improved if members of the Flat Earth Society were included in its deliberations about the space shuttle program. There are simple rules of probability involved in assessing the wisdom of the crowd. If these are explored it deflates the value of Surowiecki's thesis and suggests that it turns more on coincidence than on any real embedded causality. The probability that a large group will make better decisions than an individual rests on the collective decision-making of individuals within the group. If most members of the group make the right decision, the crowd will look smart; if a majority make the wrong choice then the crowd can look quite foolish. As Sunstein notes in his 2004 article 'Mobbed up', 'the probability of a correct answer, by a majority of the group, decreases toward zero as the size of the group increases! It follows that groups are error-prone if most of their members are likely to blunder.'

One final aspect of Surowiecki's thesis is worth mentioning as it has a direct bearing on the collective wisdom of social networking in the Web 2.0 environment. Cass Sunstein discusses the idea of 'group polarization', which results in the crowd holding to a more extreme position than the ones that individuals held when they joined the group discussion. Thai journalist Saksith Saiyasumbot calls this the 'stupidity of the horde' (Russell, 2010). As social networking sites have expanded and generated their own internal groupthink logics we tend to see more of this aggregated extremism. The opposite of wisdom can often be the result when a crowd resorts to 'groupthink' rather than 'rational dialogue' and 'peer pressure', or a core leadership group overwhelms dissenting individuals (Solomon, 2006). The result of the deliberations of these less-than-wise crowds can result in what *Tipping Point* author Malcolm Gladwell (2000) has called a 'social epidemic'—a situation in which a small but influential group is seen to be leading and attracting followers and, as the group grows, the resulting crowd takes on a legitimacy that may well be out of proportion to its likelihood of being right. Miriam Solomon suggests that in order for Surowiecki's wisdom theorem to hold, there are external calculations involved in reaching 'wise' decisions made by groups of people; for example, that they each work on the problem in isolation and then have the results averaged across the group. However, if left to its own devices and internal deliberations, a crowd may well not be so wise: 'groupthink phenomenon, which often pro-duce polarized and inaccurate decisions, are more likely when members of a group have social connections to one another' (Solomon, 2006). A further problem associated with groupthink and 'unwise' crowds is their inability to allow dissent, or opinion contrary to the developing consen-sus. However, dissent is only valuable as a corrective when it is associated with 'relevant information' and is not just contrariness for its own sake, or based on ignorance itself (Solomon, 2006). Jaron Lanier refers to some aspects of online collectivism as 'digital Maoism'.

A small amount of empirical research is now emerging that attempts to quantify the wisdom of the crowd in an online social networking and collaborative knowledge context, which allows us to further test

Surowiecki's proposition in relation to popular Web 2.0 applications such as *Wikipedia*, Flickr, blogs, Twitter, social networking sites and social bookmarking engines such as De.licio.us.[2] What Aniket Kittur (2006; 2008) and his collaborators found was that over the two-year period of their survey, there tended to be a rise in the number of less-experienced users uploading and editing copy to *Wikipedia* and that, similarly, more 'novice' recommendations appeared in the De.licio.us rankings. This led the research team to suggest that as collaborative online systems become more accepted and more users join them, influence devolves from an elite downwards to less-experienced layers of users. Thus collaborative communities tend to be in 'a state of constant change based on the prevailing opinions of the population' and the influence of the early founders tends to decrease (Kittur et al., 2006). The researchers suggest, quite usefully, that their analysis might also be applicable to online bulletin board sites, such as *Slashdot*, that have, in the past few years, begun to emerge as serious sites for community news circulation and that are often cited in the literature on citizen journalism. The collective power of the crowd is one of the driving factors of Web 2.0 according to one of its early theorists, Tim O'Reilly (2005b): 'an essential part of Web 2.0 is harnessing collective intelligence, turning the Web into a kind of global brain' and the argument continues that the wisdom of the crowd selects for quality—particularly around blog and citizen journalism sites. There is perhaps enough data now to empirically test these claims, but only a few years ago they were being taken at face value and amplified through the mainstream media, like this piece entitled 'The new wisdom of the web' from Steven Levy and Brad Stone in *Newsweek*:

> That's why some people believe that an army of bloggers can provide an alternative to even the smartest journalists, and that if millions of eyes monitor encyclopedia entries that anyone can write and rewrite (namely, the *Wikipedia*), the result will take on Britannica.

Levy and Stone (2006) go on to point out that social networking sites—particularly MySpace and Facebook—developed on the collective intelligence model, though they liken them to 'a site that easily allowed users to create their own little online treehouses, adding photos, videos, music and blogs'. Moore and Clayton's 2008 research on collaborative decision-making on the anti-phishing site *PhishTank* is also relevant as it shows that a majority of registered users are at the lower end of the spectrum in terms of submissions, while a small group contribute a vast majority of new data to the collective. Importantly, they conclude that this can in fact skew the validity of the 'crowdsource' thesis: a single highly active user's actions 'can greatly impact a system's overall accuracy'. They found that poor decision-making tended to be reinforced, and that even 'well-intentioned' users of the site could inadvertently make similar mistakes, suggesting that 'any crowd-based decision mechanism is susceptible to manipulation'. In concluding their study, Moore and Clayton suggest that the findings could be applied to other social networking and crowdsource operations online, such as blogs and other communities of interest. For example, there is a definite tendency for a 'skewed distribution' of power: a small number of contributors to make the most decisions and to influence overall outcomes. Further, they suggested that a small number of 'bad' users 'may cause significant disruption under cover of a large body of innocuous behaviour'.

It is not necessary to accept as gospel the world-changing potential of crowdsourced journalism in order to understand that social networking sites such as YouTube, Facebook and Twitter continue to put pressure on traditional methods of journalism. Despite the problems encountered in trying to codify their reporters' actions in the world of social media, mainstream media organizations are being pushed to embrace social networking or be left behind. Facebook and Twitter, in particular, can be useful marketing tools for news organizations and many have launched their own YouTube channels, including the Associated Press, the *New York Times*, the BBC, CBS, the *New Zealand Herald* and the *Wall Street Journal*. The simple reason for this mainstream media interest is one of economics—that's where the audience and eyeballs are going at the same time as television viewership is declining (Grove, 2008). Steve Grove is perhaps a little biased in this matter (he is a senior news executive with YouTube), but he's probably right about the reasons why the video-sharing site is becoming a popular news hub. YouTube provides immediate peer-to-peer feedback in the form of unofficial focus groups—communities of users that form around particular content and comment on it. Secondly, links between traditional news media and YouTube provide a convenient channel or platform for audience 'partnerships' that can also feed source material back into the mainstream outlet: 'No need for driving the satellite truck to the scene if someone is already there and sending in video of the event via their cellphone' (Grove, 2008, p. 30). Grove is a champion of the growing synergies between YouTube and the mainstream media outlets that are moving into the online space that was once only for amateurs and geeks. He sees it as a way of reinvigorating the watchdog role of MSM journalism in the digital media ecosystem. It is also a way of generating a new and productive relationship between professional and amateur newshounds through the 'major force' that YouTube has become in just a few short years. As Grove has said, 'For those who have embraced [YouTube]—and their numbers grow rapidly every day—the opportunity to influence the discussion is great. For those who haven't, they ignore the opportunity at their own peril.'

From the news industry's point of view there is one very good reason to hope that crowdsourcing works—it's free. In a political economy framework, free content that can be commodified and then sold back to the audience is attractive in terms of the bottom line. As we see with other examples of social media and bottom-up networking, the news industry works hard to incorporate crowdsourcing into its own production model—partly as a matter of economic and cultural survival and partly as a way of benefiting from open source innovation and development. As with the *Guardian* and AP examples, at some point the development work is brought in-house and commercialized. Writing on Nieman Journalism Labs in a review of the article 'The Rise of Crowdsourcing' by *Wired* reporter Jeff Howe, Tommy Tomlinson put the question of what this might mean for journalists in a straightforward way: 'How can journalists make a living when so many people are happy to do it for free? And what types of journalists stand the best chance to survive in a crowdsourced world?'

Tomlinson (2008) answers his own question: there are two types of reporters who may well survive and thrive in a world of crowdsourced news—the 'hyper-expert' and the 'renaissance journalist'. The renaissance journalist is a 'dabbler' who can 'cobble together' a career by engaging in a bit of writing, Web design and photography or video-making, supplemented by non-journalistic work. The hyper-expert has 'insight above and beyond the crowd'. Either way these postmodern types will have strong social media skills and they will need them to avoid falling victim to the new phenomenon of social surveillance.

Surveillance, journalism and social networking

These days, data about people's whereabouts, purchases, behaviour and personal lives are gathered, stored and shared on a scale that no dictator of the old school ever thought possible.

The Economist

If you think it's fun to share details of your life with friends on MySpace, Bebo or Facebook, would you feel the same knowing that weird 'lurkers' are also checking you out? Unfortunately, social networking sites are a great surveillance tool for unscrupulous observers, whether weirdos or 'normal' people, such as your employer or potential employer. In August 2010 even the Google CEO was urging people to use online pseudonyms to protect their privacy (Doesburg, 2010). As we move forward in the 21st century, into a brave new world of networking, connectivity and interactive media saturation, we also have to be aware of the increase in surveillance capability that networked computer power brings with it. According to a September 2007 article in *The Economist*, all of us will just have to get used to living with 'Big Brother'. The writer didn't mean the reality TV show of the same name, rather the all-seeing and not-so-benevolent dictator from George Orwell's nightmare novel *1984*. There is a kind of moral panic developing around social networking sites—fear and scare campaigns in the news media that focus on the unsavoury aspects of perving and stalking online. While cyber-bullying is a real problem, the moral panic is usually much worse than the problem we're encouraged to panic about, but the wave of reporting with headlines like 'Girls put their lives on the line' about police concerns that young women are putting themselves at risk by revealing personal details on sites such as Facebook underlines how such information does not remain private for long. While most social networking sites claim to be cognizant of privacy concerns and attempt to safeguard users' personal information, many of them also work with marketing firms and advertisers to serve up a fresh audience for targeted commercial messages. Unfortunately, this sharing arrangement is not always understood by people who sign up for the usually free services; it's buried in the fine print of the agreement that we all electronically 'sign' to gain access. Most of us don't read the long 'terms and conditions'; we just tick the box. We take for granted the surveillance of our Facebook and social networking profiles by the company that owns the site, but we really don't know much about what they do with that information. In a sense, we don't seem to care either; we turn a deaf ear to any discussion of the potential problems of social surveillance. In a good example of contradictions emerging within broadly accepted digital technologies, Facebook users have begun exerting pressure on the company to be more upfront and transparent about its privacy settings.

Alongside potential state-sanctioned political surveillance and commercial surveillance made possible by vast amounts of stored data available via Google and other search engines, we are also able to increase our ability to surveil our friends, colleagues, potential dates and even total strangers. We are now able to do a certain amount of this social surveillance by browsing our friends' online profiles or keeping track of their 'updates'. One reason for our complacency about surveillance is the popularity of reality-style television shows that rely on hidden cameras, or footage of crime from CCTV cameras to entertain us. This style of reality programming combines infotainment and surveillance in a way that seems to normalize it. This normalization of surveillance informs all kinds of journalistic discourses, from news programming to reality documentaries about police car chases and consumer programming that uses hidden cameras to catch tradespeople who don't do a good job. But the normalization of surveillance may also have other consequences. State monitoring of social network sites, mobile phone SMS traffic and Twitter feeds is now technically possible and—in some circumstances— politically expedient. China's 'great firewall' is one well-known example; another, discussed below, is the Iran uprising of June 2009.

Surveilling the Twitter revolution

The Ghalam News report, translated from Persian, says that the popular network 'was cut off throughout the country.' The action occurred just before midnight local time, less than nine hours before the start of elections. 'All walks of life from all over the country' are discovering that 'messages on different mobile phone networks will not send.'

Craig Kanalley

It was difficult to confirm this information during the chaotic days that followed the Iranian election in June 2009, but—true or not—it became part of the official folklore of those events (Kanalley, 2009). It seems that some confirmation came from Twitter and other social networking sites and the news was carried widely in the MSM, with little attribution. The issue of online surveillance really came to the fore during the so-called 'Twitter revolution' in Iran following hotly contested elections there on 12 June 2009. The streets of Iran exploded with protests that quickly ignited the world's interest and brought social networking sites such as Twitter, YouTube and Facebook into the front line of global politics. Unfortunately, the noise to signal ratio—when 'junk' tweets vastly outnumber genuine 'information' tweets—was so high that it was almost impossible to verify or even find real information about what was happening in Tehran and other parts of Iran. One of the hot-button issues on the Twitter threads and in the mainstream media was the ability of the Iranian security apparatus to monitor, surveil, use for misinformation, or even close down social networking sites that were spreading news of the insurrection. Writing on his *PoynterOnline* blog, Al Tompkins suggested that the use of social networking by Iranian protestors could be making it easier for the regime to track them. He mentioned a technique called 'deep packet inspection' that would allow anyone with the technology to follow online traffic to deconstruct and reconstruct the 'packets' of data that make up an email, tweet or chatroom post and then locate at least the computer from which it came—and the one it was travelling to, if not the actual sender or receiver (Tompkins, 2009). In Iran, Internet traffic is monitored from one central choke point— the offices of the monopoly Iranian telecom company. According to the Open Network Initiative group, short-message-service (SMS) was blocked on Iranian mobile phones when polling closed, perhaps because it would hinder opposition attempts to monitor the counting (rebekah, 2009). The Internet infrastructure collective CircleID was able to provide some technical data that showed how blocks of IP addresses in Iran were disabled on 13 June, but one analyst speculated that part of the reason for this might have been a higher than normal amount of global traffic pulling data out of Iran (Cowie, 2009)—something that can be explained by the global level of interest the election caused, but unusual nonetheless.

Not only does surveillance have a political dimension—as the monitoring of Internet traffic in Iran and other authoritarian states demonstrates—today it also has a huge commercial dimension too. According to the surveillance researcher David Wall (2006, p. 340), the 'new economy based on information capital(ism)' relies on surveillance and the 'exploitation of informational sites of value' as one foundation for continuing capital accumulation and profitability. This is another sense in which the media is implicated in the growth of social and commercial surveillance; the technology of interactive television is, inherently, also a tool of commercial surveillance of domestic viewing and consumption habits. As Canadian media sociologist Serra Tinic (2006) notes, the appearance of customer control through greater interactivity—channel choice, fast-forwarding through advertising and time-shifted viewing—in fact disguises the surveillance and intelligence-gathering functions that set-top boxes manage for cable and satellite television providers. Tinic argues that the power to measure audience responses to programming 'goes beyond market researchers' wildest dreams' because they can closely monitor what is being watched and then develop 'one-to-one targeted marketing' strategies based on customer preferences.

The highly commercial nature of this surveillance is daily being revealed as a less beneficial consequence of convergence culture.[3] In *Communication and New Media*, I defined the term 'surveillance economy' to describe the growing pattern of commercial surveillance but also to frame the argument that surveillance is now a central and important factor in the ongoing development and viability of the capitalist mode of production to the extent that the functionality of surveillance (observation, data-collection, data storage and data mining for commercial advantage) is now 'deeply entrenched in the production and consumption process' and combines state investment (in anti-terrorism technologies) and the commercialization of surveillance and data-mining (Hirst and Harrison, 2007). The surveillance economy leads to what Mark Andrejevic (2007) describes as 'digital enclosure': the situation where every electronic transaction 'generates information about itself'. It is a global phenomenon and has led to a situation where, as Kevin Haggerty and Richard Ericson (2006) write, 'surveillance is embedded in business enterprise'.

David Wall's work is also interesting for its explanations of various types of social surveillance, including the few surveilling the many (such as for so-called national security purposes) and the many surveilling the few (for example, online versions of the FBI's 'most wanted' list). There is a level of simultaneity and reciprocity in this synoptic surveillance regime: 'Just as the surveillers surveil their populations, then, in principle, the surveilled can surveil the surveillers' (D. S. Wall, 2006, p. 345). News organizations can take advantage of this mutuality in several ways. One is to use information gathered about visitors to news websites in a commercial capacity—popular topics are likely to receive more coverage in an effort to increase traffic; data can be accumulated and used to sell advertising space, or to customize advertising to particular stories, or even particular visitors. The second way is the use of surveillance as a journalistic tool—for example, downloading images from Facebook and other social network sites to illustrate stories, or to provide personal information about people in the news. However, this is a relatively recent phenomenon that really only began to take off when social media started to cut through into the public consciousness and appear on the journalistic radar. What is clear from this brief survey is that YouTube and social media are now embedded in convergence culture and are a steady focus of journalistic attention. For some commentators it signals 'the end' of journalism (Deuze, 2007), as everyone now has the capacity to be a reporter or editor in their own right.

---

[1] Not only are there hundreds of fixed surveillance cameras on the streets of our major urban centres, we can now surveil each other via mobile phones and wireless Internet connections. Interestingly, the contradiction inherent in surveillance also allows citizen surveillance of authority in some circumstances (street protests, demonstrations and other political action). The propaganda war that erupted when Israeli commandos intercepted an aid flotilla heading for the occupied Gaza Strip in May 2010 is a good example. The activists and the Israeli authorities both made use of YouTube to argue their version of events before a global audience (Gabbatt, 2010).

[2] See, for example, Golub and Jackson, 2007; Kittur, Chi, Pendleton, Suh and Mytkowicz, 2006; Kittur and Kraut, 2008; Moore and Clayton, 2008

[3] ibid

7

We're all journalists now. Or are we?

A new wave of open source and collaborative software, along with mobile technology, and a growing awareness of the 'wisdom of crowds' is changing the scope and definition of media.

Usha Rodriques and Emily Braham

It's almost taken for granted that in the time of Web 2.0 and social networking everyone is an instant communicator and generator of content. In fact, according to some influential commentators and academics, we—all of us—are the media now and the distinction between producer and audience that sustained the mass media through the last 60 years is now disappearing.[1] The screen has become a two-way device and the parallels with Orwell's dystopian novel *1984* are evident, but dismissed in favour of a more uplifting and utopian digital mythology of interactivity and expanding media democracy. This presents a conundrum for those who work in the news industry: 'If everyone's a journalist now, then who am I?' There's a corollary, too: 'If everyone's a journalist, then who's the audience?' If the audience is now made up of 'journalists', there's no one else left. If everyone is so busy being their own 'Daily Me', who's listening? There is potentially a lot of noise, but not much conversation. There are a lot of human headlines, but little actual dialogue, and the public sphere is in danger of becomes a tower of Babel. The wisdom of the crowd becomes the ranting of an unruly mob—as it does from time to time on social networking sites. This can be seen in instances of cyber-bullying, or when a moral outrage causes a sudden rush of blood to the heads of a handful of people who can then generate a virtual witch-hunting vigilante squad in a matter of hours, if not minutes. This is unsettling for a lot of journalists, as a 2008 survey by the Reuters Institute for the Study of Journalism indicates. The Oxford-based institute asked a number of journalists to define what being a journalist meant in their own country. The responses were varied, but core themes of public service and public interest came through, alongside some sort of defining perimeter defined by their paid/professional status within the news industry. Several respondents also mentioned the 'threat' posed by the rise of online amateur journalism and blogging.

Today, it seems, there's at least the potential for all of us to participate in the news process; Web 2.0 is all about interactivity, but it is important to distinguish between interactivity and various manifestations of what is generally known as 'citizen journalism'. In a 2005 speech to Spanish journalism students, Bill Kovach argued that digital technologies are creating the conditions for audience members to make the transition from 'passive receivers' to 'proactive consumers, who decide what they want, when they want it, and how they want it' (Kovach, 2005). However, there's a big gap between proactive consumption and citizen journalism: participation in an online discussion forum hosted by an MSM website, or even a subculture chatroom, is not an act of journalism. This increased level of interactivity and the related ability of non-journalists to submit content to mainstream sites, or even to create their own—blogs and social networking pages, for example—has attracted a good deal of academic and professional attention. However, when the literature is systematically reviewed, it is clear that there is very little agreement about what *is*, what *might be* and what is *not* 'citizen journalism'. While 'citizen journalism' is a widely used term—alongside other adjectives, such as 'alternative', 'amateur' and 'participatory'—the actual content and context of what is meant by the term varies widely from author to author.

The term 'citizen journalism', or 'citizen journalist', has been in circulation for little more than a decade. An early application was the Korean news website *OhMyNews*, which launched publicly on 22 February 2000. *OhMyNews* emerged as a means of challenging the stuffy, conservative and pro-government MSM in South Korea. Now *OhMyNews* has more than 30,000 'citizen journalists' based in nearly 100 countries. Significantly, the founder of *OhMyNews*, Oh Yeon-ho, has a very definite idea about 'citizen journalism' and it is at odds with some of the broader and looser definitions: 'Only those citizen reporters who are passionately committed to social change and reporting make our project possible' (Oh, 2006). In this construction there is a definite linkage between reporting and active political citizenship. It is important to deconstruct the concept of 'citizen journalism' to avoid what Vincent Mosco (2004, p. 43) describes as the media's (and some academics') 'near ritual adulation of cyberspace'.

User-generated news-like content

If it looks like journalism, acts like journalism, and produces the work of journalism, then it's journalism, and the people doing it are journalists. Whoever they are.

William Woo

There are many names given to descriptions of non-professional journalists today. The most common and popular over-arching terms is perhaps 'citizen journalist' (Woo, 2005). However, this terminology is slightly misleading. Citizen journalism should be regarded as a subset of a broader category: 'user-generated news-like content', or UGNC. This is a more apt description as it mirrors the generic UGC tag for all types of user-generated content. There are at least two good reasons to go with the UGNC designation: first, it is broad enough to capture any type of user-generated or non-professional material and second, the use of the term 'news-like content', rather than just 'content', signifies a particular type of material: is it news, or something closely approximating it? The term 'user-generated' is easy enough to understand: material generated by a member of, and circulated back to, the intended audience. It is an act of creation by someone who is not professionally distinguished from the audience. It is a starting point similar to Jay Rosen's working definition: 'When the people formerly known as the audience employ the press tools they have in their possession to inform one another, *that's* citizen journalism' (Rosen, 2008). The transition from one description to the other is achieved by substituting 'user-generated' for 'citizen' and 'news-like content' for 'journalism' and ensuring that we are not using *citizen* in both its political and non-political senses in an ad hoc and indiscriminate way. Rodriques and Braham (2008) illustrate this dilemma when they suggest that 'citizen' means 'ordinary person' as opposed to a citizen in the 'nation-state' sense. This is at odds with Oh Yeon-ho's explicitly political definition associated with *OhMyNews*: 'passionately committed to social change'.

User-generated news-like content is certainly created by 'the people formerly known as the audience', but it's important to also clarify what we mean by the 'news-like' signifier in the UGNC tag. The deliberate use of 'news-like' describes a wide and varied range of UGC material that appears inside and alongside readily identifiable news outlets. Some of it might be news and some of it most definitely is not. To explain this we have to go back to first principles and the simple, yet profound, question of what constitutes news and journalism. The freelance journalist who successfully turned a small newspaper into an empire, Alfred Harmsworth (Lord Northcliffe), is reputed to have uttered the immortal words about journalism: 'News is something someone wants suppressed. Everything else is just advertising.' This is perhaps a cynical and narrow view, but it is a good starting point. Harmsworth's quip, apparently made when he was owner and publisher of *The Times* newspaper, is useful because it immediately eliminates a whole swag of marketing gumpf, most public relations material and, for our purposes, the lunatic rantings of the blogosphere's outer spirals and the poisonous blather of the social media dribblejaws. However, it is not broad enough to encompass all the information that people seem to expect and enjoy—the daily goings-on that have some impact or meaning in their life. News, then, can be more than secrets revealed; it can also be common knowledge, information about events close or distant in which we take some interest. All the textbooks on the subject will refer you to a long, and growing, list of 'values' that help to shape what news is. These, too, are useful in helping to define our subject. To be news something has to be new—information that is revealed to the audience (of one, or many) for the first time.

At least some of the common news values—proximity, immediacy, impact, novelty (newness), public or human interest, conflict (never resolution?), prominence and consequence—must obviously be present in an item of information for it to be considered news. That does not mean every item must contain all, or even most, of these values, but some must be present. This must hold true for all categories of news and for all categories of journalist. Therefore, it doesn't matter if the information is presented by a professional or an amateur; if it contains enough news values, it is surely news. The problem is that the same values can also be used to define common over-the-fence gossip. This is part of the problem with social media; information circulated via Twitter or Facebook can pass through several sets of hands and become 'true' through repetition, but is it really 'news' without any verification by gatekeepers or gatewatchers?

What separates news from gossip? This is a question that has exercised the minds of journalists and editors for centuries. Quite often an item of information might start life as gossip and become news through the massaging it receives in the editorial process. What we can add is that, unlike gossip, news must be verified: 'journalists and executives alike . . . largely agree on the core principles of journalism, which include getting the facts right, getting both sides of the story and not publishing rumors' (Journalists Network, 2007). Gossip can convey rumour, half-truths and outright lies as well as truth. We have commonly come to expect news to be based on facts that are accurate and that present a true picture of what really happened. In other words, we expect our news to be checked and verified. There is a selection process involved and a certain level of editorial decision-making—even something as simple as choosing what to include and what to leave out of any particular news story. There is, in the selection and presentation of news, a certain amount of what we call 'gatekeeping'. This is not to defend as unproblematic the news produced in the system of industrial journalism. There is systemic bias and privileging of information and speaking positions within the MSM that scholars and media activists have been highly critical of for more than 30 years. However, in general we do expect news to have facts and truth embedded in it, even if it is in a distorted form.

Robert McChesney describes the current mediasphere as one of 'rich media, poor democracy'. McChesney is a tireless campaigner for change and improvement but he does not share the utopian view, expressed by many colleagues in media studies, that an explosion of user-generated content—whether news-like or not—is necessarily the best or the only answer to the problems of rich media, poor democracy. There has to be room in the media mix available in a convergence culture for the organized production of a common program of news information; to a large degree, the long-term health of democracy depends on it. The public interest is a collective interest and it should be something around which we build a common understanding and approach to social problem-solving.

Until the convergence singularity threw a digital spanner in the analogue workings of the news industry, journalists did most of the gate-keeping for us. With a few exceptions we tended to trust them to report (at least a version of) the truth. If we didn't like the 'bias' of one outlet, we could choose another—even if the range of biases was limited. In truth, up until a few years ago, whether we liked and trusted them or not we relied on journalists for all our news information. We didn't even have to think about it. Our news was like life insurance and banking: solid, reliable and not too flashy. Of course, that was before the toxic debt bloom of 2007. News was also like public transport—usually on time, not too expensive and performing a valuable social service: getting information from A to B at a reasonable cost. Apart from a few heroic or villainous figures, journalists and editors were mostly invisible too. As a member of the audience, the only time you were likely to meet one was in the unfortunate situation of a 'death-knock' when you were the unlucky relative of a deceased person of interest. Now, it would seem, if pundits like Dan Gillmor are to be believed, you are likely to run into a journalist of some sort in the ATM queue, or on the bus into town. Apparently we are all journalists, but what are we really?

In order to know who we are—the people formerly known as the audience—we need to have a pretty good idea of what a journalist is in the first place. A journalist used to be someone who supplied the news to us, usually in a regular and familiar format, perhaps an 'article', a 'bulletin' or a 'broadcast' of some description. Remember, news has never been the same thing as gossip. But remember, too, that the news was not perfect. If we leave aside the issue of quality for a moment, there are two viable definitions of a journalist in most dictionaries. The first is usually built around a professional persona: 'a person who prac-tices the occupation or profession of journalism'. The implication here in terms like 'occupation' and 'profession' is that it is a paid form of work—that is, someone who works for a salary (or freelance payment) in the news industry. Online, Thesaurus.com's definition is also explic-itly about work: 'a person who writes about factual events for a living'. A second definition is much wider and can encompass the idea of the amateur: 'a person who keeps a journal, diary, or other record of daily events' (Dictionary.com). This is very broad and, of course, can incor-porate every type of blog or online journal and diary that is accessible by the public. These two definitions are at the heart of what it means to be a journalist, but clearly they are inadequate and contradictory in the digital age, given the wide variety of situations in which some form(s) of journalism are being undertaken by a mixture of paid and unpaid individuals working inside and outside the news industry.

The elements of a definition that adequately covers what we tend to refer to as professional journalistic practice are varied, but Professor Lynette Sheridan-Burns provides a good overview of them in her book *Understanding Journalism*. Three essentials are suggested: that the person is paid for their work; that they can claim membership of a group defined by technical mastery over certain skills; and that they accept the social responsibilities that come with being a journalist (Sheridan Burns, 2002, pp. 16–19). This is a widely agreed set of conditions that define a professional journalist, but the question remains: To what extent are they essential criteria when it comes to defining a broader group, including non-professionals (alternative, citizen, amateur or accidental journalists)? A further consideration in this regard is a legal question: To what extent should non-professionals be regarded as journalists when it comes to any legal protection, such as shield laws that protect a journalist in some circumstances? To some extent the legal situation has, until recently, reflected aspects of capitalist property law in that one aspect of the definition involves a commercial relationship between the journalist and the news. The news industry is economically founded on the application of property rights. In the industrial news context both the journalist (producer) and their journalism (product) are commodified according to a series of legal precedents that reflect the rights of ownership over news as a form of property, including copyright law, privacy statutes, rules governing investment and even the US's First Amendment (Hamilton, 2003). This legal principle of news-as-property is evident in the actions of the American Society of Newspaper Editors (ASNE), which keeps a watching brief on US legislation that might impact on the business of its members. In 2007, ASNE published a briefing note on amendments to the *Free Flow of Information Act*, which—in its view—had too broad a definition of journalist and journalism that might, in an extreme case, give aid and comfort to potential terrorists. To counter this, a 'Manager's Amendment' was proposed that would restrict the definition of a journalist to someone who was 'regularly' engaged in journalistic activities and whose income was substantially derived from such activities (ASNE, 2007). In a widely reported case that contradicts this view, *Apple v. Does*, an amicus brief prepared by the Stanford Center for Internet and Society argued that a functional definition, not one based on professional status, should be the one that counts in a legal context:

> The applicability of the newsgatherers' privilege is determined not by the reporter's formal status as a 'professional journalist,' but rather by the reporter's functional conduct in gathering information with the purpose of disseminating widely to the public. (Cited in Woo, 2005)

The *Apple v. Does* case was settled in 2006 with an appeals court ruling that online journalists should have the same legal right to source confidentiality as offline reporters. According to the online rights advocates the Electronic Frontier Foundation (2006), this decision extends First Amendment privileges to amateurs as well as professional reporters. William Woo lists three elements of journalistic function that do not rely on professional status, or any necessary commercial relationship between the producer and the product. These are: activity that produces 'a journalistic work product'; work so produced that is 'aimed at an *audience*'; and that 'there is a *public benefit* to the story or work product' (Woo, 2005, emphasis in original). The most obvious point to comment on in Woo's definition is public benefit. If we can broadly equate this with public interest—in the sense of something being important for the public to know in order to make informed decisions—then it begins to narrow the parameters of our definition. Under these terms, any information that merely satisfies public curiosity would not be news. Again, it is important not to overstate this; clearly, information about Michael Jackson's death in June 2009 was newsworthy, as was information about his will, his funeral and his children. Such 'news' continues to attract interest, as does 'news' about Princess Diana more than a decade after her death. However, it is hard to see any public benefit, beyond the satisfaction of our curiosity about a pop singer and a princess who came to define a particular cultural phenomenon and whose lives and deaths have become a media circus complete with freaks, clowns and nefarious ring masters. So a journalist produces information (news) that has some (however slight) benefit for the audience it is intended for.

Thus, if we follow Woo's example, *if it quacks, it's a duck*; if it fulfils his simple criteria, then it is journalism. This might seem like a flippant response and it certainly opens the door to non-professionals, but even so there are still some qualities that a person might need to possess in order to call her/himself a journalist. Again, the textbooks are full of good advice for aspiring reporters, advice that has not changed for decades. A simple list of journalistic attributes would contain the following: an interest in the world and current affairs; the ability to write reasonably well and to have some proficiency in grammar and spelling; a sense of ethics and accuracy; an understanding of an audience and its needs; creativity and imagination; research skills; interviewing skills and some empathy; a knowledge of history and perhaps even a specialist area of knowledge. Clearly these are personal qualities that can be learned to some extent, but they are not attributes that are restricted to those engaged in journalism for monetary gain, nor can they be restricted to any professional grouping. They are skills, attributes and qualities that are open to anyone. In short, anybody who is prepared to undertake some training (either formally or informally) or to come into possession of these attributes by any means is, for all intents and purposes, a journalist. This then raises further questions about what we might call the group that consciously develops journalistic skills, but chooses to remain outside the mainstream media and hold on to its non-paid (non-professional) status.

Is it alternative journalism?

> What alternative journalism is at any given moment depends entirely on what it is responding to.
> **Chris Atton and James Hamilton**

Chris Atton and James Hamilton prefer to use a wide and descriptive term they call 'alternative journalism'. Their 2008 book *Alternative Journalism* claims to be the first 'academic book-length study' of the phenomenon; it purports to critique the very epistemology of mainstream news and seeks to address the 'imbalance of media power' that marginalizes and demonizes 'radical or non-mainstream social groups'. The central theme is that 'alternative journalism' is generally a response to capitalism and imperialism 'as the global dynamic of domination and consolidation'. Thus, alternative journalism is defined as a political and/or cultural response to globalization. Atton and Hamilton seek to identify the 'powerful dialectic' that exists between 'the use of a neoliberal new technology that is largely in the control of Western economic forces', and its deployment as a radically reforming (if not revolutionary) tool for 'globalized, social-movement-based activism'. This places a lot of responsibility on the shoulders of the 'alternative' journalists—to be at the vanguard of resistance to imperialism and global capital. Atton and Hamilton clearly position some form of political commitment in this early definition—perhaps close to the point made by Oh Yeon-ho in aligning journalism with active citizenship to produce a working definition of citizen journalism. However, they also demonstrate the common lack of clarity in this debate around definition. They firstly argue the need for some anti-systemic *ideological* stance among alternative journalists, but eventually reject this narrow view in favour of a definition that includes fanzines and community newsletters.

So, what is 'alternative journalism', because surely any definition has to have more substance than that it's a response to the cultural logic of late capitalism? According to Atton and Hamilton, alternative journalism is a broad and comparative term that embraces not only 'journalisms of politics and empowerment', but also 'those of popular culture and the everyday'. Further, it is produced 'outside mainstream media institutions and networks' and by amateurs 'who typically have little or no training or professional qualifications as journalists'. If this sounds remarkably like the definitions of citizen journalism we've encountered so far, that's because it is. In fact, alternative journalists may well be writing and reporting in their capacity as 'citizens, as members of communities, as activists or as fans'. This is a definition at odds with that supplied earlier by Rodriques and Braham, who suggested that 'citizen' is a depoliticized category.

Towards the end of *Alternative Journalism*, in an interesting chapter about 'theorizing' its practice, a few more clues as to its definition emerge. It seems that alternative journalism is about ordinary (non-elite) people; it is also by and for them. The authors suggest it might be 'native journalism', amateur reporters working to report their 'community of interest'. The most solid definition builds on the fundamental characteristics of alternative media: relative autonomy from both capital and the State; the pursuit of progressive political goals and 'horizontal communication' between members of marginalized or oppressed groups.

This is a very broad definition and one that is contested because it privileges the political citizen aspect of the binary of *citizen–journalist*. But Atton and Hamilton open it up further: '[T]here are examples of alternative journalism where professional journalists and professional techniques are employed, often in ways radically different from their conventional uses'. In other words, it seems that anything that occurs outside the mainstream news media is, by virtue of its exclusion from the MSM, 'alternative', even if it involves professional and paid reporters using conventional means of journalistic production.

It is important to understand the semantics of 'alternative' journalism. Is it the same as 'citizen journalism'? How do we differentiate it from 'amateur' or 'participatory' journalism? How close or distant to the mainstream can it be and remain 'alternative'? It is all too common in the emerging literature in this field to fudge or hedge the borders of participatory, alternative, amateur, citizen and accidental journalism. This confusion—or lack of agreed terminology perhaps—is evident in a 2008 *Australian Journalism Review* article by Colleen Murrell and Mandy Oakham in which the emergence of UGC on news media websites is described as a form of citizen journalism. But there has to be a clear distinction between the various forms of UGNC: interactive commentaries, blogs, the broadening of journalistic sources, the flow of unmoderated UGC into news websites, the amateur who writes for a local paper or news outlet and what we might properly call *citizen* journalism. Perhaps Atton and Hamilton have a point when they argue that alternative journalism tends to have a political purpose. This narrows citizen journalism to a smaller field—one characterized by news-like information that is produced outside mainstream newsrooms, with a clear positional and perhaps overtly ideological purpose in relation to its subject matter.

This view seems to be supported by Oh Yeon-ho in relation to *OhMyNews* contributors: '[citizen journalism] depends not only on the participation of the masses but on the participation of those who think critically and creatively'. Oh goes on to describe the typical *OhMyNews* contributor as a 'passionate citizen', which implies political engagement, not just ordinariness. If we can hold with this definition, it means that we can provide equally tight definitions for other forms of alternative journalism: the accidental journalist, for example, as someone who happens to be on the spot when a story breaks and provides some form of packaged content, or the amateur—an untrained, but dedicated, provider of local news. Such content will most likely be further mediated by newsroom gatekeepers, but it may include video and audio, still images and even the basics of a news story in text. These narrower definitions also help to clear up confusion about blogs and bloggers. While some blogs are clearly journalistic, most are commentary on events or stories already published in other media. Very few blogs incorporate much in the way of original reporting, interviews and so on, in what we might call a 'news-like' manner. A 2010 Pew Center report claimed that a clear 90 per cent of blogs were commenting on MSM-generated news stories (Project for Excellence in Journalism, 2010). For blogging pioneer Rebecca Blood, writing in the *Nieman Reports* (2003), there is no question that most blogs—the exceptions being perhaps blogs by journalists about the news agenda—are not journalism: 'I'm not practising journalism when I link to a news article reported by someone else and state what I think.'

Writing in the same edition of the *Nieman Reports*, journalist and blogger Paul Andrews (2003) tends to agree that most bloggers are not journalists, but he also hedges his bets. While Blood calls blogs 'participatory media', Andrews recognizes that they can impact on the news agenda and several years on from his observations we can certainly see the feedback loop is now more fully developed—and better understood by the MSM—than it was in 2003. Social media guru J. D. Lasica (2003) is more certain that blogging is a form of journalism done outside the confines of the industrial process, but is nevertheless part of an 'emerging new media ecosystem—a network of ideas'. Today there is much more discussion and analysis of blogs and a greater degree of finesse in definitions of what does and doesn't count as journalistic output (Lowrey, 2006; M. Wall, 2006). Certainly, some blogs fall into the category of user-generated news-like content, while others are no more than personal diaries. Increasingly, too, blogs within the mainstream news media are attracting more scholarly attention as they are a means of regaining some of the 'journalistic authority' that was lost in the process of confidence being drained from MSM news outlets by the Internet and social media (Carlson, 2007; Robinson, 2006).

Tanni Haas (2005) takes a slightly different view, arguing that blogging is not so different from journalism in that it adopts many of the same norms and reproduces many of the same discourses as the news industry; a small number of elite blogs also set the agenda for thousands of other bloggers in much the same way as the elite media is also the mainstream's agenda-setter. Nevertheless, there is still a wide gap between the potentiality of weblogs to replace the MSM and the reality of the semi-symbiotic and semi-parasitic relationship that currently exists between them. Most blogs are not journalism, though a few blog outlets clearly have a journalistic form; they mostly comment on news sourced elsewhere, rather than produce original reporting. News blogs—produced by MSM reporters as part of their newsroom duties—do have the potential (some of it realized) to further shift the balance in favour of social media and to make journalism more transparent. At the same time, news blogs again raise the issue of speed versus accuracy that accompanies much of the debate around the blogosphere's real impacts on journalism. While it is true that good blogs—those with a real focus on news-like information—can have a positive impact on news framing practices (Robinson, 2006), it is still too soon to believe that they will replace traditional journalism in the near future, despite this being a common belief in some circles.

It is equally common for promoters of alternative journalisms to also proclaim that the revolution to create a truly democratic media has begun. Dan Gillmor's *We, the Media* falls into this category, as does much of the material produced by Jeff Jarvis on his *BuzzMachine* blog and by many others. Quite often such digital optimists fail to look beyond the technology. The toys and the speed tend to dazzle and distract from critical analysis. While it is fair to applaud many of the experiments carried out in the name of alternative journalism—such as beat-blogging (using a blog format to cultivate contacts) and the hyper-local, or the use of Twitter and Facebook as journalistic tools—the question really remains: How alternative are they? They may well be new methods, or at least attempts to develop new methods, and they take full advantage of the new digital technologies, but too many of them fail to move beyond their small beginnings. They also raise interesting questions of political economy.

Amateurism, political economy and exploitation

> ...the less appealing side of this amateurism is the cut-price labor economy it has established as the default

mentality of the cyberworld, where sacrificial labor and self-exploitation are the order of the day.

Andrew Ross

There is another factor to consider in relation to amateurism in the news industry. It is one thing to argue that this is journalism from below, but the logic and dynamic of capitalism means that there will be serious—and probably successful—attempts to incorporate amateurism into the mainstream news media's value chain. In terms of the political economy of amateurism, Andrew Ross (2009) has argued that it in fact creates new conditions for exploitation of labour and a potential new channel of surplus value and profit for the mainstream media. Ross points out that contestants on reality TV shows often 'work' long hours for little or no pay under poor conditions and that when writers on the syndicated reality show *America's Got Talent* wanted to join a union they were fired. New York University's Sue Collins (2008) also points out that the huge global growth of reality television has displaced a highly unionized and professional workforce in Hollywood and is moving the industry towards a 'flexible' profit and cost model. Ross makes the point that these changes have occurred in sections of the 'old' media that are 'most clearly aligned with the neoliberal ethos of the jackpot economy', but in the 'world of new media, where unions have no foothold, the formula of overwork and underpayment is entirely normative' (Ross, 2009).

Ross's 'The political economy of amateurism' is a short article, but it makes some very telling points about how exploitative the world of Web 2.0 can be—for example, social network users signing away the copyright on any materials they upload to Facebook or YouTube. For the corporate players, the avalanche of user-generated content uploaded to their servers 'serves as the lucrative raw material for data mining, corporate market research, and entrepreneur hosts bent on getting bought out'. In terms of a political economy of UGC, it is important to add amateur, alternative and citizen journalism and all forms of UGNC into this mix—perhaps not when content is hosted on independent sites, but certainly when it is uploaded to CNN's *iReport* or to any other commercial website where it becomes the property of the host. As Ross points out, 'the outcome is a virtually wage-free proposition' in which users, or 'prosumers', as industry strategists call them, 'create all the surplus value' (2009). In much the same way, the incorporation of crowdsourcing into news–gathering and reporting routines does much the same thing. This is not to suggest that further developments in digital technology and social media applications won't alter journalistic practice even further, but it does imply that social media, crowdsourcing and collaborative production models will not replace mainstream news organizations or cause the *total* collapse of the news industry any time soon. Cheap labour and exploitative content farms are more likely to extend its life span.

Social networking is not (yet) journalism

> ... online journalism, including blogging, citizen journalism ... are admittedly important new developments in story-telling but, aside from a few exceptions, those telling the stories are not journalists.
>
> **Vincent Mosco**

Facebook is a useful tool for maintaining friendships across the globe, or across town; however, an attempt to use Facebook as a site for journalistic experimentation is a good example of the right idea (perhaps), but at the wrong time. While the group 'Journalists and Facebook' has over 15,000 members globally, there is very little activity on the site and most discussion board postings attract no responses. In general, the several Facebook sites established to discuss innovation and the use of social media in journalism are repositories for self-promotion rather than dialogue. It seems that neither mainstream nor alternative journalists are all that interested in the discussion, or at least have nothing useful to contribute; most of the posts are advertisements or requests for help that appear to go unanswered. Thread and discussion activity is limited to single posts mainly relating to job ads, or individuals asking other group members to follow their Twitter feeds. There is no sustained discussion of how journalists might interact with Facebook or use social media more effectively.

This leads to the rather pessimistic conclusion that the whole concept of alternative journalism is somehow flawed. Yes, as Atton and Hamilton (2008) demonstrate, alternative journalism exists in the form of ezines, fanzines, community broadcasting (though that can also have a commercial aspect) and the radical press, but these have virtually no influence, while the mainstream media, for all its flaws, does have both reach and influence. In *Alternative Journalism*, Atton and Hamilton follow the lead of other scholars in promoting *Indymedia* as the paradigm example of non-MSM, ideologically motivated citizen journalism and there's no doubt that *Indymedia* burst onto the news landscape with spectacular success in the famous 'battle for Seattle' at the 1999 World Trade Organization (WTO) meeting. However, a decade later, *Indymedia* remains a good idea that has failed in its execution and has not emerged as an alternative to the mainstream outside of a small group of anarchists and ragtag remnants of the anti-globalization movement. Its incoherent policies on editorial and free speech issues have seen it remain on the margins. It is telling that it was not *Indymedia* sites that provided alternative coverage of events in Iran during the post-election uprising of June 2009 when local and foreign media were effectively shut down. Instead it was a virtual army of amateurs (with all the attendant problems of verification and accuracy) powered by social networks and eagerly sucked up by the MSM. But, as Mosco provocatively asks: Was it journalism?

This is not to doubt that, as Murrell and Oakham (2008) argue, citizen journalism—or, if you prefer, alternative forms of journalism and user-generated news-like content—do pose a challenge to the mainstream media, but the bigger challenge is the failing political economy of the industrial journalism model. For the MSM, the challenge of UGNC and alternative journalism is the problem of incorporation; the economics of the business are a problem of survival. For all its claims to challenge the epistemology of journalism in a capitalist mode of production, alternative journalism remains a trickle next to the mighty flow of the mainstream. This is not to argue that the MSM business model is robust, or even acceptable. As recent events have highlighted, the mainstream news media (particularly newspapers) has been in spectacular financial free-fall. However, the MSM is still ideologically powerful. Television is still the most persuasive medium and no amount of hype around blogs and citizen journalism can alter that fact. Industrial journalism is still the dominant mode of news production. The issue here is again one of definition and semantics, but it is also about historical analysis.

Atton and Hamilton do not deepen their analysis of alternative journalism beyond establishing the category 'bourgeois journalism' as an ideal against which the alternative becomes the 'Other' and hence their attempt to 'historicize' alternative journalism founders. Instead, 'bourgeois' journalism is established as a fixed idea that encompasses the whole of the mass media against which the alternative must constantly struggle. The missing ingredients in their discussion of bourgeois journalism are any mention at all of the revolution that brought the bourgeoisie to power and a political economy model that explores the class nature of bourgeois journalism, its hegemonic power and the processes of combined and uneven development that created the current tensions and state of flux in which the MSM finds itself. A revolutionary class needs its own press to agitate, propagandize, organize and mobilize. The early bourgeois press played this role with great vigour in Western Europe—particularly in France and the United Kingdom—and in the New World. In *Alternative Journalism*, this whole historical movement—which is surely as significant as the rise of citizen journalism—gets only a brief mention, but it must be explored more if we are to understand why the capitalist news media today no longer plays a revolutionary, or—in most cases—even mildly reformist role in politics. The transition from a radical party press to the commercial mass production of newspapers was a necessary move by the bourgeoisie to harness the consumption of workers while at the same time distracting them with apolitical and often salacious tidbits of 'news' information that was totally stripped of any radical content. A similar historical approach to the transitions from Fourth Estate to professional and industrial modes of journalism is also necessary.

An historical account also allows us to address the question of whether or not the industrial model of journalism is finished. The bourgeois/industrial media today plays a hegemonic role. It helps to prove, test, propagate and transmit the ideologies that keep the ruling class in power. This is the fundamental political economy critique of the class-structured MSM and the ideology of professionalism in journalism (Hirst, 2010). From this critique, media democrats can conceptualize and argue for a democratic alternative that may well incorporate forms of user-generated news-like content, but to essentialize and depoliticize the problem by referring only to 'bourgeois' and 'industrial' journalism as the monolithic 'other' is a recipe for maintaining the status quo. It is only by operationalizing the concepts—through looking at the problem of combined and uneven development—that we can understand the dialectic of alternative journalisms—their tendency to both resist hegemony and to court incorporation into the mainstream.

This is the tension between *Indymedia* on one side and CNN's *iReport* on the other, and between YouTube as a 'cool teenage hang' and as a new commercial channel for the BBC and other MSM purveyors of industrial journalism.

Industrial journalism is still the dominant paradigm

> Journalism is a classic 'public good'—something society needs and people want but market forces are now incapable of generating in sufficient quality or quantity.
>
> **John Nichols and Robert McChesney**

Nichols and McChesney recognize what's wrong with the industrial model of news production: it does not satisfy the public good. Audiences know this too, but unmediated social networking, Twitter and blogs alone cannot solve the problems. The industrial model of journalistic production and its attendant ideologies of professionalism and objectivity have dominated the 20th century and were a necessary response to the needs of capital. First, all production is organized this way in a capitalist mode of production; second, the expansion of consumer society required advertising; and third, by framing the news according to its own social and cultural values the ruling class was able to inculcate these ideas into the heads of workers, ensuring the ongoing loyalty of the proletariat through cultural and ideological means. Thus, the news media has always been part of the apparatus of bourgeois hegemony. Bourgeois journalism has actually been very successful. Not only has it maintained the news industry—the production of industrial journalism—it has also consistently delivered the ideological props that maintain commodity production and capitalism as the dominant social system. Perhaps the new crisis of global capitalism will alter this; certainly, the industrial news production model seems to be faltering. Despite invoking the dialectic in the first few pages of *Alternative Journalism*, Atton and Hamilton do not carry it through as a methodology in the rest of the book. But it is precisely the historically situated contradictions within the bourgeois model of both journalism and the public sphere that have driven the rise of alternative journalism in its various forms.

What's missing from Atton and Hamilton's critique is an understanding of why the mainstream media today is so reactionary (of course there are exceptions, but they are few and far between). The key answer is that the bourgeoisie no longer needs a radical press because the main *ideological* function of the news media today is one of social control. The news media revolves around what Daniel Hallin (1989) calls the spheres of consensus and limited controversy—debate is limited to acceptable topics and boundaries, beyond which lies deviance (and perhaps alternative journalism). It seems that alternative modes of address in journalism—radical, questioning journalism—have had little, if any, real impact on capitalist hegemony, except around the margins. Today we see further attempts at incorporation, as Atton and Hamilton point out; blogs are now mainstream and embedded in most commercial news websites; the MSM is all over Twitter and social media. The incorporation of these 'alternative' news forms is necessary to capitalism for both commercial and ideological reasons. This again highlights the duality of the news commodity: the contradiction between public interest and private profit (Hirst and Patching, 2007; Taylor Jackson, 2009).

Within the massive and still dominant production system of industrial journalism there is a constant struggle between competing factions of media capital to remain ahead of their commercial rivals. This is why Rupert Murdoch bought MySpace and why he has consistently been the key media capitalist talking about news paywalls or staking out new media and social networking territory. It is also why heir-apparent James Murdoch launched a bitter attack on the BBC's online presence in September 2009. Senior Murdoch journalist Mark Day brought the fight to Australia in March 2010 with a similar attack on the Australian Broadcasting Corporation. It seems that News Corporation has launched a global war against public service journalism and the logic of capitalism pressures other media capitalists to follow suit. Each one attempts to control as much upstream, downstream and clickstream territory as they can by diversifying into film, radio, new media, telephony, media distribution, book publishing and even academic testing. Acquiring social media sites is part of this platform expansion program. It allows at least parts of the GenY clickstream to be monetized, and it ring-fences pieces of digital media real estate that competitors cannot get their hands on.

One particular and important role of the news media is to maintain the hegemony of capitalist social relations. This means that, at its most base, the news media functions to dampen, if not destroy, any enthusiasm the proletariat might have for revolution against continuing—if unstable—bourgeois rule. To be fair, some of these issues are raised in the theory chapter of *Alternative Journalism* where the Bourdieusian construction of journalism as a field of cultural production is introduced. The idea of liminal (marginal) spaces in which alternative journalisms exist is useful as it relates directly to a dialectical understanding of journalism practice. These liminal spaces represent both the margins of capital accumulation and the margins of bourgeois domination. That is why the industrial media is so keen to colonize them and to monetize the clickstream of blogs, social networking, UGNC and amateur/accidental journalism.

Ultimately, as described in *Alternative Journalism*, if bourgeois journalism is essentialized, then so too is its counterpoint—alternative journalism. Alternative journalism is such a broad category that, to some degree, it loses any real analytical or theoretical potency. Indeed, by page 131 the authors are finally dealing with the 'imprecision of a term like alternative'. Alternative journalism, in Atton and Hamilton's analysis, covers everything from Columbian community radio to the socialist press, samizdat or dissident pamphlets, music fanzines and local community media in northern UK, and these forms may or may not have a working relationship with professional journalism. There is no key attribute—social, economic, cultural or ideological—that defines alternative journalism. To some degree this diversity is a strength of loosely defined UGNC or even citizen journalism. It demonstrates that there are cultural spaces of liminality in which many forms of counter-hegemonic journalism can exist, if not flourish. The book's survey of these liminal gaps and niches demonstrates that non-mainstream media does have a rich history. What's missing is any real attempt to explain the lack of success that these alternatives have enjoyed beyond the cultural margins. One such is, of course, *Indymedia*, which has been studied in some detail,[2] but we can longer hold up *Indymedia* as a barometer of success. Activist media tends to ebb and flow around particular events, rather than present itself as a stable, useful and sustainable form of alternative journalism. With many different forms of user-generated news-like content we do not get the quality of reporting that occurs in the MSM. What we do have is an ever-increasing quantity of material, delivered at ever-higher speeds. In fact, when you actually look at the examples most often cited by the starry-eyed digital optimists, what they are praising is not the quality of the coverage, but the fact that some Tweeters may have beaten CNN to the scoop. What is being celebrated on these occasions is not quality, but the rush of speed and the hit of adrenalin that it triggers in the veins of news junkies.

---

[1] See, for example, Bowman and Willis, 2003; Bruns, 2005, 2008; Gillmor, 2006; Rodriques and Braham, 2008

[2] See, for example, Halleck, 2004; Hanke, 2005; Pickard, 2006; Platon and Deuze, 2003

8

Never mind the quality, feel the rush!

... 'news' stresses the novelty of information as its defining principle. The work of journalists therefore involves notions of speed, fast decision-making, hastiness, and working in accelerated real-time.

Mark Deuze

Journalists are used to working quickly; it is a foundation principle of reporting that being first with the news is a matter of professional pride and commercial necessity. Now, one of the most significant shifts in the world of News 2.0 is an ever-expanding need for speed. There seems to be an incessant buzz around how much 'better' things are now that news is produced more quickly and publication is almost instantaneous. The question remains though: Is the speed at which news arrives—to your inbox, or mobile phone—the most important factor? What about accuracy, completeness, breadth and balance? For Jane Singer (2003), the demands of continuous (or is that non-existent) deadlines in online journalism push reporters to work faster, but also increase the risk of ethical lapses under pressure. The buzz about speed is linked to a similar buzz about the ability of social networking sites such as Facebook, Twitter, YouTube, Flickr and others to compete with traditional news outlets. A plane crash in New York in the second week of January 2009 provides an interesting example of both the buzz and the substance of claims that social networking media can beat news organizations to the story.

Plane down—Twitter wins race to publish

http://twitpic.com/135xa There's a plane in the Hudson. I'm on the ferry going to pick up the people. Crazy. *9:36 AM Jan 16th from TwitPicjkrums*

Janis Krums

On 15 January 2009, around 3.26 in the afternoon, a plane crash-landed into the Hudson River in New York City. Ten minutes later, ferry passenger and eyewitness Janis Krums had posted a photograph to his TwitPic account and the Twitterverse was alerted to this dramatic event. The time reference in the message is '9:36 AM' on 16 January because I downloaded this tweet in a different time zone. It was 3.36 pm in New York on the 15th. Krums used his iPhone to send the images from a ferry that had been diverted to help with the rescue of the 155 souls onboard US Airways flight 1549. Everyone survived and the pilot, Chesley B. 'Sully' Sullenberger III, became a global celebrity, making the cover of *Time* magazine and a half-time appearance at the 2009 Superbowl game. But, to many, the real hero of flight 1549 was the social networking and 'micro-blogging' site Twitter. Not only did Janis Krums become the first person to post pictures and news-like content about the crash, he quickly became celebrated as the 'citizen journalist' who 'broke' the story. But Krums was simply an eyewitness with a mobile phone. Twitter also featured in the wider MSM coverage as other users became involved in an online conversation about the event.

Another interesting feature of the Hudson crash coverage was the crowdsourced material at the *NowPublic* website. A story was posted by contributor Rachel Nixon about two hours after the plane went down, significantly *slower* than the time it took the traditional news media to get on to the story. The first broadcast news was about 30 minutes after flight 1549 hit the water and the story was uploaded to the *New York Times* website about 12 minutes after the crash. So effectively we're talking about Twitter being 'faster' by a matter of a few minutes. We also have to question the value of the Twitter feed once more traditional media began to follow the story. Twitter quickly became irrelevant as the New York newspapers, radio and TV networks began to get more detail and depth. Twitter was not the primary news channel for the Hudson plane crash story. However, a few months later the Twitter-effect again became part of a news story. In this case it was coverage of a globally important story—the violent aftermath of contested presidential elections in Iran.

Iran protests—is Twitter 'more noise than signal'?

> . . . there is more information than ever: but the result isn't clarity . . . the confusion on all sides is snowballing, and even sensible voices are beginning to let their fears reign.
>
> **Bobbie Johnson**

On 12 June 2009, the voters of Iran went to the polls in an election widely tipped to be very close. The opposition presidential candidate, Mir Hossein Mousavi, was seen as very popular and likely to give the incumbent, Mahmoud Ahmadinejad, a run for his money. To the surprise and disappointment of millions of Iranians—not to mention the rest of the world—the hardline candidate declared himself the winner in a landslide. He made this claim only hours after the polls closed. The shock of this unexpected outcome led to immediate cries that the election had been unfair and that there had been widespread voting fraud. The large voter turnout was a record for an Iranian election at over 85 per cent of eligible voters and the sheer size of the turnout had been interpreted as being in Mousavi's favour. Iran erupted. On Saturday 13 June there were huge demonstrations in Revolution Square in the heart of the capital, Tehran. Militia loyal to Ahmadinejad opened fire and several protesters were killed. The protest movement grew and demonstrations became more widespread in the following days.

The regime also began a media clampdown; foreign journalists were prevented from covering the protests and some were expelled from the country. Iranians were also denied media coverage as the state-owned news organizations fell into line. In the West many people turned to cable news to find out what had happened and this is where CNN found itself being criticized. Anyone tuning in to CNN in the USA on Saturday 13 June could watch Larry King, but his show was a repeat; there was nothing on what was going on in Iran ('Twitter 1, CNN 0,' 2009). CNN recovered and, along with the BBC and other international cable news services, began to provide the best coverage they could under the circumstances. In what had become common-place by mid-2009, the major networks began to rebroadcast amateur footage from Iran that had been posted to YouTube and other social networking sites by protesters. They had little choice; the 600 or so foreign correspondents who'd descended on Tehran just before the election had their credentials withdrawn and were practically locked down in their hotels.

By 16 June social networking sites, including Twitter, had become the 'go-to' online destination for spreading news both within Iran and for the wider world. In an interesting aside, one of the most popular Twitter threads was about the failure of CNN to stay on top of the story. A Twitter feed was created specifically for this topic. In all the noise and confusion that Twitter generates around a story like this, it was hard to sort out what was real and what was merely rumour, or totally fictional. One example was the idea—tweeted and re-tweeted continuously—that the Iranian regime was tracking individual Twitter users and systematically rounding them up. Well-meaning people were tweeting things like 'If you're in Iran and protesting, wear a hat and dark sunglasses'—it hardly seemed like rocket science. A number of threads were set up using the '#' or 'hash-tag' code that makes tweets searchable and followable through various applications like Tweetdeck, Twhirl and TwitterScoop. But, ultimately, there was no way of knowing what was genuine, or where it was being tweeted from. One of the more bizarre conspiracy theories was that Israeli agents were using Twitter to destabilize Iran.

For the lay person it was hard to sort out what was legitimate and what was just an unhealthy level of paranoia. For example, on the #gr88 thread, which some bloggers claimed was one of the few legitimate feeds incorporating material from inside Iran, a constant 'RT' or 'retweet' was a call to block a certain user who, it was claimed on the thread, was a 'confirmed government agent'. A similar tone existed around the idea that Tweeters in Iran were being electronically monitored, followed and arrested. One of the wilder rumours circulating was that sections of the security apparatus were going around removing satellite dishes from people's roofs. This was later confirmed, but the other side of this security scare, of course, was that agents of the regime would infiltrate the social networking sites to spread disinformation. It appears more likely that it was being done by mischievous and bored teenagers who thought it might be funny. It seems implausible that a secret agent would establish a Twitter account with the obviously dubious handle 'AhmediNejSucks' or similar.

Cyber-activists outside Iran began setting up anonymizing servers with the aim of disguising the identity of protesters tweeting from Iran and filtering what were allegedly fake Twitter accounts. The Twitspam site took to listing what its admins considered to be dubious, fake, or inflammatory Twitter accounts suggesting they could be linked to the Iranian security forces. The site recommended users block tweets from these users. This raised an interesting issue of source validation for those following the Iran situation via social networking sites. Adam Selene wrote a blog about what he called 'Peer Source Verification', a process by which users of social networking sites assess the validity of information based on their own existing trust networks that was 'growing organically' as users of social networking sites cooperated:

> ... people around the world are using their existing trust networks, their personal relationships, common sense and a sophisticated understanding of our modern tools to ferret out who is really presenting factual information and who is spewing spam or chaff.

A lot of counter-measures were generated by a loose cyber-anarchist network. Adam Selene was posting at a site called *The Real Terrorists*. The only information listed in the 'about' page was a single line: 'We are a nation of terrorists' (Selene, 2009), obviously referring to the United States of America, not the personal politics of the *TRT* bloggers.

One Twitter source, 'PersianKiwi', seemed to be collating information from inside Iran on a regular basis and was given a lot of credibility by some observers. An Iranian friend in Auckland told me that PersianKiwi may have been several people using this account—one of whom was an Iranian for some time resident in New Zealand. He suggested that variations in language and outlook indicated that PersianKiwi was more than one person. It was not possible to verify this, but at the height of his/her/their powers PersianKiwi became a media celebrity and gathered more than 35,000 Twitter followers. The last PersianKiwi tweet was dated 25 June 2009: 'Allah—you are the creator of all and all must return to you—Allah Akbar—#Iranelection Sea of Green'. In the middle of September 2009 this cryptic message was still being re-tweeted almost hourly. PersianKiwi's Twitter account also linked to the Facebook account of defeated presidential candidate Mir Hossein Mousavi.

This case illustrates the problems with any form of reliance on Twitter as a source: it is impossible to confirm the identity of PersianKiwi, but many assumed it was one male person (constant references to 'he') and in September 2009, the rumour stood that 'he' had been arrested by the regime. There has been no confirmation of this, but as of March 2010 there were still over 30,000 people waiting for PersianKiwi to reactivate the Twitter account that bears this handle. The lack of certainty about the identity of PersianKiwi and many other purported tweets from Iran did not stop enthusiasts from declaring the events in Iran as the harbinger of a 'Twitter revolution'. One was New York University professor Clay Shirky, who described the aftermath of the Iran election on *TEDBlog* in 2009 as 'the big one', the first revolution organized and brought to the world by social media: '. . . this is it. The big one. This is the first revolution that has been catapulted onto a global stage and transformed by social media.' However, *The Guardian's* Bobbie Johnson (2009) provided some of the most sensible advice about how to deal with this fast-moving story and the rumour mill of Twitter feeds and social networking on *Technology Blog*: '. . . it's why we should be waiting for evidence before calling sabotage; and it's why amid the tumult of real-time data it's important to take a step back, and breathe deeply.'

The key factor of this case study is to establish what social networking role we're talking about in the context of a) what was actually happening in Iran and b) how social media might have assisted in the reporting of these events. One use of Twitter was its role as a social networking site inside Iran, which has around 23 million Internet users. In this context it could be a powerful tool for people to stay connected and to exchange information with friends. Of course, this would depend on how many Iranians were active on Twitter. No doubt it would be popular among students and young people and with the majority of Iran's population under 30; it's feasible to suggest a fairly good take-up of social networking among young people in the major population centres. The second role is the transfer of information out of Iran as a way of bypassing the clampdown on both local and international media. Twitter was not entirely useful in this role because of the unreliability of the information and the lack of tools to verify that the information being circulated was accurate. An example of this was the rumour, circulating on the weekend of 20 June, that Mir Hossein Mousavi had been arrested. This news was tweeted and re-tweeted for several hours on the various #Iran threads. However, it was eventually put to bed by a tweeter called 'OxfordGirl', who also had some credibility as a reliable source. In a further example of how social media still tends to rely on the MSM for accuracy and verification, OxfordGirl actually checked with the *Guardian* newsroom, which confirmed it had heard nothing of Mousavi's arrest. While that could not prove Mousavi hadn't been arrested, it is an interesting role-reversal. In February 2010 OxfordGirl was profiled in the *Guardian*. She lives in Oxfordshire and claims to be a former journalist who had worked in Tehran (Weaver, 2010). While the news media was being criticized on Twitter—for example, that CNN was way behind on the story—it was the mainstream news media that Tweeters were checking with for confirmation on major breaking news rumours. Now it seems one of the major Twitter sources was actually also a former journalist living in the UK and tweeting second-hand information, likely from MSM sources.

The third role of social networking sites was to actually spread the message among activists and concerned citizens outside Iran, who wanted to feel like they were able to help the democracy protesters. Several of these sites were created in the days after the election and one of the most significant was *Anonymous Iran*, which provided advice on cyber-protest techniques and techniques for street protests. One useful source on the *Anonymous Iran* site was a user called 'NiteOwl', who sifted a number of Twitter feeds to compile a news bulletin of sorts. NiteOwl identified himself as an Afghan called Josh Shahryar. His short, informative news-like items also contained one of the most comprehensive and ethical disclaimers ever seen on a piece of journalism, either professional or amateur:

> People inside Iran: Don't believe a WORD of what I am telling you. Do what you think is best, keeping everything in mind. I know LITTLE of what you know so make your decisions based on your OWN judgment.

This advice should have been attached to all the information coming out of Iran through social networking sites during the uprising. For several days, NiteOwl continued to provide summarized accounts of the information he was picking up from Twitter. The writing and the information appear to be genuine and, unlike much of the Twitter traffic, it was calm and not at all hyped up or over-emotional. Shahryar was always careful to note that his sources were tweets that he considered to be reliable and not mainstream media sources.

The protests appeared to take the world by surprise, but they also highlight some of the key issues in this book, in particular the blurred lines around definitions of user-generated news-like content. It was difficult to verify many of the Twitter feeds purporting to be from inside Iran; it was just as difficult on YouTube, which became an important source during the uprising. All television networks, including the big international cable services—CNN, BBC and Fox—were relying on YouTube footage of the protests from around Iran. The protesters who were consciously shooting images of their demonstrations and the actions of the security services and then uploading them to YouTube and other sites were politically motivated eyewitnesses. On the other hand, writing on *Anonymous Iran*, Josh Shahryar was acting as a citizen journalist. For the Iran protesters uploading to YouTube there was a clear political purpose to their news-gathering. Josh and the Iranians who consciously posted news-type information to social networking sites were acting as citizens in the first instance—demanding their democratic rights—and they used the tools of amateur journalism to do this. But, unlike Josh, the protesters were not able to put any news context around the video uploaded to YouTube. The small number of reporters who were familiar with Iran and with the Iranian language were able to forensically examine some YouTube videos looking for signs that would verify locations and timeframes. However, for most of us, the street scenes were dramatic but hard to interpret in any reliable news-like way. At the end of the day, it is not easy to assess the Twitter-effect entirely. *The Economist* suggested in its article 'Twitter 1, CNN 0' that the Twitter feed was overrun by perhaps well-meaning people (and a few lunatics) from outside Iran, rendering it a muddy pool at best:

> Meanwhile the much-ballyhooed Twitter swiftly degraded into pointlessness. By deluging threads like #Iranelection with cries of support for the protesters, Americans and Britons rendered the site almost useless as a source of information—something that Iran's government had tried and failed to do. Even at its best the site gave a partial, one-sided view of events. Both Twitter and YouTube are hobbled as sources of news by their clumsy search engines.

As Jack Shafer wrote in his *Slate* blog (2009), much of the time Twitter is 'more noise than signal'. Shafer's short post outlines the arguments in favour of not getting carried away with the power of Twitter and certainly debunks the digital myth that what was happening in Iran somehow constituted a 'Twitter revolution'. He points to other bloggers who had reached similar conclusions—in particular that Twitter was not and could not be a real tool for organizing protests because revolutions happen on the street, not in cyberspace. Evgeny Morozov wrote in his *Foreign Policy* blog (2009) that attempts to get Tweeters to relocate their cyberselves to Tehran only confused the real picture about who was actually on the ground in Iran. Morozov also pointed out that this action would not defeat any security apparatus sweep on known and key bloggers in Iran—information they've had for years.

In the week or so after the election and the beginning of the protest movement, there was a period of what John Hartley might describe as 'redactive' journalism and what Axel Bruns calls 'gate-watching'. The vast majority of tweets were not providing much useful or contemporary insight into what was happening in Iran; the best of them were pointing to MSM content and a small proportion were no doubt real—in the sense that they were from people on the ground in Tehran and other Iranian cities. But, importantly, the Iran election and subsequent uprising did, for a couple of weeks, force the major international networks to re-transmit material gathered and disseminated by the protesters themselves. On 20 June, CNN was catching up on itself and running long bulletins (on high rotation) on the Iran situation and the majority of footage they had was from uploaded YouTube material that they had repackaged into their *iReport* format. There is no doubt that the world woke up to Twitter during the days of the Iranian protests but the hype quickly subsided, and while sporadic protests continued well into September 2009, the Iran Twitter feeds quickly lost their relevance. The noise-to-signal ratio on the #Iran Twitter feeds was very high and there is no way that anyone could claim to be reliably informed about the situation in Iran just from following Twitter. It was surprising then when a *Christian Science Monitor* columnist nominated Twitter for the Nobel Peace Prize. Mark Pfeifle over-sells the value of Twitter, calling it 'the assignment desk, the reporter, and the producer' on the story in the absence of mainstream news reporters. It is, however, doubtful that Twitter is the 'soft weapon' (Pfeifle, 2009) of advancing democracy around the world.

Is Twitter a news tool?

Twitter then can be pure, mindless diversion, or something more useful.

Lucy Atkins

... as a medium gets faster, it gets more emotional. We feel faster than we think. But Twitter is also just a much more personal medium. Reading personal messages from individuals on the ground prompts a whole other sense of involvement.

Clay Shirky

Just what that 'something more useful' might be is not yet clear. But Clay Shirky's observation of the speed and the emotional hype of Twitter is accurate. The emotional tone of many tweets during the Iran uprisings was very evident. Tweeters outside Iran jumped onto a popular bandwagon and, without fully understanding the situation, got emotionally caught up in the hype. The role of Twitter in revealing the devastation of the January 2010 Haiti earthquake also remains unclear. When a nation's entire telecommunications infrastructure is compromised, social media must also be similarly affected. Still, it's important to acknowledge the importance of the Twitter phenomenon. Like many social networking sites it came from nowhere to prominence in no time at all, thanks to the early adopters. A week after the Iran election CNN broadcast a half-hour special report on the election by its star reporter, Christiane Amanpour, and it was interesting to note that the international news corp that was in Iran to cover the polling had good access and footage until Monday 15 June. After that date it was cut off and everyone had to rely on the amateur/citizen journalist material uploaded to YouTube and transmitted via social networking sites. Significantly, CNN was reporting material from Mousavi's Facebook page. As the second week of protests began, the mainstream news media was forced to rely on social networking sites to gain any insight at all into what was happening inside Iran. Unfortunately, the immediacy and speed of the material coming through left little room for confirmation and verification of facts, as the *Minneapolis StarTribune* website, and many others, were obliged to note in their coverage of events that were moving very quickly. As Nasser Karimi and William Kole (2009) wrote on www. startribune.com: '. . . reports from bloggers and Twitter users inside Iran could not immediately be verified.'

In the situation of an exponentially expanding and fast-moving story and in the absence of any solid, professional on-the-ground news coverage, social networking sites come to be important sources of news-like content. The footage of dead and dying protesters who had clearly been shot and the sound of gunfire were seen and heard in many Iran uprising clips posted to YouTube, but in most instances journalistic veri-fication—time, location, numbers involved—was missing. Many of the graphic YouTube videos were undated, and for anyone unfamiliar with Iranian streetscapes it was almost impossible to accurately place the images in either time or space. It's fair to say that Twitter proved to be a useful tool for reporters covering Iran, as did Facebook and YouTube, but again, with similar qualifications about accuracy and verification. The question remains: Are they a viable alternative to professional jour-nalism, or just a poor substitute when all other options are closed off?

A very public death

> To try to obtain an accurate picture of the events in Tehran by reading Twitter messages is akin to taking a drink from a fire hose—the rushing stream might wet your mouth, but it could just as likely choke you.
>
> **Daniel Flitton**

On Saturday 20 June 2009 a young Iranian woman, Neda Soltani—at the time reported to be a 16-year-old student, but later identified as a 27-year-old singer and musician—was shot and killed during pro-test marches in Iran. A 40-second video of her death was uploaded to YouTube and she quickly became the iconic—and tragic—face of the anti-government protests. A #Neda thread was established on Twitter and became a lightning rod for the emotions and frustrations being expressed globally, but it also highlighted some of the more profound issues about the way this 'revolution' was reported. Writing in Melbourne's *Age* newspaper, Daniel Flitton (2009) summarized both the 'potential for misunderstanding' and the 'great optimism' that surrounded Twitter and other social networking tools as this story unfolded. Flitton's analysis of the death of Neda Soltani also demonstrates the sheer emotionality of the Twitter phenomenon. The #Neda thread became an homage to the young woman, who was quickly elevated to martyr status. Hers was not the only death recorded in YouTube clips—there are many examples of people being shot, beaten and attacked—but it became the symbolic focus of both the optimism and the horror. It also brings into focus the problems with reliance on Twitter as a source, as Flitton noted, 'the sketchy outlines of [Neda's] tale are being painted in by those people carrying an interest'. It seems that the interest was broadly shared, particularly by those outside Iran who had been caught up in the amplified and echoing emotions that, at times, consumed the various Twitter threads on Iran. A number of disgusting online trolls injected themselves into the Twitter feeds, preying on Neda's death for their own gruesome kicks. One such troll even tweeted a link to an online porn gateway, hardly helpful to the cause. A number of others used the various #Iran threads to post anti-Obama rhetoric—clearly working to some right-wing American agenda—and others were outed as supposed Iranian government agents, or merely, perhaps, provocative idiots.

No doubt the existence of YouTube channels devoted to the Iran issue, linked to the omnipresent mobile phone culture in Tehran and other centres, made it harder for the regime to carry out its repression in secret. Indeed, it appeared to have effectively circumvented the clampdown on both local and foreign journalists. But at the same time, much of it was 'dross', which did not add to any real understanding of what was happening on the ground. There are also limits to what Twitter can achieve. The 140-character limit on tweets cannot sustain any kind of argument or analysis. Indeed, it is almost impossible to include any detail at all. On the other hand, it works well for the expression of emotions and woolly sentiment, or for spreading hate and rumour. This was summed up very nicely in a *Washington Post* piece as the 'freedom to scream' (Palfrey, Etling and Farris, 2009). The authors, one of whom also authored a longer report on the Iranian blogosphere for the Berkman Center for Internet and Society at Harvard University, made the point that online expressions of anger and emotion can be a sort of safety-valve for repressive and authoritarian regimes that safely channels activism off the streets (Kelly and Etling, 2008). The authors note that it has worked in China, Egypt and, to a lesser degree, in Burma and previously in Iran. These regimes can control the digital tap that shuts off access to the Internet, or to specific sites, including Twitter, Facebook and YouTube. The report notes that the costs of surveilling the Internet, while not totally prohibitive, are high enough to make it difficult, except under conditions of absolute duress and necessity.

In their report *Mapping Iran's Online Public*, John Kelly and Bruce Etling write: 'The Internet will not lead automatically to liberal, open public spheres in authoritarian regimes, but it will make it harder to control and more costly for authoritarian states to do so.' Thus, in Iran, for instance, Kelly and Etling found that the regime was blocking only a few blogs, even though the physical harassment, detention and judicial murder of bloggers in Iran are well documented (Curt, 2009). There are also many offline methods for sharing illicit information and in Iran one of them is known as 'taxi culture'—the sharing of a taxi with friends or strangers and exchanging gossip, political information or secrets while on the way to your destination. The point is that, despite the hype and the heightened emotional temperature around the events in Iran, to claim the events following the 12 June election as a 'Twitter revolution' are overblown and utopian. Having said that, it is perhaps also salient to pose a question raised by the Berkman Center research: Does the existence of social networking, 'the new infrastructure of the social nervous system' in Iran, bring the possibility of a more democratic public sphere—and therefore a more democratic Iran—closer? Perhaps events in Iran over the second half of June 2009 would indicate that it might. On the other hand, by early July, Iran had again been relegated to small occasional stories on the world news pages and the so-called Twitter revolution had collapsed, becoming a self-referential 'echo chamber' talking only to itself. The post-election protests did not become the 'big one' that Clay Shirky might have hoped for. However, we know from history that people learn all sorts of lessons from watching such social movements and revolutionary moments unfold. There was a small aftershock from Iran in July 2009 when YouTube footage and Twitter traffic alerted the world to an uprising by Uighur Muslims in the remote western Chinese province of Xinjiang. Dissidents will always find ways to adapt to new technologies and all media-alert people are now open to the potential that Twitter and other social media tools offer for activist communication and organizing. However, this does not make the activists journalists, or even citizen journalists; it just improves the chances that the rest of us will hear about their struggles.

Where did the Twitter revolution come from?

Graham Cluley, senior technology consultant for Sophos, a UK antivirus software company, follows 93 people on Twitter and is followed by 224. 'I was skeptical at first—I thought it was just navel-gazing,' he says.

Lucy Atkins

Twitter was founded in 2006, launching in July and growing to over six million users by the end of 2008. According to news reports at the beginning of 2009 there are upwards of 2.5 million Twitter messages ('tweets') posted each day. Twitter is described by its creators, Silicon Valley entrepreneurs Jack Dorsey, Evan Williams and Biz Stone, as a social networking and micro-blogging application. Messages sent via the service are known as 'Tweets' and are limited to 140 characters. Users can update their tweets using mobile phones or a Web browser and anyone with a Twitter account can then 'follow' any other user's updated tweets. Like many other social media applications, Twitter also links to a user's other social networking outlets, such as Facebook. It seems that many users are following their favourite celebrities via Twitter. The British actor and author Stephen Fry has been among the top-ranked celebrity Tweeters with 1.4 million followers, along with Barack Obama. By April 2010 the US President had over three million followers, around 10 per cent of people with Twitter accounts. If we return to Janis Krums for a minute, it is interesting to see that since he received some public attention with the TwitPic image from the Hudson River plane crash he has achieved his 2009 New Year's goal to have more than 1000 followers on Twitter. In April 2010 he had just over 6000 followers. He had also updated his Twitter profile to include the line: 'The Miracle on the Hudson Photo Guy'. There was also a very interesting post about how taking a simple photograph, being in the right place at the right time, has changed his life. It is a textbook example of how an eyewitness can be turned into a celebrity overnight. Krums was in high demand as the networks scrambled to catch up with the Twitter angle on the story. One insight from *The Janis Krums Blog* puts the brief burst of fame he achieved and the Twitter-as-news-outlet meme into perspective:

I think it is incredible that anyone at any point can have such an impact by simply posting a picture online. Anyone with a camera phone can report breaking news. I don't think that twittering, flickering, etc., will replace traditional news coverage. But, it can be a great aid for the traditional media channels.

The Iran case study seems to confirm Krums' thoughts and it was not the intention of Dorsey, Stone and Evans to compete with the MSM when they established Twitter. The aims were much more modest; it was to be a way for friends to stay in touch with 'real time status updates', similar to those available to share between Facebook friends. By April 2010 Twitter's founders announced that they had found a way to monetize the site's clickstream—by adding sponsored tweets and advertising on user's homepages (Arthur, 2010). The potential audience for these 'promoted' tweets is everyone who has signed up for a free Twitter account, but the actual number of followers for any single Tweeter is usually quite small. According to figures on the *TechCrunch* blog in June 2009, more than 80 per cent of Twitter accounts had fewer than 10 followers and at least 30 per cent had never actually sent a tweet message (Schonfeld, 2009). Other sources suggest that only 5 per cent of Tweeters account for over 90 per cent of the tweets (Cheng and Evans, 2009). My own 2010 survey of New Zealand journalism students also confirms that Twitter's penetration into the life and culture of digital natives is perhaps less than we might think. Less than half of respondents had Twitter accounts and most of those were inactive at the time of the survey (Hirst and Treadwell, 2010).

When Twitter began, news organizations who posted regular breaking news updates were not reaching out beyond their traditional audience base. The CNN Breaking News feed from Twitter had just over 140,000 subscribers in February 2009, or around 2 per cent of Twitter users. In September 2009, the *New Zealand Herald* had about 2500 followers, or 0.04 per cent of the Twitter community. In May 2009, even a popular network such as Fox News had only about 13,000 followers; the *New York Times* just under 70,000 and *The Guardian* fewer than 5000. A year later the numbers had exploded: Fox News just over 160,000; the *NYT* over two million; *The Guardian* over 50,000. CNN's Breaking News feed had grown to over three million users; growth in New Zealand was slower, with the *Herald* reaching 6000 followers in

April 2010. So the biggest news accounts—those with over a million or more subscribers—have around 3 per cent of Twitter's estimated 30 million users following them. Twitter has certainly become a valuable marketing channel for the MSM and it gets content out to potential readers very quickly. While news organizations are using Twitter to send updates to subscribers, there are still questions about its usefulness. For example, what can you usefully say in the 140 character message limit? There is some justification in terms of fast-breaking news—such as the Hudson River drama—but realistically, 140 characters is not much more than an extended headline.

> U.S. Supreme Court Justice Ruth Bader Ginsburg had surgery today for pancreatic cancer. 7:13 AM yesterday from CNN Alert (CNN Breaking News, 2009)

Was there a time when speed didn't matter in the news business? Probably not, is the first answer that springs to mind. Getting the news first and fast has always been one commercial driver of the news industry and a point of pride for journalists. It's also a commonplace that news will always travel at the speed of the fastest available technology. For those working in the news industry, speed is about exclusivity and being first. This matters to reporters and editors, but perhaps not so much to audiences. For the audience, timeliness is about getting the news in time, at an appropriate time and at a convenient time. It is also a value that varies with types of news. Commercially sensitive information arrives at an appropriate time if it allows those who receive it the chance to act upon it before their competitors. This has always been a hallmark and marketing principle of news agencies, going back to the earliest days of Reuters and other news agencies in the 19th century. Speed matters to journalists and editors as it is a tangible reward for their efforts to get a story before their competitors. Speed has something to do with the exclusive; being first is thought to provide a commercial edge, particularly in terms of newspapers where street sales can make a valuable contribution to cash flow on a good day. This is a big motivator for the MSM's interest in social media and alternative journalisms because the problems of maintaining profitability in the industrial news model are pressing and seemingly intractable. The search for an alternative business model explains the mainstream media's active interest in the economic potential of social media. It is the main reason why the early achievements and technology breakthroughs of sites like Twitter and pioneering models like *Indymedia* are becoming more and more commonplace across the news industry.

9

Networks, *Indymedia* and the journalism field

> Operating a team that is working remotely on the same news product requires strong communications, so unlike many other editors those at Ninemsn find much of their communication is done via MSN Instant Messenger.
>
> **Andrew Hunter**

Journalists of the near future—if they're not all replaced by a Google newsbot or cheaper amateurs armed with a camera phone and a wi-fi palm pilot—will need to be networked. Like the Australian journalist Andrew Hunter (2009), who managed three remote locations for an Australian newsroom, journalists will need to understand and adapt to, if not help to shape, what leading media scholar Manuel Castells calls the 'network society'. The networked journalist operates in an environment where the public is no longer just a formless group of receivers. In some cases they will be very well informed and any reporter who can't keep up, or stay ahead of the pack, will soon be caught out. Networked journalists will have to add value; they must report, analyze, aggregate and comment better than they did before networking. They will also have to work faster and keep an eye on audience metrics. As Andrew Hunter notes, if a story is not performing within 15 minutes of being loaded onto the Ninemsn news site it is pulled and replaced: 'It's yanked if it's not rating.' However, the idea of the networked journalist has taken on a new meaning in the age of News 2.0; it has become a term to describe collaborations between professionals and amateurs using social media, crowdsourcing and other networking tools (Flew and Wilson, 2008). It is also part of the process that is blurring the once rigid lines between consumer and producer, reducing it to a kind of porous social membrane, creating prosumers and a whole new field of amateur news-like content. In June 2010, a new networking venture for freelance journalists was launched in Australia, but with a world-wide mandate. Globizzle is a website where freelancers and amateur reporters—or, if you like, what Melbourne-based media commentator Margaret Simons calls bluntly 'content makers'—can upload stories, images, video or audio and make it available to media companies or anyone who wants to buy it. A similar venture in New Zealand, All about the story, was launched a few months earlier, but has been slow to take off.

News is increasingly positioned for a global audience; news agendas have to reflect the new global mindset. The local can become global in a very short space of time. Social networking sites such as YouTube are a key vector for the viral transmission of local stories with global impact, as the 2008 American election campaign showed more than once. A minor altercation between an Associated Press reporter and Republican hopeful Mitt Romney would normally be a footnote, but when footage of the row was uploaded to YouTube it became a virally transmitted incident that took on a life of its own (May, 2008). According to Albert May, the 2008 primary campaigns marked a qualitative shift in the way that American presidential elections are covered. He suggests the change may prove to be as significant as the shifts wrought by television in the mid-1960s. Now, argues May, politics is becoming even less about issues and more about emotions and personalities, and while YouTube may have 'democratized' politics by creating a channel for 'citizen journalism' and user-generated content, it has also become another channel for the campaign spin doctors to exploit in an effort to bypass the scrutiny of 'real' journalism. May argues that, overall, the impact of YouTube is to 'trivialize' important political news and elevate the 'bizarre'; but he also acknowledges that many younger Americans are actually engaging with political content via YouTube, rather than the traditional media. YouTube's 'news and political director', Steve Grove (2008), boasts that YouTube's global reach and ease of use is changing the face of politics, particularly in the United States—to the extent that campaigning is no longer bound 'by the traditional barriers of time and space'. Grove states that 'YouTube is now the world's largest town hall for political discussion, where voters connect with candidates—and the news media—in ways that were never before possible.'

This perhaps represents the positive side of social media, networked news and the convergence singularity. It is the hopeful sign that digital optimists cling to and emphasize. However, there is a downside too. Westminster University global media scholar Daya Thussu writes convincingly of the global infotainment sphere replacing a true public sphere of real debate and promotion of the public interest. For Thussu, the issue is not so much dumbing down public debate, but rather creating the conditions under which there is an active disengagement with politics that helps to legitimize 'neo-liberal media and communication regimes' (2007, p. 156). Despite this economic and ideological pressure towards conformity and hegemony, Thussu acknowledges that the dialectical nature of social forces also creates the spaces for resistance, including 'a transnational network of journalists and information activists' who offer some resistance to the infotainment regimes of global media oligopolies. This is, perhaps, one strength of alternative journalisms that offsets the tendency for radical and emerging cultural forms to be integrated and smothered by the dominance of capital.

Journalism and social networks

The plus side of this new media environment is more transparency in newsgathering; the downside is akin to watching sausage being made.

Albert May

Indeed, the symbiotic feedback loop between social networking and the mainstream media can sometimes seem like spectating at a sausage factory: boring and repetitive. This was brought home to me one morning when three columnists in my local newspaper were all writing about Facebook on the same day. One writer described social networking as a trend that 'demands participation', but then she confirmed Mosco's invocation of the digital mundane, agreeing that Facebook 'is not a trend any more. It just is.' Along the way we learned that the columnist is virtual friends with a series of everyday characters from her own life: 'the owner of my dog's kennel, my nephew, my hairdresser, [and] a gratifying array of ex-boyfriends'. On the business pages a regular marketing column was headlined 'Time to join the Facebook revolution'. The piece was a 'how-to' for small to medium businesses, suggesting that Facebook's 'fan page' application could be used as a free and easy-to-use marketing tool and as a 'practical, clever business use of social media'. The writer also invited readers to check out her own Facebook pages and to 'sign up as a fan'. Another columnist was also dancing around the motif of social networking in her column 'Don't be happy—be seen to be happy'. The premise of the story was that in today's celebrity-saturated world, we don't do anything without playing to an audience; the corollary, of course, is that all of us are 'peepers'. That is, we use social networking as a form of surveillance of friends and contacts. The column referenced the writer's own Facebook presence and '600-odd friends' whom she updates two or three times a day with details of her outfits, diet and reading habits. But the column was at least self-reflexive in a way that the other examples were not: 'I stop to wonder who exactly needs that information . . . And then I click "post" and sit back while it swims into the newsfeed.' It was also reflexive in that it made the uncomfortable connection between 'flirting' and 'spying' over social networks: 'Find someone new to spy on' she wrote. But the paper's gossip columnist, yet another journalist that wrote about the topic that week, displayed no self-consciousness or insights; it was plain and simple voyeurism: 'Twitter allows us to see inside people's lives—well what they want us to see.' She observed that by tweeting, celebrities could be their own 'gossip editor' and peddle their 'own chitchat' and described Twitter as 'the online place for narcissistic confessions and insightful procrasti-nation'. The column concluded with another rhetorical question about celebrities who on the one hand demand privacy, but then tweet banal details of their lives for all and sundry to read: 'Call me defensive, but doesn't that make [them] just a tad hypocritical?'

This highlights the ethical questions that must surround a journal-ist's free and easy use of Facebook and other social networking sites. It is a columnist's prerogative to disclose personal information about them-selves; but what about using social media as a source? In some cases this has happened without even the most basic fact-checking. In March 2009, a number of British news organizations were forced to apologize and pay damages to a woman after wrongly reporting that her daughter's 16th birthday in May 2008 got out of hand. Several newspapers reported that uninvited guests had turned up at Jodie Hudson's Marbella holiday house in Spain after the event was promoted on her Facebook page. According to coverage in *The Guardian*, allegations that the party had got out of hand first appeared across the national and international press, with claims that the house in Marbella had been 'trashed' or 'destroyed' by gatecrashers. Lawyers for the Hudson family successfully showed that 'only very minor damage was caused' and that Jodie had promoted the party on social networking website Bebo—not Facebook (Hirst, 2009c; Luft, 2008b). This incident supports an argument that using MySpace or Facebook to 'research' the facts is basically a lazy way to get a story, particularly if you're just taking copy from the site or not checking when someone tells you something was 'on Facebook'. A note of caution is sounded by Josh Wolf (2007), blogging at *Media Sphere* in a piece called 'Facebook and journalism': 'It's clear that Facebook is a hot site right now, but is it just the latest and greatest in a continuing evolution of social media . . . so it's anyone's guess what things will look like in the future.'

This seems to be a sensible 'wait and see' position. Media studies teacher Liz Losh, blogging at *VirtualPolitik*, also complains about shoddy journalists relying on Facebook and basically plundering content for their news stories. Losh is particularly upset at the way this is done in gruesome murder cases: 'perhaps [this is] a response to cost-cutting measures or perhaps as a salacious tactic to seem to be sharing hidden knowledge'. She makes a good point that it looks like news cobbled together in the same way students cobble together essays from *Wikipedia*.

An ethical paradox: How should journalists use social networking sites?

> How fast is too fast, when news must be more than mere glorified rumors? And how much accuracy is too much, when news must be current?
>
> **Kendyl Salcito**

There are many positives associated with the intersection of journalism and social networking: connectivity, interactivity, speed of news turn-around, enhanced distribution, conversations with audiences and the proliferation of sources (every audience member is a potential source). But there are also negatives, particularly in the form of what Kendyl Salcito of the Center for Journalism Ethics at the University of Wisconsin calls issues of 'ethical vertigo': the compromising of news values, sources, credibility and standards of both online and offline behaviour. The ethical journalistic use of social networking as a reporting tool is an important issue in the digital age and highlights some of the potential fault lines thrown up by the techno-ethical and techno-legal time gaps between technological availability and regulatory responses.

In August 2010 an Auckland-based newspaper, *The Herald on Sunday*, provided a good example of this issue in a remarkably frank account of how its staff had accessed a woman's Facebook page through first contacting one of her online 'friends' and then used posted photos and her 'comments made online' to track down her physical address. Then, using Google Maps, the paper was able to direct a reporter and a photographer to her home. The paper claimed that by cross-referencing online sources it had 'put our people on Sperling's doorstep'. What's missing here is any indication that the paper's reporters and editors had considered any ethical implications of what they were doing. That Facebook's privacy settings allow 'users to leapfrog through' one person to another is claimed as a justification, rather than a problem. There is no reflexive consideration that the paper itself is breaching someone's privacy and trust in pursuit of a story, just a claim that the paper had done it before: 'It wasn't the first time we had achieved this' (Fisher, 2010). In an email response from the paper, senior reporter David Fisher wrote that Facebook users have an individual responsibility to maintain their own privacy settings and that on this story 'it was about being honest with the readers'. I wonder if this included being honest with the 'friend' of Ms Sperling whom the paper used to 'leapfrog through' to her?

One of the first codes of ethics for reporters relating to how to manage their social networking activities was produced by the *New York Times* in January 2009. In the preamble, the *Times*' assistant managing editor Craig Whitney sets the tone and outlines the value of social networking sites for reporters: 'Facebook can help reporters do triangulation on difficult-to-research subjects. What people write on Facebook sites is publicly available information, like anything posted on any site that is not encrypted.' In this statement the *Times* is clearly establishing the principle (rightly or wrongly) that whatever is posted to social networking sites is public information and available to news organizations without the permission of the copyright holder or reference to privacy issues. Instead, the guidelines appear to be predominantly about protecting the company's brand and this is also a major concern for the business news agency Bloomberg (Carlson, 2009). The first statement in the *New York Times* code relates to political stance or controversial groups and staffers flagging their own political beliefs in cyberspace: '... do nothing that might cast doubt on your or *The Times*'s political impartiality in reporting the news.'

The Associated Press rules are similar, with the emphasis being on protecting the reputation of the brand rather than the ethical use of social networking for news-gathering (Associated Press, 2009). The *New York Times* code also calls into question the status of friendship on social networking sites: '... being a "friend" of someone on Facebook is almost meaningless and does not signify the kind of relationship that could pose a conflict of interest for a reporter or editor writing about that person.'

This 'rule' finally ends up justifying the slash and burn approach to Facebook friends. Why does the rule about this have to differ from more traditional journalistic contacts? As well as dealing only perfunctorily with privacy, there's no mention here of confidentiality. What about treating information you glean on Facebook as 'off-the-record'? If a real friend tells you something that you might think is newsworthy enough to report, would you do it without asking their permission? Would you do it by compromising their relationship with an employer or lover, for example? If you have any ethical boundaries at all, probably not. Why should information gathered through social networking sites be treated differently? There are millions of Facebookers who would disagree that their virtual friendships are almost meaningless. In an April 2010 survey of 105 New Zealand journalism students it was evident that most would regard Facebook 'friends' as real enough. They had clear rules about who they would admit as 'friends': very few would actually accept or seek 'friend requests' from 'randoms'—people they didn't already have some social connection with (Hirst and Treadwell, 2010).

In June 2009 several *New York Times* reporters tweeted comments about an internal meeting with executives on the future of the paper's online site. The reaction from *New York Times* executive editor Bill Keller reinforces an element of hypocrisy in the paper's social media policy: 'Think of it as common courtesy. *You wouldn't Twitter something you overheard at the coffee cart without asking* ... So I'd be grateful if you would lay down your BlackBerries and iPhones, and treat this as a conversation among colleagues.'

Despite the *Times'* heavy-handed approach, New York University journalism professor Jeff Jarvis makes an argument for open slather in the newsroom and for the mixing of 'business and pleasure' in a reporter's use of social media. The mention of trust in this context is noteworthy, as Jarvis writes (2009) in 'Missing the point': 'Twitter, blogs, Facebook, etc. also provide the opportunity for reporters and editors to come out from behind the institutional voice of the paper—a voice that is less and less trusted—and to become human. Of course, they should mix business and pleasure.'

There is little doubt that the MSM needs to engage with social media and the reasons are fairly obvious. Social networking is a hot trend in popular culture and is slowly earning a deserved reputation for actually being useful. Many people join sites such as Facebook to stay in touch with friends and family; social media is rapidly becoming a business medium as well and the explosion of popularity enjoyed by Twitter and others is a legitimate news story. Social media also has huge—if yet unrealized—commercial potential for the news industry. The MSM's need to connect with eyeballs that have migrated online is now part of the business reality for ailing newspapers and broadcasters. Failure to connect will only cause further economic heartache for 'big media'. Social media is also becoming a valuable—if troubled—news source for the MSM on a variety of stories. No coverage of a murder, or other tragedy it seems, is complete without some mention of the victim's or perpetrator's online networking presence—but we're still working out how to do this ethically. The growing popularity of blogs—as sources of commentary and even breaking news—means that the MSM cannot ignore what's going on in social media. But it also raises a question about the status of social networking in the broader matrix of what constitutes news and journalism. For some observers it suggests that mainstream news is finished and that professional journalists might be replaced with those we used to regard as audience. In the age of YouTube and social media, does everyone have the potential to be a journalist? Do we all in fact have the desire? One of the key examples of citizen journalism held up by the digital utopians is the *Indymedia* network, but is it all that its supporters believe it to be? The Internet platform that eventually became *Indymedia* was established in the late 1990s by Australian activists and computer wizards dissatisfied with the coverage of their political protests in the MSM. The idea was simple: if activists were not being treated fairly by mainstream news outlets, perhaps they should build their own. Activist-reporters—perhaps the first postmodern 'citizen journalists'—would create and upload their content themselves, bypassing the MSM and presenting 'news' with their own perspective and political sensibilities embedded.

The prime and decline of *Indymedia*

> ... by the time the WTO left town a global 'movement of movements,' which had pre-dated Seattle by many years in countries of the Global South, had gained worldwide attention.
>
> **John Tarleton**

In the build-up to the November 1999 World Trade Organization conference in Seattle, there was an expectation among anti-globalization activists that the mainstream media would ignore their protests and, instead, represent the ideological viewpoint of the leading capitalist nations as the 'facts' of the Seattle story. They also felt—informed by bitter experience, perhaps—that the major global news channels would portray protesters in a negative light. This feeling of hostility to the MSM fuelled the activists' desire to create an alternative model and they succeeded in turning their protests into a BYO media event. Within a year of the Seattle protests more than 30 Independent Media Centres (IMCs) emerged in other cities. One estimate made in 2006 was that IMCs operated in 150 cities and brought together around 5000 activists (Pickard, 2006, p. 316). In 2010 the network stretched to between 180 and 200 sites. It was difficult to find an accurate number because many are not listed on the *Indymedia*.org site and some appear to be defunct. Despite the hopes of *Indymedia*'s passionate founders, a dispassionate review suggests the IMCs are in decline and that it was an experiment in open-source publishing of news-like content, not a model of journalism practice (Mamadouh, 2004).

Today, many *Indymedia* sites are only updated sporadically. The New Zealand site is one of the more active, with regular updates on protest actions around the country. This book is not the place to conduct a detailed study of the IMC movement, but a random check of sites in September 2009 also showed that the Adelaide *Indymedia* site has been inactive since April 2006; the last item posted was about the jailing of the Australian (then) terror suspect David Hicks in Guantanamo Bay. At the time of writing, the Antwerp (Netherlands) site has not been updated since January 2009. The Japanese site was last updated in June 2009 with an announcement for a software action day to be held some months later, but there was no update. The post before this was dated February 2009 and was a series of excerpts from an interview with a former American Vietnam War veteran who had recently died. The original interview was posted on another IMC site hosted in San Francisco. This Bay Area site is a lot more active and news-like than others in this sample, but this highlights the inconsistency across the network. The two top posts on the Perth site were both link compilations based on mainstream news reports. A piece posted in late August 2009 by 'Hans' is a meandering and badly written opinion piece about 'world harmony' and the massacre of 'indigenous communes' (sic). The Jakarta site was updated on 10 August 2009, but the previous post was dated 30 May. It appears to be updated only sporadically, with a gap of at least two to three weeks between posts in 2009. The Vancouver collective has folded and was active for less than two years from March 2005 to January 2007. The number and quality of the posts on each city-based site also varies greatly, but it is hard to define much of the material as journalism. Others find it equally frustrating to visit *Indymedia* sites, as activist, journalist and *Indymedia* contributor Jennifer Whitney discovered in 2005. As she wrote in 'Make media, make real trouble' in the now defunct alternative journalism project *LiP Magazine*: 'Each time I try and find news among the *Indymedia* drivel, I ask myself the same question: What happens when—in our attempts not to hate the media but to be it—we end up hating the media we've become?' Whitney's insider critique is stinging; she describes the *Indymedia* technique as too often falling into 'cutting and pasting—relying on so-called experts and professionals to do what you are, evidently, too lazy or busy to do yourself' (Whitney, 2005).

So what has happened to *Indymedia*? From a promising beginning, it appears to have evolved backwards into an uneven network of independent local news and information sites that sustain small groups of activists, but with little original reporting and without any real impact on the field of journalism. Nor does *Indymedia* seem to have risen to the challenge of contesting—let alone replacing—the mainstream media it was established to compete with in 1999. Media scholar Victor Pickard

(2006) has analyzed the decline of *Indymedia* and suggests that one cause was a 'crisis' over funding in 2002. The problems developed when the Argentinean collective blocked a grant from the Ford Foundation that would have gone into the IMC's central 'bank' in Chicago–Urbana. The veto created a huge debate when it was supported by other IMC groups, creating a breakdown in the collective's consensus model and initiating a 'serious identity crisis' for the network.

On a theoretical level, Pickard characterizes *Indymedia* as a social movement built on a network model. He argues that it is 'non-hierarchical and anti-leadership to an almost dogmatic level', but nowhere does he mention that the IMC is a model of *journalism practice*. Pickard's analysis is aimed at supporting a sustainable model of organizing political activity—such as that exemplified by *Indymedia*—but he highlights two issues that tend to work dialectically against sustainability. The first is problems in the interpretation of the IMC's doctrines of open access and consensus decision-making; the second is the tension between the competing principles of 'democratizing the media and radicalizing all organizational democratic practices'. It is this dynamic and political tension between decentralization and global network coherence based on consensus decision-making that has led to the instability and unevenness evident in the global IMC network. As Pickard notes, *Indymedia* is beset with problems to do with 'power asymmetries' between the older, established branches in cities such as Seattle and the smaller, newer collectives in the global South: areas outside the major industrial regions of the world. These issues are ongoing for the IMC and do not appear to be easily resolvable as consensus and sustainability become larger issues of scale as the network expands (Mamadouh, 2004, p. 487). Pickard is ultimately hopeful that *Indymedia* can continue, but it is not a jewel in the crown of democratic media that promoters of alternative journalism practices maintain.

University of Amsterdam media researcher Virginie Mamadouh adds to Pickard's list of issues that impact on the form and structure of *Indymedia* and bring the network's sustainability into further question. There is no doubt that the technical *and* organizational backbone of *Indymedia* is the Internet, and it is also clear that many of the IMC local groups produce media content—or at least repurpose MSM content—but much of what is produced can be characterized as polemics or press releases. Only a fraction of IMC content carries a journalistic form, even in the designated newswires. Mamadouh concludes that *Indymedia* is an 'icon of the anti-globalization movement' and a 'network of grassroots movements'; she does not identify it as a news source or a network based on any identifiable principles of journalism. Independent film-maker and University of California professor DeeDee Halleck is one researcher who explicitly positions *Indymedia* as a form of journalistic output. She describes the activists as 'media makers' who contribute to a form of movement-oriented 'activist' and 'non-traditional' journalism. However, her discussion of editorial policies also highlights the problematic nature of describing *Indymedia* outputs as journalism (Halleck, 2004):

> Many of the Web sites are besieged with crank posts, occasional racist slurs and even a sort of 'left spamming'. There have been calls for heavy moderation and censorship of racist and offensive material. Most IMCs have resisted any censorship of the open newswire. Rather than remove offensive material, the response has been for people who disagree to respond to the posts themselves, which has made for some lively discussions.

It must be difficult to organize any form of regular news production when the organizational structure can be characterized as 'a horizontal network with strong anarchist sensibilities' (Halleck, 2004). This anarchist sensibility may be partly why Platon and Deuze (2003, p. 336) suggest that *Indymedia* employs a 'radically different interpretation of journalistic ideology'. The Platon and Deuze study, undertaken before the potentials of Web 2.0 were fully understood, frames *Indymedia* as a form of journalistic output that can be compared (mainly in its differences) with traditional print and broadcast media. This frame now shows its age as most MSM news outlets are today almost totally convergent in form, content and commercial structure. The potential that the IMCs held—for transcending traditional media boundaries—is now realized across most of the world's news media, and this demonstrates how a seemingly radical and oppositional discourse (and methods) can be easily subsumed into the dominant paradigm. In this case, the open-source experiment of early *Indymedia* pioneers has been incorporated and used to reinvigorate the journalistic field at a time when it seemed to be in (potentially terminal) decline. The IMCs were experimental sites for open publishing, and some of them, at least, would fit the strict definition of citizen journalism used in this book—that is, non-journalists using the techniques of news-gathering and publishing in the service of a broader political or social aim.

Platon and Deuze, as supporters of open-source journalism, attempt to locate *Indymedia* within the framework of media democracy outlined by notable theorists, including Michael Schudson and Robert McChesney, who rightly argue that the closed and exclusory conventions of traditional journalism work against a truly democratic expression of public opinion. They then go on to position *Indymedia* as the space of open-source journalism, but suggest it might also adhere to some principles of the more traditional, but short-lived, public journalism movement. Platon and Deuze (2003) argue that the ideology of the IMC collectives appears to be in conflict with the reportorial practices of the group and with the open-access principles it espouses. The journalistic production process requires some hierarchy of editorial decision-making, a structure that is missing in the *Indymedia* model. As Sara Platon and Mark Deuze write in 'Indymedia journalism': '... the ideal of transparent access for everyone to the making and distributing of news via *Indymedia* networks sometimes stands in stark contrast with the reality of having to make "traditional" editorial decisions in the day-to-day management of a news site.'

The dialectic between the open source ideals of the IMC and the practicalities of the news process are what researchers call 'active negotiation', and the key difference between *Indymedia* and the MSM (even if unevenly and sometimes haphazardly realized) is that to some imperfect degree the audience can participate in the selection and the writing of 'news' that appears on IMC websites. However, it must be made explicit that the 'audience' is not 'everyone'; it is more likely to be already motivated activists and their social circles. It is unlikely that many random page views occur, except when there is a big issue on the boil and IMC content is either linked to by other social media sites (blogs, Twitter, etc.) or where the IMC coverage itself becomes an item in the broader mediasphere. The Platon and Deuze study also suggests that there are clear similarities (at least in 2003) between the IMCs and the MSM: '[*Indymedia*] is not that much different from established forms of journalism in the kind of problems, issues and editorial discussions it faces in the practice of everyday publishing'. In concluding their survey, Platon and Deuze ask if it is likely that the 'corporate news media' could adapt or adopt the open-news and participatory principles and ideas of the online alternative media model *Indymedia* stands for. In light of events over the past five or six years, their response—'At first glance, the answer to this question seems to be: "no"'—seems a little naive. However, in their final few paragraphs Platon and Deuze anticipate many of the incorporation issues in that the IMC model might 'offer new ways of looking at journalism's function in fostering and amplifying public debate'.

Significantly, in a later work about *Indymedia*, Mark Deuze (2006, p.64) uses three criteria to identify components of an emerging digital culture based on a value system which is 'an expression of individualization, post-nationalism, and globalization'. Within this taxonomy Deuze identifies '(radical) online journalism' as 'open publishing initiatives', which include the IMCs and 'individualized story-telling' such as blogs. Further, Deuze sees *Indymedia* as a 'journalistic genre' that attempts to breakdown the hierarchies between producers and consumers and between the local and the global, through relatively autonomous, networking. In this sense it appears as an example of 'a decentralized, interactive, and plural Internet culture' (Deuze, 2006, p. 65). However, a definition of citizen journalism must account for, but cannot rely on, the active/conscious politics of the individuals or groups involved. Unfortunately, *Indymedia* has not delivered a truly sustainable global network of alternative news outlets that can pose any type of challenge to the mainstream media. In fact, to some extent the opposite has occurred: *Indymedia*'s interactive model has been copied and modified by MSM news organizations as a means of their maintaining a dominant market position by taking advantage of the Web 2.0 technologies that were pioneered by the IMCs—greater interactivity and audience participation. Recent open-source initiatives such as the content repository Globizzle also build on the original IMC principles, but in a way that monetizes the content.

Just over a decade since the 'battle for Seattle', the *Indymedia* experience seems not to have lived up to its early promise. Instead, the *Indymedia* experiment can be seen to have briefly sparked an exciting global copycat movement among frustrated activists, but the IMC movement is now a haphazard network with many broken or substandard nodes. Far from seeing the IMCs as the harbinger of a new culture of open-source news, we can rather characterize them as the artefacts of a political movement against globalization that has had brief moments of glory and long periods of relative inactivity. Or, to paraphrase Hunter

S. Thompson's 1971 novel *Fear and Loathing in Las Vegas*, perhaps the heyday of *Indymedia* (1999–2003) was the high-water mark of a period in which 'the energy of a whole generation comes to a head in a long fine flash' that seemed to promise an 'inevitable victory over the forces of Old and Evil'.

Among all the thousands of so-called alternative media sites, where is the real quality? It is true that well-established specialist sites such as *Kuro5hin* and *Slashdot* are highly regarded by aficionados and regular visitors from within their specialist communities, but you could count on one hand the alternative news sites that cover general news. There are some highly experimental sites—such as *NowPublic*—but even most of these rely on heavily cribbed and redacted MSM news, not original reporting. So, on balance the wholly positive story of *Indymedia* is a myth of the 'digital sublime' that promised 'a world without the filters and censors set up by watchful governments and profit-conscious businesses' (Mosco, 2004, p. 25). When viewed in this way—through the lens of political economy—a different picture of the legacy of the IMCs emerges. It is one that shows how the 'hard won' independence of the *Indymedia* movement is also simultaneously compromised by the logic of capital accumulation, including the incorporation of radical approaches to technology and media (Hanke, 2005; see also Bourdieu, 2003).

Alternative journalism and the field

> We return then to what is clearly a recurring question in [*Gatewatching*], then: Is it journalism?
>
> **Axel Bruns**

Axel Bruns asks this crucial question towards the end of his discussion of *Indymedia* and it remains a central question for the present. Bruns concludes that the IMC movement does constitute a form of alternative journalism and that the key difference between it and mainstream news journalism relates to questions of objectivity and trust. While the MSM does still value objectivity—though objectivity is more and more a contested construct[1]—it is really only a point of ideological difference between mainstream and alternative journalisms. A full understanding of the dialectic between the MSM and user-generated news-like content requires political economy, analysis of the processes, mechanics and techniques of news-gathering and reporting, and a critique of cultural expectations both within and outside the newsroom. There is no doubt that the establishment of the global IMC network that followed the Seattle example constituted an important development with significant impacts on both alternative and mainstream forms and cultures of journalism. However, we also have to account for the fact that over a period of 10 years there has also been a significant decline in the reach and influence of the *Indymedia* project. It has not, as its strongest supporters have claimed, mounted a sustained challenge to the 'traditional role of the news media' (Bruns, 2005, p. 105). Indeed, three years later Bruns (2008, p. 70) noted that *Indymedia* 'is no longer a catalyst' for innovation in citizen journalism. Bruns also provides an indication of another difficult set of contradictions that confronted the IMCs in the mid-2000s: How could they simultaneously maintain independence from the MSM and also from 'specific activist groups'? This highlights a greater contradiction—the apparent failure of the IMCs to continue building on their impressive initial plateau—and creates a problem for scholars of journalism and alternative media practice: How should *Indymedia* be historicized and theorized in relation to a broader scholarship of journalism?

In a critical piece of scholarship on the IMC movement, Canadian media academic Bob Hanke suggests that there are twin dangers to be avoided in scholarly work on *Indymedia*: one is the trap of 'communication populism', which might blind the researcher to issues of global divisions of labour; the second is 'positive technological determinism' that posits an emerging and inevitable democratic public sphere automatically brought into being as 'an inherent property of digital, networked media'. To overcome these deficits of scholarship, Hanke reviews the IMC experience in Ontario, using Bourdieu's observations to situate this form of alternative journalism within the dialectical spaces of the 'field' of journalism. This allows us to better understand the successes and failures of the *Indymedia* movement as the product of the limitations to radical action that the economics of production and distribution place across the entire journalistic field. As Hanke notes, the IMCs attempted to straddle the spaces of both media and activism and thus their efforts were both 'enabled and disabled' by the power relations of 'the broader journalistic field' (2005, p. 57). In part, this is a function of the tensions between activism and journalism, particularly when the dominant practice of the journalistic field is to discount the symbolic capital of political activism. This dialectic positions *Indymedia* clearly within the field of autonomous political action, influenced by anarchist ideals, but also on the margins, or in the liminal spaces, of the journalistic field. Atton and Hamilton also rework Bourdieu to some extent in order to suggest that alternative journalism inhabits a less market-driven sub-field of journalism in which cultural capital—'education, expertise, knowledge and so on' (2008, p. 131)—has a higher value than money or production capital. While this may be the case, University of Denver media scholar Adrienne Russell points out in her study of independent media in the context of the 2005 riots in Paris and other parts of France that the position of DIY and alternative practices within the journalistic field is still in a state of flux.

This flux is evident in many of the academic discussions of *Indymedia* reviewed here, including that of Axel Bruns. He is right to argue that the strength of the IMC movement lay in its ability to provide on-the-spot coverage of protests and activist events as they were unfolding. However, his account does not deal with the fact that the model appears to have hit the limits of spontaneous growth that sustained it from 1999 to around 2005. Once this limit was reached—perhaps because of cultural saturation, or the in-built problems of the IMCs dogmatic organizational fluidity—*Indymedia* began to collapse back on itself while, at the same time, many of its more innovative features began to appear in mainstream news outlets such as CNN's *iReport*. CNN has adopted the open-source principles of *Indymedia* in a shameless attempt to push eyeballs (and advertising revenue) towards its own products. According to the *iReport*.com website: '*iReport*.com is a user-generated site. That means the stories submitted by users are not edited, fact-checked or screened before they post. Only the stories marked "On CNN" have been vetted by CNN for use in CNN's global news coverage.'

Adrienne Russell (2007) suggests that Bourdieu's field theory is more relevant than ever today because of the ways in which the norms and cultural practices of professionalism are being influenced, reworked and contested by an emerging network of alternative media producers whose content can 'play loosely with standards and stream easily across editorial borders'. Further, she notes that the dialectics inherent in Bourdieu's work break along several lines, including a 'contest between old and new', which supports the historical framework outlined in Eric Klinenberg's 2005 study and in *Alternative Journalism* (Atton and Hamilton,

2008). These new entrants to the journalistic field—in this case those with an alternative approach—can be a force for 'transformation or conservation' of the dominant ideologies, practices and emotional attitudes that establish its normative terrain. As the *iReport* example shows, there is two-way traffic along the continuum of this transform–conserve dialectic. An example of this working the other way is the New York IMC that continues to produce *The Indypendent* newspaper 17 times a year. It is a publication that also, controversially in IMC circles, decided to take paid advertising. One of the key figures in this group was John Tarleton, a long-time *Indymedia* stalwart, who stated: 'People often have a fear that money will corrupt everything, and that's certainly something to be mindful of, but having no money is also really debilitating.'

The New York IMC is a good example of how the journalistic force field exerts its own pressure on alternative forms and pushes them towards adopting the dominant political-economic organizing principles of the field as a whole. It might sound trite, but there is a key axiom in political economy that comes into its own here: *money capital will trump symbolic or cultural capital every time*. The New York example illustrates the principle of combined and uneven development. *The Indypendent* is endorsed by key American leftists such as Robert McChesney and Naomi Klein; it has a free circulation of 100,000 and a highly professional Web presence—including a merchandizing arm. This is no doubt a result of geography—both physical and cultural—in the sense that New York is both large enough and diverse enough to support an active IMC collective, while other cities do not have these symbolic resources. Bob Hanke's study reminds us that there is a further instance of asymmetrical relationships in play: 'movements need media more than media needs movements'. In fact, the dominant force in the journalistic field—media capital and finance, as the *iReport* example shows—is in the strongest position to take advantage of any advances pioneered by social movement activists. Bruns makes the argument that as long as *Indymedia* could maintain growth it could approach that point of sustainability, and he is right. However, for various internal and external reasons, the IMCs have not managed to sustain a growth trajectory. The stores of cultural capital amassed by *Indymedia* in the immediate years after its symbolic victory in Seattle have now been depleted; its original points of difference—interactivity and user-generated content—are now the staples of mainstream news websites and an activist base alone is no longer enough to maintain a vibrant IMC news presence in many cities where it was once in the front lines of protest and democratic media movements.

There is not the space here to adequately deal with other examples that get frequent citations in the academic literature—for example, *Slashdot* (Slashdot.org) and *Kuro5hin* (Kuro5hin.org)—but both of these sites are really niche outlets that cater to a specific and highly motivated audience. In both cases, the audience is closely aligned to the open-source computer-code community and the majority of posted stories (or commentaries) are of specific interest to this group. *Slashdot*'s motto is 'News for nerds, stuff that matters' and *Kuro5hin* publishes according to the mantra 'technology and culture, from the trenches'. While both of these sites use forms of open-source publishing, with varying levels of editorial gatewatching, they are not news outlets in the commonly understood sense of publishing general information of use to a wide audience. They are, instead, 'virtual communities of specialists or enthusiasts' (Bruns, 2005, p. 31). *Slashdot* is open-source, but there is very little journalistic work involved in production of the site. It is a good example of Bruns' gatewatching principle, 'reporting on news stories as they are emerging elsewhere', which 'relieves its operators of the task of being traditional-style gatekeepers'. However, responsibility for content is a key editorial function that defines a journalistic outlet. As the discussion of *Indymedia* has shown, refusal to accept this responsibility creates problems of its own. In his discussion of *Slashdot*'s gatewatching function, Bruns suggests that the site's key editorial staff are not journalists 'because they do not claim independent, disinterested observership'. However, this is a very narrow conception of the differences between gatewatching and a journalistic function. While it may be one of the ideological or conceptual differences between gatewatching and journalism, it is insufficient on its own in determining what is and what isn't journalism. Finally, an important but under-theorized legacy of *Indymedia* and other experiments in open-source journalism is the incessant drive by media capital to force down the costs of content production. The news media's growing interest in monetizing online distribution channels and encouraging the proliferation of cheap 'content farms' are two examples of this new and powerful dialectic (*The Economist*, 2010a and b).

---

[1] See Hirst and Patching, 2007, for a detailed discussion of this point

10
Who pays the messenger(s)?

When it came to commercial TV or major metropolitan newspapers... They were remarkably lucrative oligopolies—quite literally licences to print money.

Mark Scott

For nearly a century the archetypal media barons held a near monopoly on the world's news with a business model that effectively controlled all access to a mass audience. It was a commercial gate through which advertisers had to pass, as well as an information gate through which news was filtered. For most of the 20th century, newspapers in large metropolitan centres were able to make money from their control over classified advertising: automobiles, real estate and employment advertising in particular. Consumer advertising has also been a key force for the last 150 years. Throughout the 20th century, many media organizations, particularly in television, were able to maintain an unprofitable and expensive news division as a brand-building loss-leader. They did so knowing that the political influence of news credibility was worth the profits foregone. The commercial, political and cultural influence that came with a respected media property is one reason why Rupert Murdoch could afford to run loss-making papers like *The Times* in London, *The Post* in New York and for many years *The Australian*. However, all this has changed in the last decade. In some cases, the traditional agenda-setting function of professional journalism and corporate news organizations is being overtaken by public relations practitioners, blogs, amateur reporting and even social networking applications such as Twitter and YouTube. At the same time, there has been a decline in revenues as newspapers, radio and television lose their audience share to the Internet.

While figures suggest that the overall readership and circulation of newspapers is remaining relatively steady, even with the perceived domination of Web-related news sources, this is of small comfort when the latest figures also show a rapid decline in advertising rates for those same papers. The 2009 data from Media Post reveals a 22 per cent decrease in overall advertising revenue between 2006 and 2009, which includes Internet, classified and traditional print advertising. While all revenue streams have decreased, the most significant decline is seen within traditional media (radio, television and newspapers). At the same time, online advertising increased by 27.5 per cent in 2005, and 17.5 per cent in 2007 until finally dropping 1.7 per cent in 2008, reflecting the global downturn in consumer and business activity. Traditional media, on the other hand, fell 3.2 per cent in 2006, 7.5 per cent in 2007 and a hefty 22 per cent in 2008 (Lin, 2009). At the time of writing, 2010 figures were showing some improvement, but without any clear signs of a permanent turnaround.

No more 'rivers of gold'

> It is now possible to contemplate a time when some major cities will no longer have a newspaper and when magazines and network-news operations will employ no more than a handful of reporters.
>
> **Walter Isaacson**

Walter Isaacson's piece appeared in *Time* magazine on Thursday 5 February 2009. Three weeks later, on Thursday 26 February, the 12th biggest newspaper in the United States was facing an uncertain future that could include closure. According to its owners, the Hearst Corporation, the *San Francisco Chronicle* was losing US$50 million a year in 2008 and facing massive redundancies, if not bankruptcy. The news came at the end of a week in which two other large American newspaper companies filed for bankruptcy, one of them the owner of the *Philadelphia Inquirer*. Talk of the 'death of newspapers' is common, and it no longer seems like idle speculation. For most informed commentators the question is 'when', not 'if'. Even optimistic commentators such as blogger Jon Austin believe that the printed media, at least, is 'doomed'. At its heart, the crisis in the news industry is all about the bottom line. The once fabled 'rivers of gold' that brought a constant stream of revenue into the coffers of newspapers have dried up as alternative forms of classified advertising have taken off—craigslist, eBay and Trade Me, for example. The global recession, which has been around for a while but really began to bite in 2008–09, also had an impact on display advertising in newspapers and magazines. The Internet has chewed into broadcasting revenues at a similar rate. Newspapers traditionally had three sources of revenue: street sales, subscriptions and advertising. Street sales and subscriptions are falling. As circulation and readership decline, so too does advertising revenue. For the past 15 years or so most news has also been available free online. It seems that the cultural logic that previously saw us pay for news has been fatally weakened. The long-held belief that online revenues would grow to replace the 'rivers of gold' has not eventuated. Now, says *Time*'s Walter Isaacson, 'when Web advertising declined in the fourth quarter of 2008, free [online content] felt like the future of journalism only in the sense that a steep cliff is the future for a herd of lemmings'.

The problem is that there has not been a one-to-one replacement of print and broadcast advertising with online revenues. The constant refrain of media executives, from Rupert Murdoch down, is that the economic model of industrial media production that created the 20th century's moguls is no longer working. In fact, there's a strong argument that the moguls and their profit-hungry investors bled the old model dry: 'publishers thought they could escape gravity and assume that what went up did not come down . . . business was getting better in spite of circulation's slow decline' (Ellis, 2010). Unfortunately as former *New Zealand Herald* editor Gavin Ellis wryly observed, that model 'has gone and will not return'. Murdoch and everyone else with an interest in the future of journalism is now scrambling, trying to find a new revenue model. This has led to a major restructuring of global media capital and a number of creative schemes to find alternative sources of revenue. At the distribution end, there has been a decade of mergers, acquisitions and closures right through the global media. The number of published newspaper titles has fallen consistently. In the UK, City University Professor Roy Greenslade has been compiling a list of newspaper closures in the

UK since the beginning of 2008. By March 2009 the number stood at 53, most of them local and regional titles. He noted that this was offset by 11 new titles, for a net loss of 42 regional mastheads. In the United States the decline is just as swift. According to media commentator Eric Alterman (2008) American newspaper companies have lost, on average, 42 per cent of their stock value since 2005. He says newspaper stocks are no longer seen as a prized asset; rather, they have become 'corporate millstones'. At the production end, less costly 'content farms' are suddenly very popular.

Paul Farhi (2006) describes the current period as a time of 'drastic change, if not grave distress' for the news industry globally. Sam Zell, head of the Tribune group, owners of the *Los Angeles Times* and the *Chicago Tribune*, described the conditions in 2008 as a 'perfect storm' for the newspaper industry. The company filed for bankruptcy in December of that year. Rupert Cornwell wrote that the 'wreckage stretches from coast to coast'. The Australian company Fairfax Media reported a loss for the first half of the 2008–09 financial year, despite a heavy round of redundancies and cost-cutting measures over the previous 18 months. According to market statements, Fairfax booked a loss of AU$365.3 million, after posting a profit of AU$196 million a year earlier. Most of the loss was a result of writing down the value of its news assets and mastheads in Melbourne and Sydney, which recorded an earnings slump of over 20 per cent. At the same time, the number of major television networks has stabilized but the operations are leaner. Cuts have been imposed on public service broadcasters as the neo-liberal mantra of 'doing more with less' has echoed around the world.

The closure of newspapers is not new. Historically there have been periods of contraction and expansion. For example, the number of British titles fell around 25 per cent between 1921 and 1948. This has led to suggestions that perhaps a 25 per cent reduction this time would be OK for the news industry (Bell, 2008). *Guardian* media commentator Emily Bell opined that the trimming of news titles is a consequence of both the global recession and the current declines in advertising revenue. She argues that the remaining newspapers might be 'more vigorous and enterprising' if competition is allowed to follow the process of attrition. However you cut it, the data tends to show that the traditional mainstream news media is suffering—perhaps even a thousand fatal cuts. The disease is an economic one. Newspapers and even network TV are unable to compete with the Internet, both in terms of attracting eyeballs (which feed advertising revenues) and in terms of keeping up with the fast pace and interactive nature of the Web. So far, the newspaper and broadcast industries have not figured out a way to remain profitable, or to increase their revenues from either online advertising or subscriptions. *Seattlepi* columnist Rupert Cornwell (2009) reports that some news companies in the US are considering a form of state patronage—taxpayer subsidies—to keep them afloat. He says this raises ethical issues about independence, but it is a sign of the drastic measures being considered to keep newspapers from succumbing to closures.

Various forms of alternative journalism have not been immune from the commercial pressures. As Atton and Hamilton suggest (2008), citizen media of all varieties face the reality that they must operate and survive in a global media ecology that is fundamentally shaped by the economic laws of capitalism. In this context, the 'limits and pressures' on alternative forms of journalism are not dissimilar to those operating to force mainstream media into downsizing, or even bankruptcy. Given that advertising revenues are also dependent on an upswing in the global economic cycle, news organizations are also seeking alternative methods of curing their economic ills. As mentioned earlier, the medicine seems to involve making consumers liable for the revenue shortfalls, but if advertising isn't going to do this in the short term, how else can the news-reading public be encouraged to put their money or, more significantly, their credit cards on the table?

At a time when the so-called 'legacy' media (traditional print and broadcast outlets) are moving to a greater online presence and shifting their brands to where customers are heading, branded websites are not yet as profitable as the old media forms used to be. There's too much competition and only a finite number of advertisers attempting to reach the same audience. Not only this, but the new age of technology has meant major newspapers and other media, which for years have led the news industry, are no longer necessarily the strongest players. According to the Alexa Top 50 websites (based on site traffic in August 2009) the highest ranking news site, BBC, is placed 45th, behind search sites such as Google and social networking sites such as Twitter and Facebook. This perhaps explains why moving with the times does not simply mean changing the long-standing advertiser-based business model to an online format. Paul Bradshaw, who teaches online journalism at Birmingham City University, says recent (2008) figures show the online readers are worth 36–55 per cent of print readers for the newspaper. Aside from this he says about 40 per cent of advertising revenue online goes to search engines. Interestingly, he makes the claim that newspapers are far from the dominant players in the online world— something they've become accustomed to in the print world for many years (Bradshaw, 2008). Advertisers and customers are quickly realizing that online searches and online marketplaces are more effective places to buy and sell than the old classified columns of the newspapers. All the legacy media are struggling to find ways to maximize their revenues online. As the ABC (Australia) CEO Mark Scott noted in early 2009, the old media is still profitable, for now, but the trend is down and the decline is structural rather than just a blip in the business cycle. He adds that poor decision-making over the past decade is also adding to the problem. The Sulzberger family's attempt to buy back shares in the *New York Times* when they were worth nearly US$50 is a good example (Bowden, 2009). Media stock buyers paid high prices when credit was cheap, but now these investments 'look pretty sick in hindsight' (Scott, 2009). The business issue of the day, then, is: What to do about this situation? As Mark Scott said, for anyone wishing to make a career in the media there are vital questions: 'What media models will operate that allow companies to recruit and employ and offer meaningful careers? What roles will there be for media professionals?' These are not just questions for investors, bankers and managing directors either; they go to the very heart of the political economy of the media—both legacy media and emerging media forms. A key question posed in *News 2.0* is: Can journalism survive the Internet? Can the organized production of public interest news continue in the absence of a sustainable, commodified form of journalism? In other words: Are the days of industrial journalism, funded from advertising revenues, subscriptions and street sales—the means by which surplus value is realized and circulated in the news business—over, and if so, what will replace this model? This is a very relevant question given that it is not yet clear whether or not Internet-based industrial journalism (in the form of 'content farms', for example) can, or will, generate sufficient revenues—from either advertising or pay-per-view—to survive as a profitable business. It is a problem for media companies globally because at the moment News

2.0 is mostly given away free on the Internet. So another obvious question is: Who pays the piper? Or, put another way: How does the piper get paid? But first: Why have we stopped paying for news?

Why did the news become free?

> By implementing the fee-based model, the online news industry runs the risk of losing the user base that they have tried so hard to build (by giving content away for free).
>
> **Iris Hsiang Chyi**

The simple reason that newspaper circulations and television news ratings are falling is that we can get the same or similar content online, at times convenient to us and free. We've stopped paying for news because the very dynamic of convergence culture—the collision of old and new media—has made it possible. Most of the early work on online news tended to focus on uses and gratifications models which suggested that convenience, interactivity and choice were motivating factors for audiences.[1] Australian journalism scholar Stephen Quinn (2004; 2005) has identified higher productivity, cost-cutting and the ability to cross-promote content as important reasons why news organizations were so keen to adopt a convergence model for online publishing. However, it seems that news organizations did not make a conscious decision to give away their content for free online, but since the floodgates were opened in the late 1990s it would be hard to turn back. According to some research, early attempts to put a subscription model in place were resisted by consumers and soon abandoned in favour of a free model that would attract eyeball attention that could then be sold to advertisers (Chyi, 2005). Savvy CEOs had quickly realized that there was a trade-off: higher subscription fees reduced traffic and, in a catch-22 scenario, a reduced advertising rate card (Prasad, Mahajan and Bronnenberg, 2003). This dilemma soon led the news media into unchartered waters and created what Quinn calls the 'defining paradox' for news organizations wishing to embrace online publishing: How can they provide content quickly—recognizing the need for speed—and still maintain the depth of coverage that discerning newsphiles demand? Quinn calls this one of the 'fundamental questions' surrounding the issue of convergence in the news industry. The Internet turned the usual economics of the news media on its head; no longer was price a determining factor for consumers, as traditional economic theory had long suggested[2]—the absence of a price barrier created a new market in which price was largely irrelevant. The subscription and street-sales model of newspapers did not translate easily into an exploding online media ecology. Even for the companies who attempted to build a paywall around their content it was a difficult business choice. When it became clear that competitors were willing to give news away online, even the staunchest of paywall operators began to waver and eventually succumbed.

The first electronic newspapers appeared in the 1970s, but they were clunky, text-driven and difficult to download over slow dial-up modems. Twenty years later, in the mid-1990s, the online publishing revolution really began to bite. In 1994, Web-based news sites associated with news-papers sprang up on several continents. By April 1996, more than 170 American newspapers had an online presence and more than 700 around the globe. By 1997 the total number had mushroomed to more than 1600. Today, newspapers that don't have at least a minimal presence online are in the minority. It is now just sensible business practice—despite the lack of up-front profitability—to be where the eyeballs are.

Early attempts to move online involved little more than 'shovel-ware', the uploading of newspaper text stories into a searchable directory. This still happens, but it is not the most common form of News 2.0 today. A decade later the most sophisticated news sites offer a variety of interactive features, including audio and video content, image slideshows, instant polling, searchable archives, feedback pages, blogs from columnists and readers and, most importantly from a business perspective, advertising. It is no longer possible for a news organization to maintain a static site that only lists stories or promotes subscriptions to the print edition; the Web has become the focus for people looking for instant and rolling updates on breaking news. Greer and Mensing's 2006 study of some 80 American newspapers between 1997 and 2003 found that all of them had significantly increased the amount of news content on their front pages, were doing more regular updates, and had links to archived databases. This is a pattern that was repeated globally until it became the industry standard. Similar findings were reported for the use of multimedia, though the take-up rate was slower and, even by 2003, less than half of Greer and Mensing's survey sample had active audio and video content. All of the sites covered had, however, lifted the level of interactivity significantly over the seven years of the study. Greer and Mensing found that there had been a steep rise in the amount and sophistication of audio-visual presentation during their study period, and suggested that it would continue to accelerate beyond 2003. In the seven years since, it is fair to say that most if not all significant news sites now have audio and video content, even if it is not provided by dedicated in-house reporters. Employing a strategy of commercial convergence, newspaper companies are either linking up with local television stations or buying in video content from the networks and news agencies.

When Greer and Mensing analyzed the business side of online newspapers in their sample they found that over 98 per cent had some form of advertising in 2003, including classifieds and real estate, but only 15 per cent were using a subscription model. The study concluded that news websites were evolving into 'stand alone' services, not just appendages of the print editions of their titles. However, some of their conclusions have not been borne out by the development of online news sites since 2003. Greer and Mensing found that in 2003 nearly half of the sites they studied required users to register before accessing content. This led them to suggest that this would become something of an industry norm and would facilitate the on-selling of customer intelligence as a way of generating revenue. This does not seem to have happened to any large degree. Many major news sites globally allow unregistered access to most of their content. Similarly, the use of a subscription model showed a dramatic upward trend in their data between 1997 and 2003—from 6 per cent to over 15 per cent—but this does not seem to have continued. On one point Greer and Mensing were spot-on: 'no one clear business model has emerged as online newspapers continue to operate at a financial loss'.

The free news model was predicated on two assumptions: that Internet users expect free content and that, over time, advertising revenues would pick up and make news websites profitable. This has not yet happened. It might slowly become the norm, but there are high cultural barriers to be overcome first. We currently expect most information on the Web to be free and it is a feature of convergence culture that the Internet encourages free access to most things. This cultural expectation will take some shifting, and it is also clear that any attempts to reimpose a paywall on free news content will have an immediate and detrimental impact on site traffic. Thus, a reduction in the all-important eyeball count will also put further downward pressure on online advertising revenues. This does not appear to have deterred some news organiz-ations from implementing subscription paywalls in late 2009 and early 2010. The other issue that emerges in the context of pay-per-view is the free circulation of pirated material. Media capital works hard to protect its valuable content and while many news organizations are attempting to rein in costs, everyone understands that serious public interest and investigative journalism does not come cheap.

Paying for the future of journalism

> ... bundling goods together can narrow the dispersion of prices consumers are willing to pay for a good, which can lead to higher revenues for producers since prices are often set in relation to the lower willingness to pay for goods in an information market.
>
> **James Hamilton**

So now we come to the business end of this discussion: How will jour-nalism, and by extension the news industry, survive the 'perfect storm' that has dented its confidence and its profits over the past 10 years or so? One potential answer is 'bundling'—which is, very simply, the aggre-gation of content into attractive packages that will appeal to a broad audience. According to media economist James Hamilton, bundling will encourage consumers to pay because it can effectively lower the unit price to a point that the market will sustain. Hamilton gives a simple example based on two fictional consumers who have different preferences for news. One might favour domestic news and the other international news, each of which can be purchased at a particular price point. But if the supplier bundles both domestic and international news into one offering at a slightly higher price, both consumers would pur-chase it, or so the theory goes. In the UK, Rupert Murdoch's strategy for paywalling the *Times* group seems to be a version of bundling. As well as access to subscriber-only news content, for a $50 annual fee users join the *Times* 'club', whose benefits include value-added extras such as discounts on events, wine, food and travel and other commercial contra-deals from Murdoch's business partners.

While this idea seems aimed at individual consumers, there is another version of bundling that works at a wider level and is perhaps more likely to be embraced. The cost of producing a news story in its original form may be quite high—taking into account wages and fixed costs—though we are seeing this cost being reduced through the outsourcing of some production to the so-called 'wise crowd' of keen amateurs and people formerly known as the audience. However, when these costs are amortized across a number of versions of the same story, the unit cost can be reduced (Hamilton, 2003). This is the strategy adopted by entrepreneurs and financiers who are backing the 'content farm' model (*The Economist*, 2010a): creating an online space to which freelance reporters and other 'content makers' upload material for free, but taking a cut of any sale price so that the costs of running the site (expenditure on server space, a small amount of marketing and limited ongoing administration) are reduced to a bare minimum.

A new type of content bundling—alongside subscription models such as the one the *Christian Science Monitor* adopted—is device bundling, which involves collaboration between media content companies and hardware producers. One such application makes *Time* magazine available on an iPad—for a price. But economists disagree about the value of bundling, particularly in an online news environment. This is mainly because of the different behaviours of online readers who might be attracted to a particular type of content and tend to read only one or two articles rather than the whole of the online offering. For example, a monthly subscription to the *Wall Street Journal* on an iPad is around US$18.00 (Perez-Pena, 2010). From this perspective an unbundled pay-per-view system could be cheaper.[3]

In this context, then, we are perhaps more likely to see an increase in different types of outsourcing and bundling across a variety of platforms and providers. We already experience this via the cross-content deals that are done between, say, a television network and a newspaper to provide video content to the newspaper's website. This is a win–win for both companies, as the TV station gets to resell expensive content that it has already produced for an all-important marginal increase in revenue and the newspaper becomes more attractive to its audience through an enhanced on-site experience. The downside is that content becomes homogenized across outlets, reducing the diversity of voices and stories over time. It can also lead to repetition of commercially successful types of stories and less risk-taking, in terms of coverage, as popular stories are repeated and recycled. Economies of scale—such as this example—also create the conditions in which monopoly and oligopoly flourish. Spreading content across several newspaper titles, for example, makes sense to beleaguered companies with outlets in several markets, and this is now an established pattern in many nations. The same logic applies to cable television operators who must undertake the expensive task of wiring up entire suburbs—it tends to work against the competitive ethos of capitalism, despite the best efforts of economists to convince us that the 'invisible hand' of the marketplace will take care of everything. According to Hamilton (2003) this advantage of size is easily transferred to the Internet economy, and despite the idealist notions that electronic information wants to be free and that we are all now newspaper moguls-in-waiting: 'The spatial model emphasizes that costs in a particular news segment limit the number of providers that can earn profits there.'

No one model can solve the problems

> ... top-tier media institutions have never adhered to a simple or single business model. They are even less likely to follow one in the future.
>
> **Jacob Weisberg**

Not only do newspapers make money from subscriptions and casual retail sales, they also aggregate an audience and sell it on to advertisers. Free-to-air television and radio have always been totally dependent on advertising for their revenue. So, it's fair to say that for the past 150 years or more news has been inseparable from advertising. However, there have been hybrid models in the marketplace, such as government-subsidized public service broadcasting (on the lines of the BBC model, for example), subscription models for radio and television and even non-profit trusts. The most famous and significant trust-controlled news organization is *The Guardian* and *The Observer* group, which is owned by the Scott Trust. The Trust reinvests its revenues to preserve the financial and editorial independence of the newspapers and websites under its control. The Trust was created in 1936 and in 1993 became a limited liability company. However, unlike most newspaper companies with shareholders, the Scott Trust does not pay dividends (Scott Trust, 2008). This is a remarkable reversal of the usual dialectic between the public and private interest that has plagued the news industry throughout the 20th century.

One of the most often cited threats to quality journalism is the decline in investigative reporting. Numerous reports suggest that funding for this is being cut, as it is generally the most time-consuming and costly of all journalistic enterprises. It's because of this that many commentators are suggesting the non-profit, publicly funded or endowed business model could be the future of investigative media; it certainly won't happen on the 'content farms', where low cost and lowest common denominator rule. Recent success with non-profit models has been illustrated with both the newsblog *Huffington Post* and the open-source document repository *Wikileaks*, both of which rely on endowments from wealthy contributors to fund investigative pieces. *The Huffington Post* relies on the philanthropic model to fund the site. For example, it raised US$25 million from Oak Investment Partners in 2008. The site, however, also relies on advertising revenue which, in 2008, doubled from previous years. In the US the political newsblog *ProPublica* relies on the philanthropic donations model. According to Savethenews.org, non-profit or low-profit models will result in news media organizations that should have more time and resourses to focus of serious journalism as opposed to cheaper forms such as celebrity news or rewritten press releases.

Non-profit and low-profit news organizations are funded in a number of ways. One of the most talked about, in terms of viability and future success, is the concept of crowd-funding, where users of the sites donate to keep the site functioning; an alternative is the small start-up based on entrepreneurial principles (Ellis, 2010). These models not only enable the organization to continue providing news, but sourcing funding from the audience rewards readers with what they want to read. *Spot. us*, *Wikileaks*, *OhMyNews* and *Chi-town Daily* are successful sites working to this model, though each with their own pitfalls. While *Chi-town* and *OhMyNews* provide content based on funds obtained, *Spot.us* only provides funding for specific story ideas, with major media companies having the right to sponsor, and have publishing rights to, whole stories while the public can fund only 25 per cent of a story. Because funding is sought for a story-pitch only, the turnover of stories is small (just over

25 in six months) and it is not possible to fund a breaking news site in this manner. Despite some obvious flaws, this model is being road-tested as a way of funding investigative journalism, with the European Fund for Investigative Journalism being set up in 2009. The philanthropic model is strongest in the US, with the Fund for Investigative Journalism as well as sites such as *Spot.us* proving relatively successful, though interestingly the concept of using different journalists to pitch stories, as opposed to a set staff, has led to one journalist disappearing from the company after the pitch was funded, with the result that the site had to pull the pitch and refund the contributors who funded it. While there is a certain level of romanticism attached to the idea of philanthropists funding good journalism, the scale of the problem—a global industry worth billions of dollars and relatively high entry costs—tends to suggest that reliance on donations is impractical for most MSM news organizations. The dictats of the market economy, and the scale of investment in plant, equipment and telecommunications infrastructure, force most CEOs to consider other models. The most obvious method within the social relations of capitalism is to make consumers pay more. There are two ways of doing this: the subscription model and the advertising model. The latter has proven itself in the past; many news executives must be hoping that it will once again rescue their bottom lines.

The commercial media exists because those with goods and services to sell need to reach a large consumer market. It is the 'selling of eye-balls' (Ehrlich, 1997) that motivates media organizations and means that the private profit-taking interest of shareholders dominates the public interest. This is the 'duality of the news commodity', the contradiction between the informational use-value of journalism and its commercial exchange-value in a capitalist economy. The size of the audience—the number of eyeballs aggregated—determines the price of a minute of television advertising time, or a column-centimetre of space in a news-paper. Aligned to this, the negotiation of advertising rates and the ratio of information to advertising in a newspaper or an hour of broadcast-ing (for example) determine the profitability of a media organization because each article or TV program comes at a cost. Without advertising there is no margin of income over expenditure, no exchange-value, no surplus to be distributed and no shareholder profits. One of the most pressing issues for the MSM is that the digital revolution has pretty much ended its monopoly of advertising revenues. We've all grown up with the idea of a 'free' Internet. By and large, we don't like paying for content—the obvious exceptions being online porn, online gambling, books, music and video downloads. Advertising has always been the hidden cost of a 'free' or subsidized news media, but that is increasingly under pressure and advertising numbers continue in free-fall.

The paywall future and the scramble to hold on to copyright

> We can no longer stand by and watch others walk off with our work under misguided legal theories.
>
> **Dean Singleton**

Dean Singleton chairs the board of one of the world's largest news-gathering operations, Associated Press (AP), and according to a story by *The Australian*'s media editor Jane Schulze in 2009, he was 'mad as hell' about the illegal aggregation of AP copy by news distributors such as Google and Yahoo. In the same article, *Wall Street Journal* editor Robert Thomson is quoted as calling news aggregators who do not pay for the material supplied to other news outlets by AP and others as 'tech tapeworms in the intestines of the Internet' (Schulze, 2009). Singleton and Thomson's outbursts highlight the troubling reality for traditional news organizations, the Internet—in particular the recirculation of news and other copyright material—is killing their business. Google head Eric Schmidt responded that search and aggregator sites were seeking to find a solution through a partnership with the mainstream providers. The biggest problem appears to be sites known as 'splogs'—short for spam blogs—which aggregate copy in an automated way and then use applications such as DoubleClick, Google's AdSense and Yahoo to place online adverts in amongst the lifted copy. The big news organizations see this as the theft of their property, and in April 2009 several news agencies and media outlets formed the Fair Syndication Consortium to tackle the problem. The consortium's solution is to negotiate with the advertising providers for a share of the revenue generated for them by the splogger sites. This money pie is estimated at between US$13 and US$51 million, depending on how it's calculated (Schonfeld, 2009).

The battle over copyright on the Internet began in the 1990s with legal challenges to amateur music-sharing sites such as Napster. The music industry won that battle and now iTunes and other online music retailers are holding their own. This is another example of how 'underground' tech innovations—in this case peer-to-peer file sharing—have been monetized by media capital. Some illegal file-sharing continues, but to some extent online music is channelled through commercial sites or user-created pages on social networking portals. This is an example of the 'techno-legal time gap' and it took the music industry nearly a decade to establish legal, regulatory and legislative barriers against peer-to-peer file-sharing. The news industry is gearing up to tackle similar issues in an environment where, as yet, there are no binding legal precedents that can be used to plug this particular hole in their revenue nets. Closing this gap is important, the industry argues, because without adequate revenue streams its investment in journalism will continue to decline. One solution, suggested as a way of maintaining copyright and increasing revenues, is to erect paywalls around what, until now, has been free general news content. While some news media have kept so-called 'premium' copy behind pay-per-view barriers for some time, it is not yet a common practice in general news. From June 2010 Murdoch's *The Times* and *Sunday Times* began charging on two rates. The first is a daily rate of £1, the second a weekly rate of £2. According to News Corporation, more of its titles in the UK and worldwide would also follow suit (Bunz, 2010b). Murdoch's move was not popular with other British newspaper figures. *The Guardian*'s editor Alan Rusbridger described paywalls as a 'sleepwalk into oblivion' (Grabiner, 2010). British PM Gordon Brown also chimed in, claiming that most people would balk at paying for online news content. After three months respected online traffic monitor comScore suggested that the *Times Online* had suffered a 50 per cent drop in traffic and that readers were spending less time on the site (Neal, 2010). However, not one to be daunted by such numbers in the short term, the octogenarian mogul also confidently announced a new venture: an e-paper that would be available (for a price) only on the iPad (Carr, 2010). Perhaps Murdoch figures that if he keeps moving, he can't be hit too hard.

A problem with paywalls is determining what you measure as 'traffic' to a site and how you quantify this to establish a scale of charges; the quantum visitor numbers, page impressions and downloads all vary. According to tech-blogger David Weir (2009), writing at *BNET*, figures are unreliable whichever metric is used. Academic and blogger Paul

Bradshaw (2008) says paywalls are not a viable option for newspapers, as any revenue made through online pay subscriptions will be devalued by the amount of income for advertisers lost through falling readership as users seek out free content elsewhere. A recent survey by New Media Age suggests only 12 per cent of newspaper readers would pay for online content. While no definitive figures are available for paywall profits at the moment, the potential casualties among UK papers were roughly worked out by Peter Kirwan from the UK's leading media publication *Press Gazette*. Using the 12 per cent figure for newspaper readers willing to pay for online content, combined with the suggested value of an online subscription (62 per cent of a similar print version) and the 2008 posted revenue of *The Times* in the UK (around £43 million), Kirwan predicted online revenues of £8 million versus print's £43 million. Other estimates are much lower, putting potential revenues for *The Times* of London as low as £2–3 million per year (Bunz, 2010). An examination of the *Christian Science Monitor*'s public data on subscriptions in the year since it launched also indicates both low volumes and low income figures: with 3000 subscribers paying US$5.75 per month, annual subscription income for the email newsletter service is only $207,000. These figures suggest the strong possibility that many papers could suffer greatly using this model, even if all of their current paper subscribers were to transfer to online. Kirwan's analysis also extends to another form of online payment that has received a lot of attention and that is based on a more open-source model of pay-per-use, known as 'micropayments'.

Micropayments: If I had a million dollars

> ... the hope is that small or nonexistent minimum charges will make it practical to sell things online for a few cents.
>
> **Michael Lesk**

One scheme being promoted as a way of news organizations regaining some of their lost revenues is 'micropayments', which is the polar opposite of 'bundling'. The idea is fairly simple: the host sites charge a fraction of a cent (or perhaps a few cents) for each visit and/or download of their content. However, while music sites such as iTunes work on a form of micropayments (about 99 cents per song), they are not yet a real fact of life for Web-based news services. They were very enthusiastically taken up—at least as an idea—during the dot.com boom at the turn of the century, but they did not really make it off the drawing board for a number of reasons. The first is straightforward: the boom went bust, and for a few years at least bricks and mortar trading was again king of the mall. The second is a little more complex and involves the transaction cost of processing a micropayment, which can often exceed the seller's profit margin. Transactions are not processed in-house but are managed by financial institutions (banks, for example) or by specialist clearing houses such as PayPal, which will want a cut of each sale. The average transaction cost is around 15 per cent on amounts less than $5, so this is the likely rate that news organizations would have to pay, but we could expect them to negotiate a discount on a high volume of transactions. The logic of micropayments is that the more traffic a site generates the more revenue it will collect, but obviously for this to work the number of unique visitors to a charging site will have to be huge. Following is a simple equation that shows just how huge.

If we assume a news website is getting 100,000 unique downloads (a single article) a day at a cost of $0.002 (two-tenths of a cent) the revenue would be $200 per day, or $73,000 over a normal year. Then we have to subtract the transaction cost. Being generous, if we assume the transaction cost has been negotiated down to 9.5 per cent, that would mean $6935 off our income, leaving us with a net balance of $66,065. That amount would just about pay the salary of a junior webmaster but would not fund a newsroom. So, we have to up the number of visitors significantly to begin making a realistic income from a micro-payment of $0.002. How significant does the increase need to be? If the site attracts a million daily visitors at two-tenths of a cent, the annual income would be $730,000; less commission, this would be a revenue stream of $660,650. That's perhaps not a bad income for a small regional news organization, but it is never going to satisfy the *New York Times* or the Melbourne *Age*. If we up the average unique daily visits to 10 million at $0.002 per visitor, we start to get a respectable $7 million in annual revenue. This is still only a fraction (about one per cent) of what a global media company might expect to make in advertising revenue and subscriptions. We can alter the numbers a little by working off the 'page impression' formula—how many individual pages (in our case stories) are accessed each day. Each time you click on a new link in your browser—say from a main page to a specific news story—you create a new 'page impression' or 'page view' in the site log. On a very busy day the *New York Times* website delivers an average of around 20 million page views; on a peak day it might reach about 36 million (Sicha, 2008). So, assuming an average of 20 million on most days and discounting this for about eight public holidays when traffic might be halved, we can calculate that the *Times* might make around $14 million annually at $0.002 per page impression. This is still a lot of money to some, so to put it into perspective we can compare it to the estimates quoted by Stephen Quinn and Deidre Quinn-Allan (2008) in their discussion of possible business models for bloggers and alternative journalists. According to O'Reilly Media research, cited in the article, most blogs (99.9 per cent) receive fewer than 5000 hits per month and can earn around $7.00 per 1000 hits from AdSense and similar services. This equates to $35 a month, or around $420 a year. Even so, $14 million is still a micro-dot in the ocean for the *New York Times*, which has annual revenues (from all sources) of around $3.24 billion a year (Alexa.com, 2009).

Given that traffic numbers and page impressions are ultimately finite the alternative is to start raising the micropayment, but at some point it becomes a real payment. For example, by raising the pay-per-view (or page impression) rate to $0.005 (half a cent) with 200,000 daily views, the annual revenue is $365,000. But 200,000 page impressions is still a lot of traffic. If we take the traffic up to one million impressions per day, the income rises to $1.825 million over a year. To earn $18 million at $0.005 per visitor a website would need to achieve over three billion page views a year.

Based on its own reported 2010 figures of 72.7 million unique visitors per month (CNN Digital, 2010), if CNN were to charge $0.005 (half a cent) for online access it would make about $4.4 million a year. CNN would have to charge 10 cents per visit to make a more respectable $87 million. So, to make micropayments work on current volumes of traffic, impressions and downloads, the rate of payment has to rise so that it is no longer a fraction of a cent. At one cent per visit, a daily page view rate of one million realizes $3.65 million. Still not a great return, unless you are a blogger, and still requiring 365 million page views per year. At five cents per visit 100,000 page views yields $1.825 million—perhaps a respectable income for a small to mid-market news outfit, if it has other sources of revenue as well such as a healthy level of paid advertising. A million daily page impressions earn you just over $18 million, and that's a respectable income in a medium metropolitan market, such as Auckland, but not in New York. New Zealand has a population of only 4.5 million, so perhaps the $18 million is a pipedream. At a payment level of $0.10 (10 cents), a million daily downloads draws down $36.5 million a year and a commission for the transaction agency of $332,500. But at that level, how many subscribers, or micropayers, are you going to have? If you take the micropayment higher obviously the income stream increases, but the attractiveness of the value proposition for the consumer drops proportionately. At $5 per download, a million hits a day brings in $1.8 billion a year. But who's going to pay $5 an article for their news fix? This is similar to the problem *The Times* group faces in the UK; £1 per day is a lot of money, even if it's not much more than the price of a paper copy.

On a simple correlation between the average cost of a newspaper subscription (assume around $1.20 per day) taken six days a week for 48 weeks a year and micropayments, the average news consumer may come out in front. A six-day-a-week subscription would cost $345.60 for 48 weeks and if our average consumer reads 12 articles per day they would read around 3456 articles. That works out at 10 cents per article. So, theoretically, if our average reader transferred their subscription to a micropayment system, at any price below 10 cents an article he/she would be in front. For example, at a micropayment of $0.002, the average cost of reading 3456 articles over 12 months would be $6.91. Even at one cent per read, it would still only cost 10 per cent of a paper subscription to read the same number of articles online ($34.56 as against $345.60). In terms of market economics we could argue that a bundling arrangement might work here if it is marginally less than a paper subscription but more than can be charged for micropayments. If we plug Peter Kirwan's formula in here (subscribers would pay 62 per cent of a paper subscription for online access) our hypothetical paper could charge about $210 for an online subscription. If a newspaper has 100,000 paper subscribers at $345.60 it would earn $34.56 million a year; transferring all subscribers to an online rate of $210 would mean a loss of $13.5 million. Some of that might be offset by a small rise in advertising revenues but it is unlikely that all of it would, at least in the short to medium term. If we now use the figure quoted earlier that only 12 per cent of paper subscribers would take up an online subscription (perhaps reflecting the average age of newspaper readers), the model looks very weak indeed: on this calculation the annual revenue drops to a very sick-looking $2.5 million.

If we now assume our online reader likes to visit several news websites or read more than 12 items a day, their overall cost starts to rise. For example, if our reader visits three news websites a day from Monday to Friday (during working hours) and reads an average of 30 articles (ten per site) at $0.002 per item, that would only be $14.40 per year. This is not a big jump from paying nothing, as at present, but it is a big cultural shift for consumers accustomed to reading news online for free. At two cents per article, our average reader would be spending $144 a year for his/her news fix. At five cents an item, the cost ($360) is roughly the same as a subscription to a daily newspaper at $1.20 per day ($345.60). At ten cents a read the cost rises to $720 per year, nearly double the price of a newspaper subscription.

A newspaper like the *New York Times* (perhaps the biggest news brand in the world) averages around 168 million unique visitors a year (a monthly average of 14 million), so a micropayment of one cent per page view would net $1.68 million per year. If each visitor read ten articles at one cent, that's $16.8 million. Or, ten articles at ten cents each would yield $168 million. Maybe it's do-able at that rate from the company's perspective. That, at least, is the view of supporters of the micropayment system. Jon Austin is such a believer. He has recently argued, in a long blog post at *The same rowdy crowd* (Austin, 2009), that micropayments can work for online news content, and he believes that we could see variable pricing—some material is worth a few cents, some less than one cent per read. According to Austin, perhaps the only thing standing in the way of micropayments becoming standard for online news delivery is the cost of collecting all those fractions of cents. Even then, Austin argues, a 'clearing house' system of reconciliations could smooth out any problems.

That said, paywalls are being regarded by many as the solution to the falling newspaper market, and Rupert Murdoch has announced that all his papers will eventually be running a paywall model. But not all newspaper publishers are behind him. In a survey conducted by industry experts Greg Harmon and Greg Swanson for the American Press Institute it was found that only 51 per cent of American publishers believed paywalls were a viable option. Of those considering charging for content, only 22 per cent were charging at the time or planned to by the end of 2009, with the rest considering doing so in 2010 or later. The same research found 19 per cent of these publishers will charge for premium content only, leaving the remainder of the site with free access. The remaining 81 per cent said they would charge a combination of subscriptions, pay-per-story charges and daily charges (Mutter, 2009). A large number of media commentators disagree with the news managers who believe paywall systems will work and suggest this model is not enough to ensure a paper's survival. Readers are fickle and the online availability of free news is vast. For example, Michael Gluckstadt (2009) asked if the people would pay for an online only version of the *Baltimore Sun*: 'Is there any evidence to show that citizens of Baltimore would be willing to pay $120 a year for a quality news product, instead of receiving their news from television, blogs, social networks, other news websites, mobile alerts, etc. for free?'

To make online paywalls work, news executives and company boards must be able to guarantee a supply of content that is unlikely to be found anywhere else and will have to consider making up the lost revenue by offering additional pay services such as dating (*Daily Mail, The Telegraph*), Bingo or other gambling services (*The Sun, The Mirror, Daily Mail*) and shopping (*Daily Express, Daily Mail, The Telegraph, The Times*). It will also require aggressive control of copyright and leakage of material to other sites. Though numerous business models are being talked about within the industry, two things are being made clear from research and discussions. The first is that simply moving online, yet running the same business model of funding through advertising, will not work. With news companies in danger of losing their dominance in the online world, new revenue models need to be validated in order for them to survive. It also seems clear that no one method will work successfully on its own. Some knowledgeable industry insiders suggest that paywalls and micropayments alone will not work without strong niche content or value-added extras to lure subscribers, as well as advertising funds and extra paid services. For non-breaking news, however, it would seem the concepts of crowd-funding and non-profit organizations are leading the trend for future sites. That said, the majority of these are also backed up by additional services and advertising.

Before leaving this issue, it is worth briefly mentioning the 'Who pays?' question in relation to citizen and alternative journalism forms as well. While sites like *Spot.us* attempt to fill this gap through a micropayment-like system of small donations to fund individual stories, outside of a handful of large and well-supported sites like *Huffington Post*, most alternative news sources on the Web are still struggling to make money. Even a large and popular site like *OhMyNews* in Korea breaks even, rather than making huge profits, but it only pays contributors a pittance—well below established freelance rates. As Stephen Quinn and Deidre Quinn-Allan suggest, this is because site traffic rates are very low and they do not aggregate enough eyeballs to attract serious advertising incomes. To some extent, alternative news sites are a victim of their own anti-establishment philosophy and that of the Internet pioneers who believed that access and information should remain free. At the end of the day alternative journalism sites that rely on user-generated news-like content cannot compete with the large industrially organized global and national news organizations. *Indymedia* and other independent sites are not stealing huge audiences from the MSM, but perhaps the pro-am models like *OhMyNews* are the best bet. Quinn and Quinn-Allan have presented the most realistic assessment to date of the potential of user-generated news-like content, and in their 2008 article they are not overly optimistic about alternative journalism succeeding in the short-term, at least not financially:

> Given the paucity of business models for blogging and citizen jour-nalism, [their] lack of desire for financial success is probably a good thing . . . most blogs have the lifespan of a blowfly . . . like blow-flies . . . [they] make a lot of noise. But they are not likely to replace journalism.

This is a harsh description of bloggers and a brave prediction, but one thing we can confidently suggest is that the public will always seek out the news and information it is interested in. Although branded news sites are currently outside the top 50 global Web destinations, the future of online journalism is not so much doomed as perhaps in need of a short, sharp intervention. Writing in the *Columbia Journalism Review*, David Simon (2009) suggested that all the proprietors should 'meet in a bathroom' and 'talk bluntly for 15 minutes' to reach a decision that they would all, at the same time on the same day, build their paywalls and start charging for content. This is not likely to happen—American anti-monopoly laws would certainly get in the way—but the fact that this is being seriously talked about begs the final question: Can journalism survive the predations of the Internet?

---

[1] See, for example, Althaus and Tewkesbury, 2000; Tewkesbury, 2003

[2] See Hamilton, 2003 and Meyer, 2004 for an explication of market-based economics in relation to the news industry

[3] See Stahl et al., 2004 for an outline of this view

11

Can journalism survive the Internet?

It has been argued that spaces for political engagement and/or participation have expanded in a digital mediascape. But often these spaces allow for no more than 'clickable' participation on short-term and rapidly shifting issues that do not lend themselves to long-standing commitments or deeply held loyalties but a following that is also fleeting and momentary.

Natalia Fenton

There is a concern among media professionals, media managers, academics and the general public that either the news industry or professional journalism, or perhaps both, might not have a future at all. Throughout *News 2.0* I have argued that digital technologies are important in the change process, but they are only one element. While technology is perhaps the most visible aspect of the 'perfect storm' shaking up the global news industry, I have also cautioned against succumbing to the 'digital sublime' and basing our analysis on technological determinism. My reasoning is that, from a political economy perspective, it is hard to imagine any form of journalism within the capitalist industrial news model that is not commodified—content farms and monetized UGNC are no different. Capitalism is a resilient—if destructive—economic system, so it is worth paying some attention to what one of the world's leading media capitalists is up to. Rupert Murdoch is outspoken and bold in his interventions, and for the past decade he has been one of the leading capitalist thinkers in relation to Web 2.0 social networking and News 2.0. He doesn't always make the right choices—such as buying MySpace just before Facebook took off—but Murdoch is not afraid to make left-field decisions in order to stay in front of his competitors; recent biographies of Murdoch make this point (Chenoweth, 2001; Wolff, 2003, 2008). In August 2009, Murdoch gave a speech in which he outlined his methodology for dealing with the crisis of profitability in the news business: 'As I always have said before, the traditional income and business model has to change rapidly to ensure that our journalistic enterprises can return to their old margins of profitability.' In short, Murdoch could not see a future in which News Corporation would not be a major force in the global news industry. Murdoch sees no end to the commodity form of journalism and the industrial news model. He could be right: the alternative forms of journalism—user-generated news-like content—are not yet mature or robust enough to overturn the dominant paradigm; in fact, we've seen how they can be easily subsumed into industrial production models. Outside of complete collapse of the global media economy, it is unlikely that there will be a short-term future without the media's industrial giants. In that context, the real issue is about the potential loss of public service journalism.

Important figures like Robert McChesney continue to argue for public service broadcasting that relies on some form of government subsidy, and this argument has been extended to newspapers as well. However, many public service broadcasters—even PBS in the US—are really mixed models that also rely on commodified income streams, if not direct advertising. They are also compromised by the general cultural form of the capitalist media industry. There are very few strictly non-commercial models in broadcasting—and virtually none in news publishing—outside of BBC-like national radio networks. The patronage model, or innovations such as the Globizzle copy exchange, for online distribution can work on a local level and may replace some income for freelancers, but it is not going to work at the same scale as industrial journalism. It is therefore impossible to end this book with anything really solid in terms of an answer to the problems of commodity form news and profitability in the news business, but media capitalists like Rupert Murdoch are determined not to just give their business away. There is also a sense of frustration that the Internet may not have delivered on its promise of greater democratic participation in public life, or even in the news media—via practices like user-generated news-like content (Fenton 2009). This is the reality we face, what Dan Schiller (2009) calls an 'actually existing information society'. Schiller is not a digital optimist; he questions the received wisdom that somehow the Internet will lead inexorably to some imagined and utopian future:

> I reject the reassurances of those proponents of the digital who point to the Internet as if to revealed truth. Just how, exactly—in which ways—does 'the Internet' remedy or reverse the trends to defund public institutions and toward surveillance, privatization, and commodification?

On the other side of the ledger, Adrienne Russell (2009) argues that journalism is going through a boom period of 'innovation and expansion', which is hidden from wide view by the news media's gloomy reports of its own demise. There are some signs that this is the case and it's not surprising that the news media has been moodily reporting its own last days. The weight of opinion during 2008–09 was that 'old media' was on the way to extinction. On the basis of evidence to date, however, it is possible to also conclude it will be some time yet before anyone is reading the last rites over the mainstream media. While the 'bottom up' model has broken through, alternative journalism is not in a position to really challenge the news industry. In fact, many people would like the news industry to improve rather than disappear under a smorgasbord of badly written and badly argued blogs and shallow 140-character 'tweets'.

Thousands of newspaper features, columns and opinion pieces have been written in newspapers and magazines around the world that explore the crisis in journalism and the news media. They each ask: What do we do? Not just what do we do about journalism, but also about democratic discourse more broadly. Do we actually have an opportunity to move beyond the appearance of mediated democracy—such as voting for one or another contestant in a reality TV talent quest? Robert McChesney says the 'critical juncture' is both a threat and an opportunity: good journalism and democratic political discourse are two sides of the same coin. Some think the future is one of amateur and bottom-up journalism that totally bypasses the legacy news media; others argue for a 'pro-am' model of structured collaboration between professionals and amateurs (the people we used to call audience); still others hope for some sort of revival in the fortunes of professional journalism—they would argue that amateurs can never do as good a job. Supporters of alternative journalisms retort, 'But you didn't do a good job anyway!' and are they right to do so. So, what happens next?

Perhaps it's too early to tell: there will be a state of flux for some time. Legacy media will continue—in some form—for perhaps another generation. History tells us that old media do not die quickly but, like the dinosaurs, they will perhaps one day be extinct. But, if the commodity form of news dies it is difficult to see how it might be replaced within a capitalist economy. It would be nice to think that information can be 'free' in every sense: free from censorship, free from corruption, free from bias and lies and, importantly, free in terms of price too. However, the more likely option appears to be a new business model that retains the commodity-form relations of production and seeks to extract value and profits from the packaging and selling of news in a different way. Content farms are attracting attention because they are cheap— at Demand.com writers get $5 per article—and they appear to satisfy some crudely measured audience demand. But nobody could seriously argue that they are an adequate replacement for quality journalism.

From gatekeeper to referee?

> A journalist standing by the gate—opening it to allow this 'fact' to pass but closing it to other information that has not been verified—looks silly because on either side of the gate the fence is down and unfiltered, indiscriminate information is flooding through. Instead of gatekeepers, journalists now become referees.
>
> **Bill Kovach**

The journalist as 'referee'? An interesting idea, but what did Bill Kovach have in mind here? It seems that he was not talking about anything as simple as a football game or a boxing match. He doesn't mean referee in the sense of adjudicating fair play, but more in the sense of providing a point of trust and a reference for quality: 'we must construct our work to offer them the referee's advice: this information has been checked and verified; this information has been found to be untrue;

this is self-interested propaganda; this is being reported but we have yet to be able to verify the information' (Kovach, 2005). However, how is this substantially different from a gatekeeping function? The verification processes of gatekeeping have never been perfect; they have always been understood to be an honest attempt, to the best of the abilities of the journalist/editor. Everyone knows that mistakes get made; the expectation has always been that they would be quickly corrected. Kovach offers another suggestion about the emerging role of the journalist: 'to help consumers construct their own news package'. He adds that this requires a rebuilding of the relationship of trust between producer and consumer that we have seen is sadly lacking today: 'we must build a more transparent relationship with our audience.' In other words, the world still needs journalists.

This might well seem like a commonplace truism to many; to others it will appear to be a straight-out endorsement of the shaky status quo and a denial of the digital revolution, convergence culture and 'bottom-up' alternative journalism. However, it is a statement worth defending. The promise of convergence—for journalists in the news industry at least—was access to a better range of tools, more interactive platforms and new ways of constructing a news narrative. To some it represented an 'intersection of ideals' (Quinn, 2005), but it is a process driven by competing social forces—forces that have shaped the news industry for the past 200 years. The fundamental contradiction between the commodity 'news' and the public interest or informational function of the social category 'news' has not disappeared. In *Losing the News* (2009), Pulitzer prize-winner Alex Jones has described the information function of news as the 'iron core' of journalism in its role as a social force that promotes democratic public discourse. This is why, despite its many imperfections, we still need organized and paid-for journalism in one form or another. The human desire for news of the world is not diminished in a convergence culture. The production methods and delivery systems of the future may look very different—even from today's perspective from within a digital society. Newspapers have a half-life that is still uncertain; radio and television, while weakened, seem to have a future; but long-term, it is the digital (and portable) screen that seems set to be the dominant media platform.

It won't be the one-way screen of the television that we have grown so accustomed to over the past 80 years; it may not even be the familiar screen of the desktop or laptop computer. The dominant screen will be highly portable and quite small; most likely it will resemble a Kindle or an iPad; eventually it will be a wearable device of some description. It might even be a heads-up display that we see scrolling across our eye through a pair of 'frames' worn like common spectacles, but wireless and full of computing and communications power. Whatever form the next generations of screens take, the real issue is what we will see and how we will evaluate it. One real benefit of Web 2.0 and social networking has been the development of circles of trust—extending them to online forums and information verification. This can help us to deal with information overload and may also assist us to deal with the low signal-to-noise ratio on social media such as Twitter feeds. But, as events like the Iran protests of June 2009 show, there are limits to what can be achieved in these individuated circumstances. The public interest belongs to all of us—it is by its nature a collective interest. News has always provided a common and collective approach to issues of trust and public interest, despite its many flaws.

For some, the age of industrial journalism, the commercial print news industry and the broadcast model of media delivery appears to be almost over. The final shape of the new media landscape may take some time to emerge as no media form dies out suddenly; competing technologies may battle for years until one triumphs over the other (Beta/VHS is one good example). McChesney thinks the digital singularity, now under way, may yet have another decade or even another generation to play out before the future becomes clear. We can already see some global trends emerging: the atomization of audiences and a more narrowcast way of presenting both news and entertainment information within a commercial package; for example, the advent of 'mobisodes' and 'snack' content streamed to mobile phones. Whatever the outcome, the conditions laid out by Robert McChesney for a 'critical juncture' are in place. The question is really about how the collective 'we'—those of us with a commitment to democratic media forms—react to the singularity.

The first condition for change is a revolutionary matrix of communication technologies that undermines the existing system in a process of combined and uneven development, which is obvious in the transition from analogue to digital modes and the emergence of convergence culture. The second is media content—and in particular, journalism—a discredited and 'illegitimate' practice in the eyes of the general populace. McChesney's third condition was not apparent when he wrote *Communication Revolution* in 2007, but today we can be certain it exists: 'There is a major political crisis—severe social disequilibrium—in which the existing order is no longer working and there are major movements for social reform'. We have seen this systemic instability emerge through the financial collapse in 2008-09 and attendant political crises across the world—from Iceland through the European heartland, in the former Eastern Bloc, across Central and Latin America, in all parts of Asia, Africa and the Middle East and even in the heart of the capitalist world, North America. We can add a fourth dimension to this matrix of conditions: the predominance of spin in our news media to the extent that it seems we are in a constant and permanent round of political campaigning.

The 'permanent campaign' thesis is not new; its genesis was during the Carter presidency in the 1970s, though some political historians believe it has been around since at least the American Civil War in the 1860s. The modern—or, if you like, postmodern—version of the permanent campaign is a product of the media age in which we live and is premised on the fact that from the mid-1960s on television changed everything, including the rules of politics. As American political adviser and commentator Joe Klein argued in 2005 in relation to the US presidency: 'The pressure to "win" the daily news cycle—to control the news—has overwhelmed the more reflective, statesmanlike aspects of the office'. This climate of permanent campaigning and personalizing politics has help to actually *depoliticize* the coverage of politics. The focus on personality has devalued debates about policy and turned the Press Corp in the world's political capitals into what some describe as 'stenographic' journalism, blurring the line between reporter and publicist. Unfortunately, Klein is right when he suggests that the news media is complicit in this shift—the permanent campaign is more exciting and lends itself to soundbites and short television news items. It also allows opinion writers licence to speculate, rather than just provide an analysis of mundane policy and procedural news.

One aspect of the permanent campaign mode worth commenting on is the use of telecommunications technology, such as prerecorded messages that are automatically directed to certain electorates. This is now commonplace in Western democracies, though the effectiveness of such tactics in the face of growing voter cynicism must be questioned. However, permanent campaigning has been taken to new heights in the United States thanks to the Barack Obama election machine that since January 2009 has maintained its momentum in the post–election period (Murray, 2009). In reality, Obama's advisers know that they must continue campaigning for four years if their candidate is to win a second term in the White House. Writing on the *Washington Post* staff blog site, correspondent Dana Milbank (2009) noted how the use of focus groups, email list campaigns, membership rallies and the permanent mobilization of party workers and volunteers characterizes the Obama White House. Another technological element of note is the Obama camp's use of YouTube and social networking to keep the permanent campaign alive. The problem with the permanent campaign is that it relies on populist rhetoric to keep people mobilized and it confuses real government and leadership with the more overtly political campaign period: it uses the offices and resources of government to boost and maintain the popularity of the leadership, which does not necessarily match the public interest or the public need. According to Professor James Thurber (2009) of the Center for Congressional and Presidential Studies, the process of a permanent campaign is 'the use of governmental policy to build and keep public approval by politicians in their drive to win and sustain partisan control'. With the technological assistance of social networking, YouTube and machine–assisted telecommunications messaging, permanent campaigning has become an entrenched fixture in our public life. It seems to be no more than a cynical hijacking of the public sphere by well-funded political operatives crowding out any real chance for democratic engagement. It certainly appears to sideline the values of strong, independent journalism, but does it also have to mean that we are stuck in a world of bad journalism and distrust?

A journalism of emancipation?

> . . . how should one nowadays imagine an emancipating kind of journalism that tries to explain, unmask, or even counteract the mechanisms of the contemporary global capitalist system?
>
> **Peter Berglez**

Journalism should always be, at one level, about emancipation—in other words, about *freedom*. Freedom from tyranny springs to mind, as does freedom of expression and opinion, freedom to enjoy life with a good level of material comfort, creative freedom and freedom from racism and sexism and an end to ideologies we associate with the oppression and repression of basic human rights. Swedish researcher Peter Berglez writes (2006) that to take an interest in these issues is the 'political-democratic' purpose of journalism studies. This is why the rise of alternative journalism forms and user-generated news-like content is so interesting and appealing. On first glance it seems like an emancipatory social practice that leads to greater democracy. Indeed, Atton and Hamilton (2008) make opposition to the oppressive structures of the MSM a key ingredient in the definitions of alternative journalism that pose 'a challenge to the political economy of mass communication itself through its alternative democratic structures'. However, the process of combined and uneven development—the dialectic between the news industry and the alternative reportorial community—means that there is no certain trajectory or predetermined outcome that would lead to a more democratic mediasphere.

So the final question to be resolved in this book is: What to do next? Robert McChesney wrote hopefully in 2007 about the growing American movement for policy change and reform in the mediasphere. In other parts of the world the reform and public service media movement appears to be stagnant or going backwards. There are a few hopeful signs, and perhaps user-generated news-like content and alternative journalism trends are two of them. However, as McChesney suggests, one possible—and likely—outcome is the incorporation of so-called citizen journalism and UGC into the corporate machinery of big media. Convergence has created conditions favourable to big media and the news industry by raising the productivity of reporters and editors working across several platforms and by pushing them to incorporate user-generated news-like material into their offerings. Outsourcing the production of content to freelancers, 'smart' crowds or content farms, lowering costs through the use of centralised sub-editing operations and monetizing the free labour of enthusiastic amateurs are innovations powered by digital convergence, but they also provide a commercial lifeline to the sinking news industry. If anything, McChesney suggests that the Internet has accelerated the process of consolidation for media capital. Perhaps there's more room for optimism if we look for collective solutions involving greater collaboration and conversations between news producers and what's left of the audience.

There is a live and vital debate going on about alternative business models, but there are no guarantees that a not-for-profit model will emerge as the new paradigm for a political economy of the media. It is more likely, in the framework of global capitalism, that media companies will cling to their monopolies. While it is technically and theoretically possible for everyone (at least in the affluent nations of the world) to become a mini-mogul, a more realistic view is that tomorrow's mini-moguls are going to be the children and grandchildren of Rupert Murdoch. The family dynasty shows no signs of giving up its wealth or power (Wolff, 2008). What is not clear is how the future commercial news market will be structured. Murdoch made the point in his 2006 speech to the Worshipful Company of Stationers and Newspaper Makers that 'content is king', but also that owning the content and the distribution channels will be the key to financial success. In this he was right and it will always be the case no matter what business model, or more likely what mix of business models, is adopted. Murdoch may be an old man but his eye is on the future, particularly on the generation of iPod users and digital natives: 'This is a generation, now popularly referred to as the "MySpace generation", talking to itself in a world without frontiers'.

A digital native is someone who has grown up in the age of convergence, for whom a mobile phone, an iPod and online gaming are second nature. Digital natives can type before they can write with a pen. The future certainly belongs to the digital natives. What will they do with it? One argument is that we might see the very idea of a professional journalist (as defined in this book) disappear entirely within a generation or two. Technological determinists might argue that the Internet will lead to a 'golden age' of democratic media in which anyone with a computer, a mobile phone and a digital camera can become their own one-person media service. However, political economy seems to indicate that, rather than create a society of citizen journalists, the trend is towards even greater concentration of ownership and control. The problem we have here is that while everyone—taking into account the digital divide—can perhaps add to the digital information flow, most of us will only contribute noise rather than clear signals. If we are all to be 'gatewatchers' it implies that there are gates worth watching and that most information will, at some point, pass through them. However, if everyone's creating their own version of 'multiperspectival' news, how do we sort useful information from the inevitable megabytes of junk? Perhaps we will still need some trusted, paid and even branded gate-keepers, referees and gatewatchers. This could be the not-too-distant future of the industrial media.

There are also mixed opinions about the value and longevity of the so-called 'citizen journalist'. There are many examples of 'bystander' or 'eyewitness' accounts and recordings of newsworthy events being integrated into mainstream media, particularly in television and online media. However, outside of CNN's *iReport*, it is perhaps not happening with the speed or with the volume of content predicted by the digital optimists. During the 12 months of Masters student Vincent Murwira's study *The Open Newsroom*, he only found one example of UGC making it onto New Zealand television news. His other examples were limited to 'wild weather' still pictures used during the weather segment of bulletins (Murwira, 2009). At one level, digital convergence and the emergence of tens of millions of blog sites and communal virtual spaces, such as MySpace and YouTube, seems to negate any argument that professional journalism can maintain anything like its current form. The number of journalists working professionally today continues to shrink as the total number of media outlets also drops. It appears that we can all add our own thoughts, impressions, opinions and ideas to the global public sphere that has grown in cyberspace on the back of the digital revolution. In this context it might be hard to sustain any argument that the professional journalist has any future at all. This might make it seem redundant that a book like this has even been written. However, most blogs and UGC sites (outside of the big brands like YouTube) have a limited life online, and some research suggests that most blogs disappear after a couple of posts and don't last more than a couple of months. Many Twitter accounts are inactive or hardly used at all; Bebo was facing closure in April 2010. Despite the utopian sentiments and digital mythology, perhaps we don't all want to be amateur journalists or to talk to each other constantly, but we are interested in regular and reliable content online. We are also interested in connecting and interacting online through popular social media sites, 'though one would hesitate to call this journalism' (Quinn and Quinn-Allan, 2008, p. 81).

Journalism and the future of citizenship—why the public interest still matters

The prediction that citizen journalism will usher in a new golden era as it subsumes traditional news platforms needs to be challenged.

Stephen Quinn and Deidre Quinn-Allan

Taking up this challenge has been a central purpose of *News 2.0*, but at the same time it is important to capture and support the positive developments that have arisen in the first few years of convergence culture and Web 2.0. Therefore, it is worth restating another truth: for the past 60 years the global media industry has, at times, obscured the real public interest, or disguised the sectional interests of the rich and powerful as the general interest of the population. This can only happen when the news media is compliant with the demands of the powerful, when journalists ignore their role as the intellectuals of the everyday and when reporters forget their obligation to truth and trust. Journalists, whether professional or amateur, must always remember that they have a critical role: it is their job (whether paid or unpaid) to 'disclose, record, question, entertain, suggest and remember' (MEAA, 1997). The structures and constraints of industrial journalism—covering most of the 20th century—work against this ideal and dialectically created a journalism that was, in many instances, no more than the churning of ideologies on behalf of the rich and the powerful. It is perhaps too early in the dialectic cycles of the digital revolution to know whether the shifting boundaries of the reportorial community (Hirst and Harrison, 2007) and the blurring of distinctions between producer and consumer will lead to a growth in democratic media and the regeneration of the public sphere. What is more certain (in a world of certain uncertainty) is that today—as ever—a democratic public needs a reportorial community—whether professional or amateur—that is equipped with the skills to challenge the status quo. Democracy needs a loud and collective voice.

In this regard, the efforts of the social media and alternative journalism pioneers are important and must be supported, but so too must the efforts of those who are working hard to improve journalism in the mainstream. It is a mistake to dismiss the system of industrial news production out of hand; it is going to remain important and dominant in the public sphere for the foreseeable future. While the economic system of the MSM is dominated by a few monopolistic companies—who will do almost anything to ensure their own survival—it is wrong to assume that every reporter and editor is ideologically committed to the status quo, or to the values of Rupert Murdoch or Silvio Berlusconi. The journalistic field is a contested terrain of power relationships and real social forces—including those fighting for more 'bottom up' control and influence. Developing an alliance of progressive forces inside and outside of the news industry offers the best chance to realize a vision of a motivated and engaged public capturing control of the journalistic means of production.

'Pessimism of the intellect, optimism of the will'

> ... changes in the way of thinking, in beliefs, and in opinions, do not occur in quick and generalized 'explosions'; they usually occur in 'subsequent combinations' according to the most varied formula.
>
> **Antonio Gramsci**

To a large degree the industrial mass media has failed us. It is, first and foremost, a media for selling us consumer goods and selling us a way of life that perpetuates consumerism and poverty in equal measures. The duality of the news commodity ensures that its information function seamlessly reproduces the 'hegemony' of the ruling class. The news and entertainment media normalizes, on a global scale, the rule of capital. The challenge is to enable all of us to shift our view of the world out of its grip and to regain our active citizenship. The question is how. According to the Italian journalist and revolutionary Antonio Gramsci, it is reasonable to be pessimistic—or perhaps 'realistic'—about the prospects for democratic change in a capitalist society. Gramsci recognized the imbalance in economic, cultural and political power in his own society. In relation to the mass media of his day, Gramsci understood that the cost of new technologies (wire services, the telegraph and telephone) pushed newspaper owners into the arms of local industrialists and eventually into the Fascist party of Mussolini (Forgacs and Nowell-Smith, 1985b, p. 386). The differentials in power between political and economic elites and the rest of us are as great today as they were 100 years ago; as I have argued in these pages, the commercial power of the news monopolies has been shaken by UGNC and convergence, but it is quite capable of recovering lost ground and retaining its leading role.

Gramsci began his journalism career in 1915 and worked for a series of influential left-wing Italian newspapers until his arrest and imprisonment in November 1926. He was freed from detention in April 1937, but died less than a week later from injuries and illnesses sustained while incarcerated (Rosengarten, 2010). The period during which Gramsci was a newspaper reporter, columnist and editor was a time of intense workers' struggle—the Bolshevik revolution in Russia (1917), the 1921 workers' uprisings in Turin and other Italian cities and the British General Strike of 1926. Throughout these events Gramsci was a central figure in the Italian communist party (PCI) and the international communist movement. During the 10 years he spent in various prisons, Gramsci wrote his famous *Prison Notebooks* (1992a, 1992b) and the phrase 'pessimism of the intellect, optimism of the will' is the most quoted line from these voluminous writings.

What Gramsci meant by this enigmatic and contradictory phrase was that it is important to maintain a sense of optimism about the power of ordinary people to make change—if they are organised and willing to sacrifice—but at the same time, it is necessary to recognize that the conditions in which social movements operate are not always conducive to radicalism. Certainly, that was the situation in Europe during Gramsci's life; Italian, Spanish and German fascism were able to crush workers' organizations and the revolutionary period ended in defeat when, in the late 1930s, the republican movement in Spain was overrun by General Franco, Mussolini ruled Italy with an iron fist and Hitler's Germany embarked on a path of military expansion that led to the Second World War.

Gramsci's insight echoes Marx's phrase about the need to confront the world 'with sober senses', but this does not detract from its enduring truth and I would argue that it is also applicable to the current state of the news media. It helps to realize that the industrial model of news production is not yet finished. It is grounded in the political economy of capitalism, and without a systemic catastrophe or revolutionary moment it will continue to adapt to the prevailing conditions—including sublimating user-generated and 'bottom up' news-like content to its needs. We also need some 'optimism', otherwise depression and nihilism result. One source of optimism is the fact that news is no longer a 'lecture', but

a 'conversation' as Dan Gillmor has suggested. In this climate, professional and amateur members of the reportorial community have begun
to talk and to learn from each other, as well as from the audience. In his
own writings on journalism Gramsci recognized the important edu-
cative or 'didactic' role that it could play. He argued for a form of what
he called 'integral journalism' that would not only inform and entertain
the public, but also 'create and develop' the political ideas of the audience, to 'arouse its public and progressively enlarge it' (Gramsci, 1985,
p. 408). There is a direct link from Gramsci to the arguments of Dan
Gillmor ('we the media'), Jay Rosen ('the people formerly known as the
audience'), Vincent Mosco ('the digital sublime') and Robert McChesney's calls for democratization of the media; it lies the contradictions and
dialectic between the powerful and the powerless. Gramsci was explor-
ing ideas that would empower those in 'subaltern' positions—it is the
same struggle we face today in attempting to remake the global media
system. The link is evident in the Web-like structure of Gramsci's work
in the *Prison Notebooks* because, as his editors have noted, the 'coherence'
of the text:

> is not linear . . . it is established through multiple branchings out,
> with arguments that double back on themselves and reconnect lat-
> erally rather than in sequence . . . They require a different sort of
> suspended attention, an openness of reading to match their open-
> ness of writing. (Forgacs and Nowell-Smith, 1985a, p. 10)

Gramsci had a great interest in the relationship between journalism,
civil society (citizenship), economics, culture and politics. It is precisely
these issues that inform the arguments of this book and that are generally being discussed by many of the writers, editors and news owners,
bloggers and journalists cited in *News 2.0*. We can be optimistic about
this conversation if we also take note of this insight from Karl Marx
(1852)—himself a journalist of some note:

> [People] make history, but not under conditions of their own
> choosing, but under conditions directly inherited from the past.

This refers to the role of human agency in historical change and it is
very relevant today. We cannot change the historical circumstances nor

turn back the clock, and we cannot wish away the current conditions, but we can take advantage of the 'critical juncture' that we have been presented with. It is in our power to change the world, but it won't be easy.

One of the most important lessons from Gramsci's political note-books is that a collective public must be active before it can become activist and take on the political tasks of changing the world. In media terms, this means that a passive audience will not question that the received and highly ideological 'common sense' that is manufactured and delivered to us is easily digestible chunks of news and entertain-ment. The activation of the 'people we used to call the audience' is one really positive result of technological convergence and the rise of social media, blogging and user-generated news-like content. This may also be a positive pressure on journalists themselves. John Hartley has suggested journalists will be the last to know about the crisis they are facing—as we've addressed—but it is clear that reporters and editors are critically aware of their circumstances. They are not ignorant and many are begin-ning to engage with UGNC and blogging and amateur journalism from the 'bottom up'. What I think holds them back is the ideology of profes-sionalism that prevents news workers from recognizing their own class location (as workers) and their real class interests. At the same time, the news industry creates the social conditions for the hegemonic realiza-tion of an ideology that disguises the general class nature of capitalism. But it is this common class interest that journalists share with the bulk of their audience. Stripped of its ideological trappings, the public inter-est is the collective class interests of the global proletariat. The working class has not disappeared; capitalism is still the globally dominant mode of production; the network society, or 'information economy', is just its latest manifestation. My radical suggestion is to argue and agitate for workers' control of the newsroom and the news production process. I first raised this idea a decade ago (Hirst, 2001):

> It is possible to argue that a fully developed working-class journal-ism would be of more public service and lead to more public good than the reporting that passes for informed social critique today. It is hard to predict the ultimate impact such a move might have on the nature of journalism, but one might argue that class-conscious journalism is better journalism.

It might not yet be time, but collective control of the news process—by news producers and the people we used to call the audience—is the only real and sustainable way to defend and extend the public interest in news. We can do little about the singularity of convergence culture—the future has already crashed into our present. The dominant paradigm of industrial journalism is weakened by this and by the twin crises of declining profits and trust. But if we are to take advantage of the 'critical juncture' we also have to recognize that the ideals of journalism 'from below' and the democratic potential of social media are still only loosely formed, fragile and in danger of being consumed as industrial news capital fights for its life. In our favour is the realization that the tools enabling audience control over news-like content are quickly losing their novelty and newness: they are moving—as Vincent Mosco said they would—from the digital sublime to the mundane and the everyday. When this happens, these technologies lose their mystique and we can more easily use them to our advantage.

Carpe diem.

Bibliography

ABI Research (2009, November). *Pay TV Market Overview*. Retrieved 1 September 2010, from http://cable.tmcnet.com/topics/cable/articles/71112-global-pay-tv-subscribers-will-hit-over-730.htm.

Ahlers, D. (2006). News consumption and the new electronic media. *Press/Politics, 11*(1), 29–52.

Albarran, A. B., Anderson, T., Garcia Bejar, L., Bussart, A. L., Daggett, E., Gibson, S., et al. (2007). What happened to our audience? Radio and new technology uses and gratifications among young adult users. *Journal of Radio Studies, 14*(2), 92–101.

Alexa.com (2009). *nytimes.com traffic stats*. Retrieved 11 September 2009, from www.alexa.com/siteinfo/nytimes.com.

Alterman, E. (2008). Out of Print: The death and life of the American newspaper. *The New Yorker*, 31 March. Retrieved 27 February 2009, from www.newyorker.com/reporting/2008/03/31/080331fa_fact_alterman.

Althaus, S. L. & Tewkesbury, D. (2000). Patterns of Internet and traditional news media use in a networked community. *Political Communication* (17), 21–45.

Andersen, M. (2009). Four crowdsourcing lessons from the *Guardian*'s (spectacular) expenses-scandal experiment. *Nieman Journalism Lab*. Retrieved 14 September 2009, from www.niemanlab.org/2009/06/four-crowdsourcing-lessons-from-the-guardians-spectacular-expenses-scandal-experiment.

Andrejevic, M. (2007). *iSpy: Surveillance and Power in the Interactive Era*. Lawrence, Kansas: University Press of Kansas.

Andrews, P. (2003). Is blogging journalism? *Nieman Reports*, 63.

Andrews, R. (2009, 9 May). So much for online-only; Finnish web paper back in print. *Paid Content*. Retrieved 16 May 2009, from www.paidcontent.co.uk/

entry/419-so-much-for-online-only-finnish-web-paper-back-in-print.

Arango, T. (2009, 27 April). Fall in newspaper sales accelerates to pass 7%. *New York Times*. Retrieved 25 July 2009, from www.nytimes.com/2009/04/28/business/media/28paper.html.

Arthur, C. (2009, 9 June). Are downloads really killing the music industry? Or is it something else? Retrieved 1 September 2010, from www.guardian.co.uk/news/datablog/2009/jun/09/games-dvd-music-downloads-piracy.

——(2010). Twitter unveils 'promoted tweets' ad plan. *guardian.co.uk*. Retrieved 14 April 2010, from www.guardian.co.uk/technology/2010/apr/13/twitter advertising-google.

Artz, L. (2006). On the material and the dialectic: Toward a class analysis of communication. In L. Artz, S. Macek & D. Cloud (Eds), *Marxism and Communication Studies: The point is to change it* (pp. 5–51). New York: Peter Lang.

ASNE (2007, 2 November). *Definition of journalist*. Retrieved 15 December 2008, from www.asne.org/index.cfm?id=6775.

Associated Press (2009). Social Networking Q&A. Associated Press.

Atkins, L. (2009). How to Twitter: why the world is Twitter crazy. *telegraph.co.uk*. Retrieved 6 February 2009, from www.telegraph.co.uk/scienceandtechnology/technology/twitter/4523494/How-to-Twitter-why-the-world-is-Twitter-crazy.html.

Atkins, M. (2008). *Australia's most trusted professions 2008*. Retrieved 17 July 2008, from www.readersdigest.com.au/content/australia-most-trusted-professions-2008.

Atton, C. (2003). What is 'Alternative' Journalism? *Journalism, 4*(3), 267–72.

Atton, C. & Hamilton, J. (2008). *Alternative Journalism*. London: Sage.

Austin, J. (2009, 23 January). Fixing the Newspaper Business or 'Do I have to do everything around here? *The same rowdy crowd*. Retrieved 27 February 2009, from http://thesamerowdycrowd.wordpress.com/2009/01/23/fixing-the-newspaper-business-or-do-i-have-to-do-everything-around-here.

Ayish, M. I. (2002). Political communication on Arab world television: Evolving patterns. *Political Communication* (19), 137–54.

Bahry, L. Y. (2001). The new Arab media phenomenon: Qatar's Al-Jazeera. *MiddleEast Policy, 8*(2), 88–99.

Bakker, P. (2009). Halfway 2009: Closures and circulation in decline. *Newspaper Innovation*. Retrieved 25 July 2009, from www.newspaperinnovation.com/index.php/2009/07/06/halfway-2009-closures-circulation-decline.

Barnett, T. (2008, 20 August). One picture worth a thousand lies. *New Zealand Herald*, p. A15.

Baume, P. (2009, 13 April). How technology is changing journalism. *The Australian*, p. 31.

Bell, E. (2008, 20 October). Amid the carnage, why should we be immune? *guardian.co.uk*. Retrieved 27 February 2009, from www.guardian.co.uk/media/2008/oct/20/pressandpublishing-emilybell.

Benson, R. (2006). News media as 'journalistic field': What Bordieu adds to New Institutionalism and vice versa. *Political Communication* (23), 187–202.

Berglez, P. (2006). *The Materiality of Media Discourse: On capitalism and journalistic modes of writing* (Vol. 4). Orebro: Univeristetsbibliotekt.

Blood, R. (2003). Weblogs and journalism: Do they connect? *Nieman Reports*, 61–3.

Bocanegra, M. (2000). *Jeff Perlstein interview*. Retrieved 15 August 2008, from http://depts.washington.edu/wtohist/interviews/Perlstein.pdf.

Bollenbache, J. (2009). *McCormick Media Matters*. Retrieved 25 July 2009, from http://mccormickmediamatters.blogspot.com/2009/06/newspaper-circulation-up-13-worldwide.html.

Bond, P. (1999). What is 'uneven development?' In P. O'Hara (Ed.), *The Encyclopaedia of Political Economy*. London: Routledge.

Bourdieu, P. (1998). *On Television and Journalism* (P. Parkhurst, Trans.). London: Pluto Press.

——(2003). *Firing back: Against the tyranny of the market 2*. New York: The New Press.

——(2005). The political field, the social science field, and the journalistic field. In R. Benson & E. Neveu (Eds), *Bourdieu and the Journalistic Field* (pp. 19–47). Cambridge: Polity Press.

Bowden, M. (2009, May). The Inheritance. *Vanity Fair*, 114–21, 165–70.

Bowman, S. & Willis, C. (2003). *We Media: How audiences are shaping the future of news and information*. Reston, VA: The Media Center at the American Press Institute.

Bradshaw, P. (2008). Making money from journalism: New media business models (A model for the 21st century). *Online Journalism Blog*. Retrieved 12 September 2009, from http://onlinejournalismblog.com/2008/01/28/making-money-from-journalism-newmedia-business-models-a-model-for-the-21st-century-newsroom-pt5.

Bradsher, K. (2009, 12 August). China's trash problem may also be the world's. *New York Times*. Retrieved 26 June 2010, from http://query.nytimes.com/gst/fullpage.html?res=9800E1DD113DF931A2575BC0A96F9C8B63.

Braverman, H. (1974). *Labor and Monopoly Capital: The degradation of work in the Twentieth Century*. New York: Monthly Review Press.

Bruns, A. (2005). *Gatewatching: Collaborative online news production*. New York: Peter Lang.

——(2008). *Blogs, Wikipedia, Second Life and Beyond: From production to produsage*. New York: Peter Lang.

Bunz, M. (2010a, 30 March). In the US, algorithms are already reporting the news. *guardian.co.uk*. Retrieved 1 September 2010, from www.guardian.co.uk/media/pda/2010/mar/30/digital-media-algorithms-reporting-journalism.

——(2010b, 26 March). *Times* and *Sunday Times* websites to start charging from June. *guardian.co.uk*. Retrieved 28 March 2010, from www.guardian.co.uk/media/2010/mar/26/times-website-paywall.

Byrne, S. (2005, 3 September). Be seen, read, heard. *Sydney Morning Herald*, p. 4.

Callahan, S. (2003). New challenges of globalization for journalism. *Journal of Mass Media Ethics, 18*(1), 3–15.

Canning, S. (2009, 13 April). Alliances set for shake-up. *The Australian*, p. 28.

Carlson, M. (2007). Blogs add journalistic authority: The role of blogs in US election day 2004 coverage. *Journalism Studies, 8*(2), 264–79.

Carlson, N. (2009). Bloomberg's insane Twitter rules for employees. *Silicon Alley Insider*. Retrieved 13 September 2009, from www.businessinsider.com/bloomberg-lps-insane-twitter-rules-for-employees-2009-5.

Carlyle, T. (1869). *Heroes and Hero-Worship* (Vol. XII). London: Chapman and Hall.

Carpentier, N. (2005). Identity, contingency and rigidity: the (counter-) hegemonic constructions of the identity of the media professional. *Journalism, 6*(2), 199–219.

Carr, P. (2010, 15 August). Murdoch's new iPaper: One last tragic roll of the digital dice. *Tech Crunch*. Retrieved 1 September 2010, from http://techcrunch.com/2010/08/15/crazy-like-a-fox.

Carter, C. (2009). Growing up corporate: News, citizenship and young people today. *Television & New Media, 10*(1), 34–6.

Castells, M. (1999). *The Information Age: Economy, Society and Culture—End of Millennium* (revised and updated ed. Vol. 3). Oxford & Malden, MA: Blackwell.

——(2000). *The Information Age: Economy, Society and Culture—The rise of the network society* (Second ed. Vol. 1). Oxford & Malden, MA: Blackwell.

——(2002). *The Internet Galaxy: Reflections on the Internet, business and society*. New York: Oxford University Press.

Cha, M., Kwak, H., Rodriguez, P., Ahn, Y.-Y. & Moon, S. (2007). *I tube, you tube, everybody tubes: Analyzing the world's largest user generated content video system*. Paper presented at the IMc'07, San Diego, CA. Retrieved 14 April 2009, from http://an.kaist.ac.kr/traces/papers/imc131-cha.pdf.

Chalaby, J. K. (2003). Television for a new global order: Transnational television networks and the formation of global systems. *Gazette: International Journal for Communication Studies, 65*(6), 457–72.

Champagne, P. (2005). The 'double dependency': The journalistic field between politics and markets. In R. Benson & E. Neveu (Eds), *Bourdieu and the Journalistic Field* (pp. 48–63). Cambridge: Polity Press.

Cheng, A. & Evans, M. (2009, June). *An in-depth look inside the Twitter world.* Retrieved 6 April 2010, from www.sysomos.com/insidetwitter.

Chenoweth, N. (2001). *Virtual Murdoch: Reality Wars on the Information Highway.* London: Secker & Warburg.

Chitty, N. (2000). A matrix model for framing news media reality. In A. Malek & A. P. Kavoori (Eds), *The Global Dynamics of News: Studies in international news coverage and news agenda* (pp. 13–30). Stamford, CT: Ablex Publishing.

Choire (2009, October 26). *A graphic history of newspaper circulation over the last two decades.* Retrieved 11 March 2010, from www.theawl.com/2009/10/a-graphic-history-of-newspaper-circulation-over-the-last-two-decades.

Chyi, I. H. (2005). Willingness to pay for online news: An empirical study on the viability of the subscription model. *Journal of Media Economics, 18*(2), 131–42.

Cloud, J. (2006, 16 December). The Gurus of YouTube. *Time.* Retrieved 21 December 2008, from www.time.com/time/magazine/article/0,9171,1570721,00.html.

CNN Breaking News (2009, 5 February). *U.S. Supreme Court Justice Ruth Bader Ginsburg had surgery today for pancreatic cancer.* Retrieved 6 February 2009, from http://twitter.com/cnnbrk.

CNN Digital (2010, 23 August). CNN digital No. 1 in Online news for 23 months and mobile news for 42 months. Retrieved 1 September 2010, from www.cnnasiapacific.com/press/en/content/586.

CNN *iReport* (n.d.). About. Retrieved 1 August 2009, from www.ireport.com/about.jspa.

Cockburn, A. (2003, 18 August). Judy Miller's war. *Counterpunch.* Retrieved 27 April 2008, from www.counterpunch.org/cockburn08182003.html.

Cohn, D. (2009). Moving past a pitch—When reporters go missing. *Spot.us.* Retrieved 9 September, from http://blog.spot.us/2009/05/13/moving-past-a-pitch-when-reporters-go-missing/#more-1863.

Collins, S. (2008). Making the most out of 15 minutes. *Television & New Media, 9*(2), 87–110.

Connolly, L., Lipkin, D., Riazati, S. & Bruin senior staff (2006, 15 November). Breaking News: Student shot with Taser by UCPD officers. *The Daily Bruin.* Retrieved 18 November 2008, from http://dailybruin.com/news/articles.asp?id=38958.

Cook, D. (2008, 28 October). Monitor shifts from print to Web-based strategy. *Christian Science Monitor.* Retrieved 2 February 2009, from www.csmonitor.com/2008/1029/p25s01-usgn.html.

Cornwell, R. (2009, 23 February). Heroic age of U.S. newspapers ends with a whimper. *Seattlepi.com.* Retrieved 27 February, from http://seattlepi.nwsource.com/opinion/401115_cornwellonline24.html.

Cowie, J. (2009, 14 June). *A closer look at Iran's state of Internet, strange transit changes in wake of controversial election.* Retrieved 23 June 2009, from www.circleid.com/posts/20090614_closer_look_at_iran_internet_strange_changes.

Crouch, I. (2009). The Associated Press tries crowdsourcing Sotomayor coverage. *Nieman Journalism Lab.* Retrieved 15 September 2008, from www.niemanlab.org/2009/07/the-associated-press-tries-courtside-crowdsourcing-sotomayor-coverage.

Crikey.com & ACIJ (2010, 15 March). *Spinning the Media.* Retrieved 3 April 2010, from www.crikey.com.au/spinning-the-media.

Currah, A. (2009). *What's Happening to our News? An investigation into the likely impact of the digital revolution on the economics of news publishing in the UK.* Oxford: Reuters Institute for the Study of Journalism.

Curt (2009, 18 March). Omid Reza Misayafi has died in prison. Committee to Protect Bloggers, Retrieved 23 June 2009, from http://committeetoprotectbloggers.org/2009/03/18/omir-reza-misayafi-has-died-in-prison.

Davies, N. (2008a). *Flat Earth News.* London: Chatto & Windus.

——(2008b, 4 February). Our media have become mass producers of distortion. *guardian.co.uk.* Retrieved 17 September 2008, from www.guardian.co.uk/commentisfree/2008/feb/04/comment.pressandpublishing.

Davis, M. (2007). *Planet of Slums.* London: Verso.

Day, M. (2009, 13 April). Questions, but landscape changed forever. *The Australian,* p. 28.

Deahl, R. (2009, 28 January). *Journalist turned entrepreneur?* Retrieved 30 January 2009, from http://mediacareers.about.com/b/2009/01/28/journalist-turned-entrepreneur.htm.

Deuze, M. (2005). What is journalism?: Professional identity and ideology of journalism reconsidered. *Journalism, 6*(4), 442–64.

——(2006). Participation, remediation, briccolage: Considering principal components of a digital culture. *The Information Society* (22), 63–75.

——(2007). *Media Work.* Cambridge: Polity Press.

——(2008). Understanding journalism as network: How it changes, and how it remains the same. *Westminster Papers in Communication and Culture, 5*(2), 4-23.

Deuze, M., Bruns, A., & Neuberger, C. (2007). Preparing for an age of participatory news. *Journalism Practice, 1*(3), 322–38.

Dillon, L. (2009). Using social network sites as sources—have journalists gone too far? *Communities: Interactive Media.* Retrieved 13 September 2009, from www.cemp.ac.uk/communities/interactivemedia/interactivemedia/using-social-network-sites-as sources-have-journalists-gone-too-far.

Dimock, M. (2007, 19 July). *Who do you trust for war news?* Retrieved 19 July 2008, from http://pewresearch.org/pubs/445/who-do-y0u-trust-for-war-news.

Dodd, J. (2010, 14 April). Reports of newspapers' death greatly exaggerated. *New Zealand Herald.*

Doesburg, A. (2010, 27 August). What's in a name? Too much to throw away. *nzherald.co.nz.* Retrieved 1 September 2010, from www.nzherald.co.nz/business/news/article.cfm?c_id=3&objectid=10669217.

Donsbach, W., Rentsch, M. & Mende, A.-M. (2009, 21–25 May). *The Ethics Gap: Why Germans have little esteem and no trust in journalists.* Paper presented at the International Communication Association, Dresden.

Druick, Z. (2009). Dialogic absurdity: TV news parody as critique of genre. *Television & New Media, 10*(3), 294–308.

Dyer-Witheford, N. (1999). *Cyber-Marx; Cycles and circuits of struggle in high-technology capitalism.* Urbana and Chicago: University of Illinois Press.

——(2002). E-capital and the many-headed hydra. In G. Elmer (Ed.), *Critical Perspectives on the Internet* (p. 129). Lanham, MD: Rowman & Littlefield.

The Economist (2007, 1 October). Learning to live with Big Brother. *New Zealand Herald,* pp. A14–15.

——(2009, 18 June). Twitter 1, CNN 0. *The Economist.* Retrieved 20 June 2009, from www.economist.com/world/mideast-africa/displaystory.cfm?story_id=13856224.

——(2010a, 7 May). All the news that's cheap to upload. *The Business Herald,* p. 16.

——(2010b). Emperors and beggars: Can technology help make online content pay? *The Economist.* Retrieved 27 June 2010, from www.economist.com/node/16010291?story_id=16010291.

Edelman Trust Barometer & Strategy One (2010). *Annual global opinion leaders study.* New York: Edelman.

Edmonds, R. (2007, 3 December). *Pulling the plug on print.* Retrieved 29 April 2009, from www.poynter.org/column.asp?id=123&aid=133814.

——(2009, 6 March). Christian Science Monitor *prepares for online magazine relaunch this month.* Retrieved 29 April 2009, from www.poynter.org/column.asp?id=123&aid=159614.

Ehrlich, M. C. (1997). The Competitive Ethos in Television Newswork. In D. Berkowitz (Ed.), *Social Meanings of News: A text-reader* (pp. 301–20). Thousand Oaks, CA: Sage.

Electronic Frontier Foundation (2006). *Apple v. Does.* Retrieved 1 September 2010, from www.eff.org/cases/apple-v-does.

Ellis, G. (2010, 1 September). Paying the piper. *nzherald.co.nz.* Retrieved 1 September 2010, from www.nzherald.co.nz/nz/news/article.cfm?c_id=1&objectid=10668571.

el-Nawawy, M. (2003). Why Al-Jazeera is the most popular network in the Arab world. *Television Quarterly* (34), 10–15.

ENP Newswire (2005, 7 November). YouTube receives $3.5M in funding from Sequoia Capital. Retrieved 23 June 2006, from http://factiva.com.

Farhi, P. (2006). Under Siege. *American Journalism Review* (February/March). Retrieved 7 September 2010, from www.ajr.org/Article.asp?id=4043.

Fenton, N. (2009). Getting political in a global, digital age. *Television & New Media, 10*(1), 55–7.

Fisher, D. (2010, 22 August). Tracking the cyber footprint. *Herald on Sunday,* pp. 40–1.

Fjaervik, S. (2006, 11 June). *Guardian puts web first: or do they?* Retrieved 8 October 2008, from www.poynter.org/column.asp?id=31&aid=102695.

Flew, T. (2009, 16–17 July). *Democracy, Participation and Convergent Media: Case studies in contemporary online news journalism in Australia.* Paper presented at the Journalism in the 21st Century conference: Between globalization and national identity, University of Melbourne. http://eprints.qut.edu.au/26380/2/c26380.pdf.

Flew, T. & Wilson, J. (2008). Journalism as social networking: The Australian youdecide project and the 2007 federal election. Brisbane: Queensland University of Technology.

Flitton, D. (2009, 23 June). A very public death. *The Age.* Retrieved 23 June 2009, from www.theage.com.au/world/a-very-public-death-20090622-ctyb.html?page=-1.

foibl.es (2009). *Guardian*: 'MP paler than we might have led you to believe'. *Foibl.es.* Retrieved 14 September 2009, from http://foiblesblog.wordpress.com/2009/06/21/guardian-mp-paler-than-we-might-have-led-you-to-believe.

Forgacs, D. (Ed.) (2000 (1988)). *The Antonio Gramsci Reader: Selected writings 1916–1935.* New York: New York University Press.

Forgacs, D. & Nowell-Smith, G. (1985a). General Introduction (W. Boel-hower, Trans.). In D. Forgacs & G. Nowell-Smith (Eds), *Antonio Gramsci: Selections from cultural writings* (pp. 1–15). Cambridge, MA: Harvard University Press.

——(Eds) (1985b). *Antonio Gramsci: Selections from cultural writings.* Cambridge, MA: Harvard University Press.

Freeman, B. & Chapman, S. (2007). Is 'YouTube' telling or selling you something? Tobacco content on the YouTube video-sharing website. *Tobacco Control* (16), 207–10.

Freepress (2009). Nonprofit, low-profit and cooperative models. *Savethenews.org.* Retrieved 10 September 2009, from www.savethenews.org/new_models/nonprofit_and_lowprofit.

Gabbatt, A. (2010, 31 May). Israel attacks Gaza flotilla—live coverage. *guardian. co.uk*. Retrieved 27 June 2010, from http://www.guardian.co.uk/world/ blog/2010/may/31/israel-troops-gaza-ships.

Gant, S. (2007). *We're All Journalists Now: The transformation of the press and reshaping of the law in the Internet Age*. New York: Free Press.

Garson, B. (1988). *The Electronic Sweatshop: How computers are transforming the office of the future into the factory of the past*. New York: Simon & Schuster.

Gillmor, D. (2005). Where citizens and journalists intersect. *Nieman Reports, 59*(4), 11–13.

——(2006). *We, the Media: Grassroots journalism by the people, for the people*. New York: O'Reilly.

Gladwell, M. (2000). *The Tipping Point*. New York: Little, Brown & Co.

Glaser, M. (2008, 30 January). In digital age, journalism students need business, entrepreneurial skills. *Mediashift*. Retrieved 14 March 2009, from www.pbs.org/mediashift/2008/01/in-digital-age journalism-students-need-business-entrepreneurial-skills030.html.

Gluckstadt, M. (2009). Beware the paywall. *The Faster Times*. Retrieved 12 September 2009, from http://thefastertimes.com/businessofnews/ 2009/08/14/beware-the-paywall.

Gollust, D. (2006, 23 May). US denies torture of detainees at Guantanamo. *Global Security*. Retrieved 27 June 2008, from www.globalsecurity.org/ security/library/news/2006/05/swec-060523-voa03.htm.

Golub, B. & Jackson, M. O. (2007). *Naive Learning in Social Networks: Convergence, influence and the wisdom of crowds*. California Institute of Technology, Pasadena: Stanford University.

Grabiner, A. (2010). *Guardian* editor attacks online news paywalls. *ArtsLondon news*. Retrieved 6 February 2010, from www.artslondonnews.co.uk/ 20100125-guardian-editor-paywalls.

Gramsci, A. (1985). Integral Journalism (W. Boelhower, Trans.). In D. Forgacs & G. Nowell-Smith (Eds.), *Antonio Gramsci: Selections from cultural writings* (pp. 408-9). Cambridge, MA: Harvard University Press.

——(1992a). *Prison Notebooks* (J. A. Buttegieg & A. Callari, Trans. Vol. 1). New York: Columbia University Press.

——(1992b). *Prison Notebooks* (J. A. Buttegieg & A. Callari, Trans. Vol. 2). New York: Columbia University Press.

Grant-Adamson, A. (2007, 12 January). Can the parish pump save local newspapers? *Wordblog*. Retrieved 13 March 2008, from www.wordblog.co.uk/ 2007/01/12/can-parish-pump-save-local-newspapers.

Green, H., Lowry, T. & Yang, C. (2005, March 3). The new radio revolution. *Businessweek*. Retrieved 4 April 2010, from www.businessweek.com/ technology/content/mar2005/tc2005033_0336_tc024.htm.

Greenslade, R. (2009, 19 February). Britain's vanishing newspapers. *guardian.co.uk*. Retrieved 27 February 2009, from www.guardian.co.uk/media/greenslade/2009/feb/19/local-newspapers-newspapers.

Greer, J. D. & Mensing, D. (2006). The evolution of online newspapers: A longitudinal content analysis 1997–2003. In X. Li (Ed.), *Internet Newspapers: Making of a mainstream medium* (pp. 13–32). Mahwah, NJ: Lawrence Erlbaum Associates.

Grossman, B. (2009). The state of TV news: That's the way it is. *Broadcasting & Cable, 139*(29), 8.

Grove, S. (2008). YouTube: The flattening of politics. *Nieman Reports* (summer), 28–30.

Guillen, M. F. & Suarez, S. L. (2005). Explaining the global digital divide: Economic, political and sociological drivers of cross-national internet use. *Social Forces, 84*(2), 681–708.

Haas, T. (2005). From 'public journalism' to the 'public's journalism'? Rhetoric and reality in the discourse on weblogs. *Journalism Studies, 6*(3), 387–96.

Haggerty, K. D. & Ericson, R. V. (Eds.). (2006). *The New Politics of Surveillance and Visibility*. Toronto: University of Toronto Press.

Halleck, D. D. (2004, 5–7 January). *Indymedia: Building an international activist internet network*. Paper presented at the 2nd international symposium of interactive media design. http://newmedia.yeditepe.edu.tr/pdfs/isimd_04/12.pdf.

Hallin, D. C. (1989). *The 'Uncensord War': The media and Vietnam*. Berkeley: University of California Press.

Hallin, D. C. & Mancini, P. (2004). *Comparing Media Systems: Three models of media and politics*. Cambridge: Cambridge University Press.

Hamilton, J. (2003). *All the News that's Fit to Sell: How the market transforms information into news*. Boston: Princeton University Press.

Hamilton, N. & Jones, M. (2009, August 17). A look at levels of public trust in the professions. *Minnesota Lawyer*. Retrieved 10 March 2010, from www.stthomas.edu/ethicalleadership/pdfs/Minn_Lawyer_Public_T.pdf.

Hanke, B. (2005). For a political economy of *Indymedia* practice. *Canadian Journal of Communication, 30*(1), 41–64.

Hargreaves, I. (1999). The ethical boundaries of reporting. In M. Ungersma (Ed.), *Reporters and the Reported: The 1999 Vauxhall lectures on contemporary issues in British journalism* (pp. 1–15). Cardiff: Centre for Journalism Studies.

——(2003). *Journalism: Truth or Dare?* Oxford: Oxford University Press.

Hartley, J. (2008a). Journalism as a Human Right: The cultural approach to journalism. In M. Loffelholz & D. Weaver (Eds.), *Global Journalism Research: Theories, methods, findings, future* (pp. 39–51). Malden, MA: Blackwell Publishing.

——(2008b). The supremacy of ignorance over instruction and of numbers over knowledge. *Journalism Studies, 9*(5), 679–91.

Harvey, D. (2006). *Spaces of Global Capitalism: Towards a theory of uneven geographical development*. London: Verso.

Harvey, M. (2009, 14 April). Video treat online for music fans. *The Australian*, p. 12.

Heald, E. (2009). EFIJ: funding for European investigative journalism that breaks through national barriers. *Editors Web Blog*. Retrieved 10 September 2009, from www.editorsweblog.org/analysis/2009/02/efij_funding_for_european_investigative.php.

Heaton, T. L. (2003, October 2003). TV news in a postmodern world: the rise of the independent video journalist. *Digital Journalist*. Retrieved 8 November 2003, from www.digitaljournalist.org.issue0310/tvpomo.html.

Henry, N. (2007a). *American Carnival: Journalism under siege in an age of new media*. Berkeley: University of California Press.

——(2007b, 29 May). The decline of news. *San Francisco Chronicle*. http://www.sfgate.com/cgi-bin/article.cgi?file=/chronicle/archive/2007/05/29/EDGFKQ20N61.DTL.

Herman, E. S., & Chomsky, N. (1988). *Manufacturing Consent: The political economy of the mass media*. New York: Pantheon.

Hesmondhalgh, D. (2006). Bourdieu, the media and cultural production. *Media Culture & Society, 28*(2), 211–31.

Hiltzik, M. A. & Hsu, T. (2008, 29 October). *Christian Science Monitor* to discontinue daily print edition. *Los Angeles Times*. Retrieved 2 February 2009, from http://articles.latimes.com/2008/oct/29/business/fi-monitor29.

Hirschman, D. (2010, 31 March). So what do you do, John Yemma, editor of the *Christian Science Monitor? Media Bistro*. Retrieved 4 April 2010, from www.mediabistro.com/articles/cache/a10833.asp.

Hirst, M. (1993). Class, mass news media and the 1993 election. *Australian Journal of Communication, 20*(2), 28–43.

——(1997). MEAA Code of Ethics for journalists: an historical and theoretical overview. *Media International Australia* (83), 63–77.

——(1998a). From Gonzo to Pomo: Hunting new journalism down under. In M. Breen (Ed.), *Journalism Theory and Practice*. Sydney: McLeay Press.

——(1998b). Looking out from Terra Nullius: Journalism, Modernity and the 'Vacant Lot'. *Asia Pacific Media Educator* (4).

——(2001). Journalism in Australia: hard yakka? In S. Tapsall & C. Varley (Eds), *Journalism: Theory in practice* (pp. 55–70). Melbourne: Oxford University Press.

——(2003). *Grey Collar Journalism: The social relations of news production*. Bathurst, NSW: Charles Sturt University.

——(2008a). A day in the life of Ashley Dupre: Celebrity callgirl to callgirl celebrity. *Ethical Martini*. Retrieved 13 September 2009, from http://

ethicalmartini.blogspot.com/2008/03/day-in-life-of-ashley-dupre-celebrity.html.

——(2008b). Facebook and the news. *Ethical Martini*. Retrieved 20 January 2010, from http://ethicalmartini.blogspot.com/2008/01/facebook-and-news.html.

——(2008c). This is real, or 'what the?' *Ethical Martini*. Retrieved 13 July 2009, from http://ethicalmartini.wordpress.com/2008/07/13/this-is-realor-what-the.

——(2009a). Facebook vigilantes 'just can't get enough'. *Ethical Martini*. Retrieved 13 April 2009, from http://ethicalmartini.wordpress.com/2009/02/18/facebook-vigilantes-just-cant-get-enough.

——(2009b). Social networking and the *NYT*—be careful what you sign-up for. *Ethical Martini*. Retrieved 13 April 2009, from http://ethicalmartini.wordpress.com/2009/02/03/social-networking-and-the-nyt.

——(2009c). 'Sorry' is indeed the hardest word: Facebook faux pas leads to apology. *Ethical Martini*. Retrieved 13 April 2009, from http://ethicalmartini.wordpress.com/2009/03/06/sorry-is-indeed-the-hardest-word-facebook-faux-pas-leads-to-apology.

——(2009d). The witches of Facebook—lynch mobs dribble-jaws' style. *Ethical Martini*. Retrieved 13 April 2009, from http://ethicalmartini.wordpress.com/2009/02/17/the-witches-of-facebook-lynchmobs-dribblejaws-style.

——(2009e). Old habitus die hard, diehards just get older, goldfish bite back. *Ethical Martini*. Retrieved 29 May 2009, from http://ethicalmartini.wordpress.com/2009/05/29/old-habitus-die-hard-diehards-just-get-older.

——(2010). Journalism education 'Down Under': A tale of two paradigms. *Journalism Studies, 11*(1).

Hirst, M. & Harrison, J. (2007). *Communication and New Media: Broadcast to Narrowcast*. Melbourne: Oxford University Press.

Hirst, M. & Patching, R. (2007). *Journalism Ethics: Arguments & cases* (2nd ed.) Melbourne, Oxford: Oxford University Press.

Hirst, M. & Treadwell, G. (2010). *'Blogs bother me': Social media, journalism and the curriculum*. Paper presented at the World Journalism Education Congress, Rhodes University, Grahamstown, South Africa, 5–7 July. Retrieved 13 July 2010, from http://aut.academia.edu/MartinHirst/Papers/200695/Blogs-bother-me--Social-media-and-the-journalism-curriculum.

Hopkins, C. (2009, 18 March). *Omid Reza Misayafi has died in prison*. Retrieved 23 June 2009, from http://committeetoprotectbloggers.org/2009/03/18/omir-reza-misayafi-has-died-in-prison.

Horne, D. (1994). A marketplace of ideas? In J. Schultz (Ed.), *Not Just Another Business* (pp. 7–10). Sydney: Pluto Press.

Huberman, B. A., Romero, D. M. & Wu, F. (2008). *Crowdsourcing, Attention and Productivity*. Palo Alto, CA: HP Laboratories.

Hume, T. (2009, 26 April). Just a mo while we drink to Susan. *Sunday Star Times*, p. A4.

Hunter, A. (2009, 13 April). E-messaging hooks up Nine's virtual newsroom. *The Australian*, p. 27.

Hutchins, B. & Rowe, D. (2009). From broadcast scarcity to digital plenitude: The changing dynamics of the media sport content economy. *Television & New Media, 10*(4), 354–70.

The Indypendent (n.d.). About our newspaper. Retrieved 15 April 2010, from www.indypendent.org/?pagename=about.

Internet World Stats (2010, 30 June). *Internet usage statistics*. Retrieved 12 August 2010, from www.internetworldstats.com/stats.htm.

Isaacson, W. (2009). How to save your newspaper. *Time*. Retrieved 27 February 2009, from www.time.com/time/business/article/0,8599,1877191,00.html.

Jackson, R. (2007, 28 April). Essential qualifications of a good journalist. *Journalists.net*. Retrieved 15 December 2008, from http://journalists.net/news/Journalism-Training/journalists-qualities.html.

Jameson, F. (1991). *Postmodernism or, The cultural logic of late capitalism*. Durham: Duke University Press.

——(1998). Marxism and Postmodernism. In *The Cultural Turn: Selected writings on the postmodern, 1983–1998* (pp. 33–49). London, New York: Verso.

——(2009). *Valences of the Dialectic*. London: Verso.

Jarvis, J. (2007). The web is preeminent. *BuzzMachine*. Retrieved 3 March 2009, from www.buzzmachine.com/2007/03/07/the-web-is-preeminent.

——(2009). Missing the point. *BuzzMachine*. Retrieved 13 September 2009, from www.buzzmachine.com/2009/05/13/missing-the-point-2.

Jenkins, H. (2006). *Convergence Culture: Where old and new media collide*. New York: New York University Press.

Johnson, B. (2009, 17 June). Net response to Iran shows we are all newsmakers now. *guardian.co.uk*. Retrieved 17 June 2009, from www.guardian.co.uk/technology/blog/2009/jun/17/twitter-socialnetworking.

Johnson, T. J. & Fahmy, S. (2008). The CNN of the Arab world or a shill for terrorists: How support for press freedom and political ideology predict credibility of Al-Jazeera among its audience. *The International Communication Gazette, 70*(5), 338–60.

Jones, A. S. (2009). *Losing the News: The future of news that feeds democracy*. New York: Oxford University Press.

journalism.co.uk (2008). Publishers must put digital at centre of business models, says Sly Bailey. *Journalism.co.uk*. Retrieved 9 October 2008, from www.journalism.co.uk.

Journalists Network (2007, 28 April). What makes it journalism? Who are the journalists? *journalists.net*. Retrieved 15 December 2008, from http://journalists.net/news/index.php?news=2602.

Kakutani, N. (2008). Is Jon Stewart the most trusted man in America? *New York Times*. Retrieved 15 August 2008, from www.nytimes.com/2008/08/17/arts/television/17kaku.html.

Kanalley, C. (2009, 11 June). SMS system down in Iran just hours before election. Breakingtweets.com. Retrieved 23 June 2009, from www.breakingtweets.com/2009/06/11/sms-system-down-in-iran-just-hours-before-election.

Karimi, N. & Kole, W. J. (2009, 21 June). Iran braces for possible fresh violence after bloody clashes between protestors, police. *StarTribune.com*. Retrieved 21 June 2009, from www.startribune.com/world/48697647.html?elr=KArks:DCiUBcy7hUiD3aPc:_Yyc:aUU.

Keane, M. & Moran, A. (2008). Television's new engines. *Television & New Media, 9*(2), 155–69.

Keen, A. (2007). *The Cult of the Amateur: How today's internet is killing our culture.* London, Boston: Nicholas Brealey.

Kelly, J. & Etling, B. (2008). *Mapping Iran's Online Public: Politics and culture in the Persian blogosphere.* Boston: Berkman Center for Internet and Society.

Kerwin, J. (2006). Op-Ed: Why I don't trust the police. *The Stanford Daily Online*. Retrieved 18 November 2007, from http://daily.stanford.edu/article/2006/11/17/opedWhyIDontTrustThePolice.

Khouri, R. G. (2007). The Arab story: The big one waiting to be told. *Nieman Reports, 61*(2), 10–11.

Kirwan, P. (2009a, 17 April). Crunch time for newspapers. *wired.co.uk*. Retrieved 17 April 2009, from www.wired.co.uk/news/archive/2009-04/17/crunch-time-for-british-newspapers.aspx.

——(2009b). The economics of paywall publishing: It's a niche thing. *Press Gazette*. Retrieved 12 September 2009, from http://blogs.pressgazette.co.uk/mediamoney/2009/05/20/the-economics-of-paywall-publishing-its-a-niche-thing.

——(2009c, 2 April). The great transition. *wired.co.uk*. Retrieved 17 April 2009, from www.wired.co.uk/news/archive/2009-04/01/peter-kirwan-the-great-transition.aspx.

Kittur, A., Chi, E., Pendleton, B. A., Suh, B. & Mytkowicz, T. (2006). *Power of the few vs wisdom of the crowd: Wikipedia and the rise of the bourgeoisie.* Paper presented at the SIGCHI (Special Interest Group on Computer Human Interaction) conference 2007.

Kittur, A. & Kraut, R. E. (2008, 8–12 November). *Harnessing the wisdom of crowds in Wikipedia: Quality through coordination.* Paper presented at the ACM (Association for Computer Machinery) conference 2008, San Diego.

Klein, J. (2005, 30 October). The perils of the permanent campaign. *Time*. Retrieved 17 April 2009, from www.time.com/time/columnist/klein/article/0,9565,1124237,00.html.

Klinenberg, E. (2005). Channelling into the journalistic field: Youth activism and the media justice movement. In R. Benson & E. Neveu (Eds.), *Bourdieu and the Journalistic Field* (pp. 174–92). Cambridge: Polity Press.

Koblin, J. (2009). Twitter culture wars at *The Times*: 'We need a zone of trust,' Bill Keller tells staff. *New York Observer*. Retrieved 13 September 2009, from www.observer.com/2009/media/twitter culture-wars-itimesi.

Kovach, B. (2005, 1 February). A new journalism for democracy in a new age, Madrid, Spain. *journalism.org*. Retrieved 17 April 2009, from www.journalism.org/node/298.

Kraft, D. (2006, 2 January). Satire that spares nothing, not even God and country. *New York Times*. Retrieved 14 July 2008, from www.nytimes.com/2006/01/02/international/middleeast/02telaviv.html.

Kramer, S. D. (2009). *HuffPo* changes CEOs: Betsy Morgan being replaced by SoftBank's Eric Hippeau. *Paid Content*. Retrieved 9 September 2009, from http://paidcontent.org/article/419-huffpo-changes-ceos-betsy-morgan-being-by-softbank-eric-hi.

Krause, E. A. (1971). *The Sociology of Occupations*. Boston: Little, Brown & Company.

Kraverts, D. (2009). AP issues strict Facebook, Twitter guidelines to staff. *Wired*. Retrieved 13 September 2009, from www.wired.com/threatlevel/2009/06/facebookfollow.

Kruse, H. (2009). Betting on News Corporation: Interactive media, gambling and global information flows. *Television & New Media, 10*(2), 179–94.

Kunelius, R. & Ruusunoksa, L. (2008). Mapping professional imagination. *Journalism Studies, 9*(5), 662–78.

Kwak, K.-S. (2008). Restructuring the satellite television industry in Japan. *Television & New Media, 9*(1), 62–84.

Lanier, J. (2010). *You are not a gadget: A manifesto*. Camberwell, VIC: Allen Lane.

Lasica, J. D. (2003). Blogs and journalism need each other. *Nieman Reports*, 70–4.

Lawton, B. (2007, 19 July). A spectacularly successful failure. *Digital Edge*. Retrieved 1 May 2009, from www.naa.org/blog/digitaledge/1/2007/07/A-Spectacularly-Successful-Failure.cfm.

Lesk, M. (2004). Micropayments: An idea whose time has passed twice? *IEEE Security & Privacy*, 61–3.

Levy, S. & Stone, B. (2006, 3 April). The new wisdom of the web. *Newsweek;MSNBC.com*. Retrieved 11 October 2009, from www.msnbc.msn.com/id/12015774/site/newsweek/page/3.

Lin, E. (2009, 8 September). Internet up 37.5% while traditional media down 30% from 2006 to 2009. *sfnblog.com*. Retrieved 14 September 2009, from www.sfnblog.com/industry_trends/2009/09/internet_up_375_while_traditional_media.php.

Losh, L. (2007, 18 August). Facebook Journalism. *VirtualPolitik*. Retrieved 15 April 2009, from http://virtualpolitik.blogspot.com/2007/08/facebook-journalism.html.

Love, R. (2007, March/April). Before Jon Stewart. *Columbia Journalism Review*. Retrieved 19 July 2008, from www.cjr.org/feature/before_jon_stewart.php.

Lowrey, W. (2006). Mapping the journalism-blogging relationship. *Journalism, 7*(4), 477–500.

Luft, O. (2008a). AFP reporters barred from using Wikipedia and Facebook as sources. *journalism.co.uk*. Retrieved 13 September 2009, from www.journalism.co.uk/2/articles/530941.php.

——(2008b, 4 March). Papers sorry for 'Facebook party' story. *guardian.co.uk*. Retrieved 7 March 2008, from www.guardian.co.uk/media/2009/mar/04/papers-sorry-for-facebook-party-story.

Lynch, M. (2003). Beyond the Arab street: Iraq and the Arab public sphere. *Politics and Society, 31*(1), 55–91.

Lynn, C. (2008, 28 April). Top tech bloggers define WEB 2.0. *Socialtnt.com*. Retrieved 14 January 2009, from http://socialtnt.com/2008/04/28/tech-bloggers-define-web-20.

Mamadouh, V. (2004). Internet, scale and the global grassroots: Geographies of the *Indymedia* network of independent media centres. *Tijdschrift voor Economische en Sociale Geografie* [*Review of Economic and Social Geography*], *95*(5), 482–97.

Manjoo, F. (2008). *True Enough: Learning to live in a post-fact society*. Hoboken, NJ: John Wiley & Sons.

Martin, J. (2006, May). Arab journalism comes of age. *Middle East,* 50–4.

Marx, K., (1852). *The Eighteenth Brumaire of Louis Bonaparte*. Marx and Engels Internet Archive. Retrieved 1 September 2010, from www.marxists.org/archive/marx/works/1852/18th-brumaire/ch01.htm.

——(1990 (1867)). *Das Kapital* (Penguin Classics ed.,Vol. 1). London: Penguin.

Marx, K. & Engels, F. (1973 (1872)). *Manifesto of the Communist Party*. Moscow: Progress Publishers.

May, A. L. (2008, Summer). Campaign 2008: It's on YouTube. *Nieman Reports,* 24–8.

McChesney, R. W. (2000). *Rich Media, Poor Democracy: Communication politics in dubious times* (New Press Paperback ed.). New York: The New Press.

——(2001). Global media, neoliberalism and imperialism. *Monthly Review, 52*(10).

——(2007). *Communication Revolution: Critical junctures and the future of media.* New York, London: The New Press.

——(2008a). The new economy: Myth and reality. In *The Political Economy of Media: Enduring issues, emerging dilemmas* (pp. 291–304). New York: Monthly Review Press.

——(2008b). *The Political Economy of Media: Enduring issues, emerging dilemmas.* New York: Monthly Review Press.

——(2008c). The problem of journalism. In *The Political Economy of Media: Enduring issues, emerging dilemmas* (pp. 25–66). New York: Monthly Review Press.

McChesney, R. W. & Schiller, D. (2003). *The political economy of international communications: Foundations for the emerging global debate about media ownership and regulation* (Technology, Business and Society Programme Paper No. 11). Geneva, Switzerland: United Nations Research Institute for Social Development.

MacManus, R. (2009, 13 December). Content Farms: Why media, blogs & Google should be worried. Retrieved 27 June 2010, from www.readwriteweb. com/archives/content_farms_impact.php.

McMasters, P. (2003). Blurring the line between journalist and publicist. *Nieman Reports.* Retrieved 16 September 2009, from www.nieman.harvard. edu/reportsitem.aspx?id=101223.

McNair, B. (1998). *The Sociology of Journalism.* London: Arnold.

MEAA (1997). *Ethics in journalism / report of the Ethics Review Committee, Media Entertainment and Arts Alliance, Australian Journalists' Association Section.* Carlton, VIC: Melbourne University Press.

Meehan, E. R. (2007). Deregulation and integrated oligopolies: Television at the turn of the century. In G. Murdock & J. Wasko (Eds.), *Media in the Age of Marketization* (pp. 11–32). Cresskill, NJ: Hampton Press.

Mellor, N. (2005). *The Making of Arab News.* Oxford: Rowman & Littlefield.

——(2008). Arab journalists as cultural intermediaries. *Press/Politics, 13*(4), 465–83.

Menezes, E. (2009). *Journalism in the Americas.* Retrieved 25 July 2009, from http://knightcenter.utexas.edu/blog/?q=en/node/3393.

Merrill, J. C. (1989). *The Dialectic in Journalism: Toward a responsible use of press freedom.* Baton Rouge: Lousiana State University Press.

Meyer, P. (1995). Public journalism and the problem of objectivity. Retrieved 8 March 2007, from www.unc.edu/~pmeyer/ire95pj.htm.

——(2004). *The Vanishing Newspaper: Saving journalism in the Information Age.* Columbia, MO: University of Missouri Press.

Milbank, D. (2009, 2 April). Bricka Bracka Firecracker, Sis Boom Bah! *Washington Post.* Retrieved 17 April 2009, from www.washingtonpost.com/ wpdyn/content/article/2009/04/01/AR2009040104218.html.

Miles, H. (2005). *Al-Jazeera: How Arab TV News Challenged the World*. London: Abacus.

Moore, T. & Clayton, R. (2008). Evaluating the wisdom of crowds in assessing phishing websites. *Financial Cryptography and Data Security*, 16–30.

Morozov, E. (2009, 16 June). More on Twitter and protests in Tehran. *Foreign Policy*. Retrieved 20 June 2009, from http://neteffect.foreignpolicy.com/posts/2009/06/16/more_on_twitter_and_protests_in_tehran.

Mosco, V. (1988). Introduction: Information in the Pay-per Society. In V. Mosco & J. Wasko (Eds), *The Political Economy of Information*. Madison, WI: University of Wisconsin Press.

——(1996). *The Political Economy of Communication: Rethinking and renewal*. London: Sage.

——(2004). *The Digital Sublime: Myth, power and cyberspace*. Boston: The MIT Press.

——(2009). The future of journalism. *Journalism, 10*(3), 350–2.

Murdoch, R. (2005, 13 April). *Speech to the American Society of Newspaper Editors*. Retrieved 1 November 2005, from www.newscorp.com/news/news_247.html.

——(2006). Murdoch speech at Stationers Hall: full text. *timesonline.co.uk*. Retrieved 14 September 2009, from http://business.timesonline.co.uk/tol/business/industry_sectors/media/article740587.ece.

Murdock, G. & Wasko, J. (Eds.). (2007). *Media in the Age of Marketization*. Cresskill, NJ: Hampton Press.

Murray, M. (2009, 17 March). First 100 Days: The permanent campaign. *First Read*. Retrieved 17 April 2009, from http://firstread.msnbc.msn.com/archive/2009/03/17/1839051.aspx.

Murrell, C. & Oakham, M. (2008). Gatekeepers: going, going, gone—the challenge of citizen journalism to traditional practice. *Australian Journalism Review, 30*(2), 11–21.

Murwira, V. (2009). *The Open Newsroom*. Retrieved 9 March 2010, from www.theopennewsroom.com.

Museum of Broadcast Communications (2008). *That Was the Week That Was*. Retrieved 12 June 2008, from www.museum.tv/archives/etv/T/htmlT/thatwasthe/thatwasthe.htm.

Muthukumaraswamy, K. (2009). When the media meet crowds of wisdom. *Journalism Practice, iFirst Article*, 1–18.

Mutter, A. D. (2009). Only 51% of pubs think pay walls will fly. *Reflections of a Newsosaur*. Retrieved 14 September 2009, from http://newsosaur.blogspot.com/2009/09/only-51-of-pubs-think-pay-walls-will.html.

National Union of Journalists (2008a, 30 September). ITV announces 40 per cent cut to regional news staff. *nuj.org.uk*. Retrieved 9 October 2008, from www.nuj.org.uk/innerPagenuj.html?docid=932.

——(2008b, 6 October). London Newsquest redundancies threaten titles' quality. *nuj.org.uk*. Retrieved October 9 2008, from www.nuj.org.uk/innerPagenuj.html?docid=936.

Neal, D. (2010, 17 August). Pay wall causes 50 per cent drop in *Times* visitors. *V3.co.uk*. Retrieved 1 September 2010, from www.v3.co.uk/v3/news/2268285/times-sees-user-numbers-halve.

Neus, E. (2005, 11 August). New and notable on the Web. *Gannet News Service*. Retrieved 16 November 2006, from www.usatoday.com/tech.

News One (2010, 2 March). Minority journalists: Media does a poor job covering race issues. *newsone.com*. Retrieved 10 March 2010, from http://newsone.com/nation/news-one-staff/minority-journalists-media-does-poor-job-covering-race-issues.

Newspaper Works (2009). Newspaper circulation steady. *The Newspaper Works*. Retrieved 25 July 2009, from www.thenewspaperworks.com.au/go/news/newspaper-circulation-steady/41eccc96-5056 887e-a67db501c400393c.

New Zealand Herald (2010, 14 August). It's Black and White: *Herald*'s most read. *The Weekend Herald*.

Nichols, J. & McChesney, R. W. (2005). *Tragedy & Farce: How the American media sell wars, spin elections, and destroy democracy*. New York: New Press.

——(2010). How to save journalism. *Common Dreams.org*. Retrieved 13 January 2010, from www.commondreams.org/print/51378.

Novack, G. (1972). The law of uneven and combined development. In G. Novack (Ed.), *Understanding History: Marxist essays*. New York: Pathfinder Press.

O'Brien, D. & Fitzgerald, B. (2006). Digital copyright law in a YouTube world. *Internet Law Bulletin, 9*(6&7), 71–4. Retrieved 27 November 2008, from http://eprints.qut.edu.au/7505/1/7505.pdf.

O'Connell, D. (2009, 2 August). Guardian Media Group plots closure of *Observer* newspaper. *Timesonline.co.uk*. Retrieved 7 October 2009, from http://business.timesonline.co.uk/tol/business/industry_sectors/media/article6736037.ece.

O'Harrow, Jr. R. (2005). *No Place to Hide*. New York: Free Press.

O'Reilly, T. (2005a, 5 August). Not 2.0? *radar.oreilly.com*. Retrieved 14 June 2008, from http://radar.oreilly.com/archives/2005/08/not-20.html.

——(2005b, 30 September). What is Web 2.0? *radar.oreilly.com*. Retrieved 14 April 2009, from www.oreillynet.com/pub/a/oreilly/tim/news/2005/09/30/what-is-web-20.html.

——(2006, 10 December). Web 2.0 Compact definition: Trying again. *radar.oreilly.com*. Retrieved 14 June 2008, from http://radar.oreilly.com/archives/2006/12/web-20-compact-definition-tryi.html.

Oakham, M. (2006). In our own image? The socialisation of journalism's new recruits. *Australian Journalism Review, 28*(1), 183–97.

Oh, Y.-h. (2006, 11 July). Welcome to Korea and OhmyNews. *OhmyNews*. Retrieved 12 April 2009, from http://english.ohmynews.com/articleview/article_view.asp?article_class=11&no=304539&rel_no=1.

Oliver, L. (2008, 24 September). Teeside Evening Gazette to recruit 1,000 citizen journalists for hyperlocal sites. *journalism.co.uk*. Retrieved 9 October 2008, from www.journalism.co.uk/2/articles/532405.php.

——(2009). *The Roanoke Times*: Ethical guidelines for social media. *journalism.co.uk*. Retrieved 13 September 2009, from www.journalism.co.uk/5/articles/533328.php.

Orwell, G. (2004 (1946)). Why I write. In S. Orwell & I. Angus (Eds), *Orwell: An age like this 1920–1940* (2 ed., Vol. 1, pp. 1–10). Jaffrey, NH: Nonpareil.

Palfrey, J., Etling, B. & Farris, R. (2009, 21 June). Reading Twitter in Tehran? *Washington Post*. Retrieved 23 June 2009, from www.washingtonpost.com/wpdyn/content/article/2009/06/19/AR2009061901598.html.

Palloix, C. (1976). The labour process: From Fordism to neo-Fordism (J. Mepham & M. Soneuscher, Trans.). In C. Palloix (Ed.), *The Labour Process & Class Strategies*. London: Conference of Socialist Economists.

Papacharissi, Z. & de Fatima Oliveira, M. (2008). News frames terrorism: A comparative analysis of frames employed in terrorism coverage in U.S. and U.K. newspapers. *Press/Politics, 13*(1), 52–74.

Pavlik, J.V. (1994). Citizen access, involvement, and freedom of expression in an electronic environment. In F. Williams & J.V. Pavlik (Eds), *People's Right to Know: Media, democracy, and the information highway*. Mahwah, NJ: Lawrence Erlbaum.

——(2001). *Journalism and New Media*. New York: Columbia University Press.

Pavlik, J.V. & Feiner, S. K. (1998, Fall). *Implications of the mobile journalist workstation for print media*. Retrieved 25 March 2004, from www.futureprint.kent.edu/articles/pavlik01.htm.

Perez-Pena, R. (2009, October 26). US newspaper circulation falls 10%. *nytimes.com*. Retrieved 15 March 2010, from www.nytimes.com/2009/10/27/business/media/27audit.html.

——(2010). The *Times* of London to charge online. *Media Decoder*. Retrieved 28 March 2010, from http://mediadecoder.blogs.nytimes.com/2010/03/26/the-times-of-london-to-charge-online.

Peskin, D. (2003). Introduction. In S. Bowman & C. Willis (Eds), *We Media: How audiences are shaping the future of news and information* (p. v). Reston, VA: The Media Center at the American Press Institute. Retrieved 11 July 2008, from www.hypergene.net/wemedia/download/we_media.pdf.

Pew Research Center (2009). *Press Accuracy Rating Hits Two Decade Low*. Washington DC: The Pew Research Center for the people and the press.

Pfeifle, M. (2009, 6 July). A Nobel Peace Prize for Twitter. *csmonitor.com*. Retrieved 2 August 2009, from www.csmonitor.com/2009/0706/p09s02-coop.html.

Physicians for Human Rights (2008). *Broken laws, broken lives*. Retrieved 4 July 2008, from http://physiciansforhumanrights.org/library/report-2008-06-18.html.

Pickard, V. W. (2006). United yet autonomous: Indymedia and the struggle to sustain a radical democratic network. *Media Culture & Society, 28*(3), 315–36.

Pilger, J. (1991). *Distant Voices*. London: Vantage.

Pintak, L. (2009). Border guards of the 'imagined' watan: Arab journalists and the new Arab consciousness. *The Middle East Journal, 63*(2), 191–213.

Pintak, L. & Ginges, J. (2008). The mission of Arab journalism: Creating change in a time of turmoil. *Press/Politics, 13*(3), 193–227.

——(2009). Inside the Arab newsroom. *Journalism Studies, 10*(2), 157–77.

Platon, S. & Deuze, M. (2003). Indymedia journalism: A radical way of making, selecting and sharing news? *Journalism, 4*(3), 336–55.

Ponsford, D. (2010, 12 March). Feb ABCs: Qualities plunge but Star and Sun are up. *Press Gazette*. Retrieved 15 March 2010, from www.pressgazette.co.uk/story.asp?sectioncode=1&storycode=45172&c=1.

Posetti, J. (2009a). How journalists balance work, personal lives on Twitter. *MediaShift*. Retrieved 13 September 2009, from www.pbs.org/mediashift/2009/06/how-journalists-balance-work-personal-lives-on-twitter159.html.

——(2009b). Rules of engagement for journalists on Twitter. *MediaShift*. Retrieved 13 September 2009, from www.pbs.org/mediashift/2009/06/rules-of-engagement-for-journalists-on-twitter170.html.

Poulantzas, N. (1975). *Classes in Contemporary Capitalism* (D. Fernbach, Trans.). London: New Left Books.

PoynterOnline (2009, 19 January). *New York Times'* policy of Facebook and other social networking sites. *poynter.org*. Retrieved 15 February 2009, from www.poynter.org/content/content_view.asp?id=157136.

Prasad, A., Mahajan, V. & Bronnenberg, B. (2003). Advertising versus pay-per-view in electronic media. *International Journal of Research in Marketing, 20*(1), 13–30.

Prensky, M. (2001). Digital natives, digital immigrants. *On the Horizon, 9*(5).

Press Trust of India (2007). Newspaper circulation up: India, China lead. *Business Standard*. Retrieved 25 July 2009, from www.business-standard.com/india/news/newspaper-circulation-up-india-china-lead/23172/on.

Project for Excellence in Journalism (2004, 15 March). *The State of the News Media 2004*. Retrieved 19 July 2008, from www.stateofthemedia.com/2004.

——(2006, 15 March). *The State of the News Media 2006*. Retrieved 19 July 2008, from www.stateofthemedia.com/2006.

——(2008, 8 May). Journalism, satire or just laughs? *'The Daily Show with Jon Stewart,'* examined. *journalism.org.* Retrieved 14 August 2008, from www.journalism.org/node/10953.

——(2010, 23 May). New Media, Old Media: The blogosphere. *journalism.org.* Retrieved 15 August 2010, from www.journalism.org/analysis_report/blogosphere#fn2

Purdum, T. (2002, 8 October). Threats and responses: Stern tones, direct appeal. *New York Times.*

Quinn, S. (2005). Convergence's fundamental question. *Journalism Studies, 6*(1), 29–38.

Quinn, S. & Quinn-Allan, D. (2008). Where is the business model for citizen journalism? *Australian Journalism Review, 30*(2), 75–83.

Reader's Digest (2008a). *2008 New Zealand's most trusted people.* Retrieved 19 July 2008, from www.readersdigest.co.nz/content/2008-new-zealands-most-trusted-people-list.

——(2008b). *2008 New Zealand's most trusted professions.* Retrieved 19 July 2008, from www.readersdigest.co.nz/content/2008-new-zealands-most-trusted-profressions-list.

Reality Digital (2007). Lonely Planet teams with Reality Digital to launch LonelyPlanet.tv. *Press Release.* Retrieved 14 November 2007, from www.realitydigital.com/press_release_040207.htm.

rebekah (2009, 23 June). Cracking down on digital communication and political organizing in Iran. *Open Net.* Retrieved 15 June 2009, from http://opennet.net/blog/2009/06/cracking-down-digitalcommunication-and-political-organizing-iran.

Reed, R. (1988). From hot metal to cold type printing technology. In E. Willis (Ed.), *Studies in Society* (pp. 35–50). Sydney: Allen & Unwin.

——(1999). Journalism & technology practice since the Second World War. In A. Curthoys & J. Schultz (Eds), *Journalism: Print, politics and popular culture* (pp. 218–28). Brisbane: Queensland University Press.

Reuters (2007). US agency apologises for news conference on fires. *Reuters Alertnet.org.* Retrieved 12 January 2009, from www.alertnet.org/thenews/newsdesk/N26366100.htm.

——(2009). News Corp. ends its free London paper. *nytimes.com.* Retrieved 19 September 2009, from www.nytimes.com/2009/08/21/business/media/21paper.html.

Reuters Institute (2008, 12 December). *Definitions of Journalism.* Retrieved 12 February 2009, from http://reutersinstitute.politics.ox.ac.uk/research/definitions-of-journalism.html.

Rice, R. E. & Katz, J. E. (2003). Comparing internet and mobile phone usage: digital divides of usage, adoption and dropouts. *Telecommunications Policy* (27), 597–623.

Robinson, S. (2006). The mission of the j-blog: Recapturing journalistic authority online. *Journalism, 7*(1), 65–83.

Rodriques, U. M. & Braham, E. (2008). Citizen journalism and the public sphere: a study of the status of citizen journalism in Australia. *Australian Journalism Review, 30*(2), 49–60.

Rosen, J. (1999). *What Are Journalists For?* New Haven, London: Yale University Press.

——(2008, 14 July). A most useful definition of citizen journalism. *Press Think.* Retrieved 12 March 2009, from http://journalism.nyu.edu/pubzone/weblogs/pressthink/2008/07/14/a_most_useful_d.html.

Rosengarten, F. (2010, 10 May). An Introduction to Gramsci's Life and Thought. *International Gramsci Society.* Retrieved 12 July 2010, from www.internationalgramscisociety.org/about_gramsci/biograpy.html.

Ross, A. (2009). The political economy of amateurism. *Television & New Media, 10*(1), 136–7.

Rothman, W. (2010). BP digitally alters press photo, confesses it's a fake. *msn.com.* Retrieved 1 September 2010, from www.msnbc.msn.com/id/38333456/ns/technology_and_science-tech_and_gadgets.

Rugh, W. A. (2004). *Arab Mass Media: Newspapers, radio and television in Arab politics.* Santa Barbara, CA: Greenwood Press.

Rushton, K. (2009). Murdoch speech signals the start of a perfect BBC storm. *Broadcast.* Retrieved 14 September 2009, from www.broadcastnow.co.uk/news/broadcasters/murdoch-speech-signals-the-start-of-a-perfect-bbc-storm/5005190.article?referrer=RSS.

Russell, A. (2007). Digital communication networks and the journalistic field: The 2005 French riots. *Critical Studies in Media Communication, 24*(4), 285–302.

——(2009). News bust; news boom. *Journalism, 10*(3), 365–7.

Russell, J. (2010, 7 May). Social media and technology in Asia. *Asian Correspondent.* Retrieved 13 August 2010, from http://us.asiancorrespondent.com/jon-russell/2010/05/07/top-journalists-in-thailand-talk-social-media.

Salcito, K. (n.d.). *Online journalism ethics: New media trends.* Retrieved 13 September 2009, from www.journalismethics.ca/online_journalism_ethics/new_media_trends.htm.

——(n.d.) *Online journalism ethics: Speed and accuracy.* Retrieved 13 September 2009, from www.journalismethics.ca/online_journalism_ethics/speed_and_accuracy.htm.

Sauls, S. J. & Greer, D. (2007). Radio and localism: Has the FCC dropped the ball? *Journal of Radio Studies, 14*(1), 37–48.

Schaefer, T. M. (2006). When terrorism hits home. Domestic newspaper coverage of the 1998 and 2002 terror attacks in Kenya. *Studies in Conflict and Terrorism, 29*(6), 577–89.

Schiller, D. (2000). *Digital Capitalism: Networking the global market system.* Cambridge, MA: The MIT Press.

——(2009). Actually existing information society. *Television & New Media, 10*(1), 147–8.

Schleifer, S. A. (2004). Arab satellite TV news: Up, down and out. In R. D. Berenger (Ed.), *Global Media Goes to War: Role of news and entertainment media during the 2003 Iraq war* (pp. 223–8). Spokane, WA: Marquette Books.

Schonfeld, E. (2009, 21 April). Should ad networks pay publishers for stolen content? The Fair Syndication Consortium thinks so. *Tech Crunch.* Retrieved 22 February 2009, from www.techcrunch.com/2009/04/21/should-ad-networks-pay-publishers-for-stolen-content-the-fair-syndication-consortium-thinks-so.

——(2009, 6 June). On Twitter, most people are sheep: 80 per cent of accounts have fewer than 10 followers. *Tech Crunch.* Retrieved 3 April 2010, from http://techcrunch.com/2009/06/06/on-twitter-most-people-are-sheep-80-percent-of-accounts-have-fewer-than-10-followers.

Schultz, J. (1998). *Reviving the Fourth Estate: Democracy, accountability and the media.* Melbourne: Cambridge University Press.

Schulze, J. (2009, 13 April). News service backs call for content fees. *The Australian,* p. 31.

Scott, M. (2009, 9 April). *Annual Media Studies Lecture,* La Trobe University. Retrieved 9 April 2009, from www.abc.net.au/corp/pubs/documents/ABC_MD_Mark_Scott_LaTrobe_Annual_Media_Lecture_08_04_09.pdf.

Scott Trust (2008, 8 October). *Scott Trust updates structure.* Retrieved 17 March 2009, from www.gmgplc.co.uk/media/pressreleases/tabid/213/default.aspx?pressreleaseid=121&cid=viewdetails.

Selene, A. (2009, 17 June). Peer Source Verification. *therealterrorists.com.* Retrieved 18 June 2009, from www.therealterrorists.com/2009/06/peer-source-verification.

Selwyn, N. (2004). Reconsidering political and popular understandings of the digital divide. *New Media & Society, 6*(3), 341–62.

Shafer, J. (2009, 17 June). Doubting Twitter. *Slate.* Retrieved 20 June 2009, from www.slate.com/id/2220736.

Shapiro, S. M. (2005, 2 January). The war inside the Arab newsroom. *New York Times.*

Sheridan Burns, L. (2002). *Understanding Journalism.* London: Sage.

Sicha, C. (2008). 'Times' web traffic peaks . . . and peaks again. *New York Observer.* Retrieved 15 September 2009, from www.observer.com/2008/Times-web-traffic-peaks-mdash-and-peaks-again.

Silk, C. (2009, 3 August). The future of the *Observer* hangs in the balance as Guardian Media Group reviews its long-term strategy. *Editors Weblog*. Retrieved 5 August 2009, from www.editorsweblog.org/newspaper/2009/08/the_future_of_the_observer_hangs_in_the.php.

Simon, D. (2009). Build the wall. *Columbia Journalism Review*. Retrieved 16 September 2009, from www.cjr.org/feature/build_the_wall_1.php?page=all.

Simons, M. (2010, 29 June). Media content community goes global—boon to freelancers. *Crikey.com*. Retrieved 30 June 2010, from www.crikey.com.au/topic/globizzle/.

Singer, J. B. (2003). Who are these guys? The online challenge to the notion of journalistic professionalism. *Journalism, 4*(2), 139–63.

Sissons, H. (2006). *Practical Journalism: How to write news* (1st ed.). London, Thousand Oaks, CA: Sage.

Smedinghoff, G. (2007, May/June). The art, philosophy, and science of data. *Contingencies*, 36–42.

Smith, E. (2009, 30 July). *Paper Cuts*. Retrieved 30 July 2009, from http://graphicdesignr.net/papercuts.

Solomon, M. (2006). Groupthink versus the wisdom of crowds: the social epistemology of deliberation. *The Southern Journal of Philosophy* (44), 28–42.

Sparks, C. (2006). Contradictions in capitalist media practices. In L. Artz, S. Macek & D. Cloud (Eds), *Marxism and Communication Studies: The point is to change it* (pp. 111–32). New York: Peter Lang.

Stahl, F., Schafer, M.-F. & Maass, W. (2004). Strategies for selling paid content on newspaper and magazine web sites: An empirical analysis of bundling and splitting news and magazine articles. *International Journal on Media Management, 6*(1&2), 59–66.

Starr, J. (2008, 23 January). Reporters, privacy settings and other people's Bebo profiles. *Evolving Newsroom*. Retrieved 13 September 2009, from http://evolvingnewsroom.co.nz/reporters-privacy-settings-and-other-peoples-bebo-profiles.

Stevens, J. (2002, April). Backpack journalism is here to stay. *Online Journalism Review*. Retrieved 20 November 2003, from www.ojr.org/ojr/workplace/1017771575.php.

Stone, M. (2002, 2 April). The backpack journalist is a 'mush of mediocrity'. *Online Journalism Review*. Retrieved 20 November 2003, from www.ojr.org.ojr/workplace/1017771634.php.

Stross, C. (2003). After the future imploded. In C. Stross (Ed.), *Toast* (pp. 9–20). Holicong, PA: Cosmos Books.

——(2004). *Singularity Sky*. London: Orbit.

Sunstein, C. R. (2004, 24 June). Mobbed up. *New Republic*. Retrieved 15 April 2009, from www.tnr.com/article/politics/the-tnr-archives-cass-r-sunstein.

Surowiecki, J. (2005). *The Wisdom of Crowds: Why the many are smarter than the few and how collective wisdom shapes business, economies, societies and nations.* New York: Doubleday Books.

Sweney, M. (2006, 7 June). Guardian to offer news online first. *guardian.co.uk.* Retrieved 8 October 2008, from www.guardian.co.uk/media/2006/jun/07/theguardian.pressandpublishing.

Tarleton, J. (2009, 20 November). Why Seattle still matters: 1999 WTO protests exposed deep flaws in global capitalism that remain unaddressed. *The Indypendent.* Retrieved 10 Feb 2010, from www.realbattleinseattle.org/node/181.

Taylor Jackson, P. (2009). News as a contested commodity: A clash of capitalist and journalistic imperatives. *Journal of Mass Media Ethics, 24*(2&3), 146–63.

TEDBlog (2009, 16 June). *Q&A with Clay Shirky on Twitter and Iran.* Retrieved 17 June 2009, from http://blog.ted.com/2009/06/qa_with_clay_sh.php?utm_campaign=ted&utm_content=site-basic&utm_medium=on.ted.com-copypaste&utm_source=twitter.com.

Tewkesbury, D. (2003). What do Americans really want to know? Tracking behaviour of news readers on the Internet. *Journal of Communication Inquiry, 53*(4), 694–710.

Thomas, A. O. (2003). Reviewing policies on satellite broadcasts in East Asia: New technology, political economy and civil society. *Knowledge, Technology & Policy, 16*(3), 103–12.

Thompson, K. (2008a, 28 August). Australia: Fairfax Media to outsource part of editorial production. *Editors Weblog.* Retrieved 8 October 2008, from www.editorsweblog.org/newsrooms_and_journalism/2008/08/australia_fairfax_media_to_outsource_par.php.

——(2008b, 2 October). Turning the newsroom on its head—Interview with Trinity Mirror's Neil Benson. *Editors Weblog.* Retrieved 8 October 2008, from www.editorsweblog.org/analysis/2008/10/turning_the_newsroom_on_its_head_intervi.php.

——(2008c, 3 October). US: Newsroom revamp and redesign for Tampa Tribune. *Editors Weblog.* Retrieved 8 October 2008, from www.editorsweblog.org/multimedia/2008/10/us_newsroom_revamp_and_redesign_for_tamp.php.

Thurber, J. (2009). *Is the permanent campaign alive and well after 9/11?* Retrieved 17 April 2009, from www.spa.american.edu/ccps/getpdf.php?table=publications&ID=47.

Thurman, N. & Myllylahti, M. (2009). Taking the paper out of news. A case study of *Taloussanomat*, Europe's first online-only newspaper. *Journalism Studies, iFirst Article,* 1–18.

Thussu, D. K. (2007). *News as Entertainment: The rise of global infotainment.* London: Sage.

Tinic, S. (2006). (En)visioning the televisual audience: Revisiting questions of power in the age of interactive television. In K. D. Haggerty & R. V. Ericson (Eds), *Green College Thematic Lecture Series* (pp. 308–26). Toronto: University of Toronto Press.

Tomlinson, T. (2008). Lab Book Club: A time for hyper-experts and Renaissance reporters. *Nieman Journalism Lab*. Retrieved 15 September 2009, from www.niemanlab.org/2008/11/lab-book-club-a-time-for-renaissance-reporters-and-hyper-experts.

Tompkins, A. (2009, 22 June). Iranian Government uses new technology to monitor information about political turmoil. *PoynterOnline*. Retrieved 23 June 2009, from www.poynter.org/column.asp?id=2&aid=165548.

Townend, J. (2008, 30 September). Trinity Mirror Birmingham chapel calls off strike action. *journalism.co.uk*. Retrieved 8 October 2008, from www.journalism.co.uk/2/articles/532421.php.

Tripunitara, M. & Messerges, T. (2007). Resolving the micropayment problem. *Computer, 40*(2), 104–6.

Trotsky, L. (1977). *The History of the Russian Revolution* (M. Eastman, Trans.). London: Pluto Press.

Truemorist (2009, 17 April). Ashton Kutcher Punks Twitter: A giant million follower PR stunt. *Now Public*. Retrieved 21 April 2009, from www.nowpublic.com/culture/ashton-kutcher-punks-twitter-giant-million-follower-pr-stunt.

Underwood, D. (1993). *When MBAs Rule the Newsroom: How the marketers and the managers are reshaping today's media*. New York: Columbia University Press.

Vendeland, K. (2008, 12 March). Trinity Mirror's hyperlocal experiment going national. *Editors Weblog*. Retrieved 13 March 2008, from www.editorsweblog.org/web_20/2008/03/uk_trinty_mirrors_hyperlocal_experiment.php.

Volkmer, I. (2003). The global network society and the global public sphere. *Development, 46*(1), 9–16.

Von Drehle, D. (2009, 30 March). The Moment: 3/17/09: Seattle. *Time*, 5.

Waisbord, S. (2004). McTV: Understanding the global popularity of television formats. *Television & New Media, 5*(4), 359–83.

Wall, D. S. (2006). Surveillant Internet technologies and the growth in information capitalism: Spams and public trust in the information society. In K. D. Haggerty & R.V. Ericson (Eds), *Green College Thematic Lecture Series* (pp. 340–62). Toronto: University of Toronto Press.

Wall, M. (2006). 'Blogs of war': Weblogs as news. *Journalism, 6*(2), 153–72.

Walters, P. (2007, 26 July). Facebook: What's in it for journalists? *Poynter Institute*. Retrieved 15 April 2009, from www.poynter.org/column.asp?id=101&aid=127211.

Wasko, J. (2009). Global media studies. *Television & New Media, 10*(1), 167–8.

Wayne, M. (2003). *Marxism and Media Studies: Key concepts and contemporary trends.* London: Pluto Press.

Weaver, D. & Loffelholz, M. (2008). Questioning national, cultural and disciplinary boundaries: A call for global journalism research. In M. Loffelholz & D. Weaver (Eds), *Global Journalism Research: Theories, methods, findings, future* (pp. 3–12). Malden, MA, Oxford UK: Blackwell Publishing.

Weaver, M. (2010). Oxfordgirl vs Ahadinajad: the Twitter user taking on the Iranian regime. *guardian.co.uk.* Retrieved 7 April 2010, from www.guardian.co.uk/world/2010/feb/10/oxfordgirl-ahmadinejad-twitter-iran.

WebWire (2009, 7 May). *Sanoma News expands its rationalisation programme.* Retrieved 16 May 2009, from www.webwire.com/ViewPressRel.asp?aId=94463.

Weir, D. (2009). The dirty truths about web traffic. *BNET.* Retrieved 14 September 2009, from http://industry.bnet.com/media/10003921/the-dirty-truths-about-web-traffic.

Weisberg, J. (2009, 2 March). Dubious new models for news. *Newsweek.* Retrieved 17 March 2009, from www.newsweek.com/id/18504/output/print.

Weprin, A. (2009). Network news: One click away. *Broadcasting & Cable, 139*(8), 10.

Wheen, F. (2004). *How Mumbo-jumbo Conquered the World: A short history of modern delusions.* London: Fourth Estate.

Whitney, J. (2005, 15 June). Make media, make real trouble: What's wrong (and right) with *Indymedia. LiP Magazine, Summer.* Retrieved 13 April 2010, from www.lipmagazine.org/articles/featwhitney_indymedia_p.html.

Wilde, O. (1891). The soul of man under socialism. Retrieved 17 February 2009, from http://libcom.org/library/soul-of-man-under-socialism-oscar-wilde.

Williams, R. (1980). Base and superstructure in Marxist cultural theory. In R. Williams (Ed.), *Problems in Materialism and Culture: Selected essays* (pp. 50–63). London: Verso.

——(1989). *Keywords: A vocabulary of culture and society* (Third ed.). London: Fontana Press.

Wilson, K. (2008, Feb/March). In your Facebook. *American Journalism Review.* Retrieved 15 April 2009, from www.ajr.org/Article.asp?id=4465.

Wilson, K. R., Wallin, J. S. & Reiser, C. (2005). Social stratification and the digital divide. *Public Administration and Public Policy, 111*, 173–84.

Winton, R., Lin Il, R.-G., Proctor, C. & Times Staff Writers (2006, 18 November). UCLA orders outside probe of Taser arrest. *LA Times online.* Retrieved 18 November 2008, from www.latimes.com/news/local/la-me-taser18nov18,0,4080498.story?coll=la-home-headlines.

Wolf, J. (2007, 1 August). Facebook and journalism. *cnet.com*. Retrieved 15 April 2009, from http://news.cnet.com/8301-13508_3-9753328-19.html.

Wolfe, T. (1973). The new journalism. In T. Wolfe & E. W. Johnson (Eds), *The New Journalism*. New York: Harper & Row.

Wolff, M. (2003). *Autumn of the Moguls: My misadventures with the titans, poseurs, and money guys who mastered and messed up big media* (1st ed.). New York: HarperBusiness.

——(2008). *The Man who Owns the News: Inside the secret world of Rupert Murdoch*. New York: Random House.

Woo, W. F. (2005, Winter). Defining a journalist's function. *Nieman Reports*. Retrieved 15 February 2009, from www.nieman.harvard.edu/reportsitem. aspx?id=100569.

World Association of Newspapers (WAN) (2008, 2 June). *Global Press Trends: Newspapers are a growth business*. Retrieved 21 April 2009, from www. wan-press.org/article17377.html.

——(2009, 27 May). *Newspaper circulation grows despite economic downturn: WAN*. Retrieved 30 May 2009, from www.wan-press.org/article18148.html.

Zavisca, J. & Sallaz, J. J. (2008). From the margins to the mainstream: The curious convergence of Pierre Bourdieu and US sociology. *Sociologica* (2), 1–21.

Zelizer, B. (2004). *Taking Journalism Seriously: News and the academy*. Thousand Oaks, CA: Sage.

Index